50% OFF Online NHA Phlebotomy Prep Course!

Dear Customer,

We consider it an honor and a privilege that you chose our NHA Phlebotomy Study Guide. As a way of showing our appreciation and to help us better serve you, we have partnered with Mometrix Test Preparation to offer you **50% off their online NHA Phlebotomy Prep Course**. Many NHA Phlebotomy courses are needlessly expensive and don't deliver enough value. With their course, you get access to the best NHA Phlebotomy prep material, and **you only pay half price**.

Mometrix has structured their online course to perfectly complement your printed study guide. The NHA Phlebotomy Prep Course contains **in-depth lessons** that cover all the most important topics, over **800 practice questions** to ensure you feel prepared, and more than **300 digital flashcards**, so you can study while you're on the go.

Online NHA Phlebotomy Prep Course

Topics Included:
- Safety and Compliance
    - Laboratory Safety and Quality Control
    - Laboratory Infection Control
- Patient Preparation
    - Laboratory Orders
    - Medical Terminology
- Routine Blood Collections
    - Blood Collection Additives and Collection Tubes
    - Specific Blood Tests
- Special Collections
- Processing

Course Features:
- NHA Phlebotomy Study Guide
    - Get content that complements our best-selling study guide.
- Full-Length Practice Tests
    - With over 800 practice questions, you can test yourself again and again.
- Mobile Friendly
    - If you need to study on the go, the course is easily accessible from your mobile device.
- NHA Phlebotomy Flashcards
    - Our course includes a flashcard mode with over 300 content cards to help you study.

To receive this discount, visit them at mometrix.com/university/nha-phlebotomy or simply scan this QR code with your smartphone. At the checkout page, enter the discount code: **NHA50TPB**

If you have any questions or concerns, please contact them at support@mometrix.com.

Sincerely,

 in partnership with

FREE Test Taking Tips Video/DVD Offer

To better serve you, we created videos covering test taking tips that we want to give you for FREE. **These videos cover world-class tips that will help you succeed on your test.**

We just ask that you send us feedback about this product. Please let us know what you thought about it—whether good, bad, or indifferent.

To get your **FREE videos**, you can use the QR code below or email freevideos@studyguideteam.com with "Free Videos" in the subject line and the following information in the body of the email:

   a. The title of your product

   b. Your product rating on a scale of 1-5, with 5 being the highest

   c. Your feedback about the product

If you have any questions or concerns, please don't hesitate to contact us at info@studyguideteam.com.

Thank you!

NHA Phlebotomy Study Guide 2025-2026

3 Practice Exams and Prep Book
[Includes Detailed Answer Explanations]

Lydia Morrison

Copyright © 2024 by TPB Publishing

All rights reserved. No part of this publication may be reproduced, distributed, or transmitted in any form or by any means, including photocopying, recording, or other electronic or mechanical methods, without the prior written permission of the publisher, except in the case of brief quotations embodied in critical reviews and certain other noncommercial uses permitted by copyright law.

Written and edited by TPB Publishing.

TPB Publishing is not associated with or endorsed by any official testing organization. TPB Publishing is a publisher of unofficial educational products. All test and organization names are trademarks of their respective owners. Content in this book is included for utilitarian purposes only and does not constitute an endorsement by TPB Publishing of any particular point of view.

Interested in buying more than 10 copies of our product? Contact us about bulk discounts:
bulkorders@studyguideteam.com

ISBN 13: 9781637752548

Table of Contents

Welcome — 1
   FREE Videos/DVD OFFER — 1
Quick Overview — 2
Test-Taking Strategies — 3
Audiobook Access — 7
Introduction to the CPT Exam — 8
Study Prep Plan for the NHA Phlebotomy Exam — 10
Core Knowledge — 15
Safety and Compliance — 29
Patient Preparation — 42
Routine Blood Collections — 54
Special Collections — 78
Processing — 90
Practice Test — 99
Answer Explanations — 117
Practice Test — 130
Answer Explanations — 147
Practice Test — 159
Answer Explanations — 176

Welcome

Dear Reader,

Welcome to your new Test Prep Books study guide! We are pleased that you chose us to help you prepare for your exam. There are many study options to choose from, and we appreciate you choosing us. Studying can be a daunting task, but we have designed a smart, effective study guide to help prepare you for what lies ahead.

Whether you're a parent helping your child learn and grow, a high school student working hard to get into your dream college, or a nursing student studying for a complex exam, we want to help give you the tools you need to succeed. We hope this study guide gives you the skills and the confidence to thrive, and we can't thank you enough for allowing us to be part of your journey.

In an effort to continue to improve our products, we welcome feedback from our customers. We look forward to hearing from you. Suggestions, success stories, and criticisms can all be communicated by emailing us at info@studyguideteam.com.

Sincerely,
Test Prep Books Team

FREE Videos/DVD OFFER

Doing well on your exam requires both knowing the test content and understanding how to use that knowledge to do well on the test. We offer completely FREE test taking tip videos. **These videos cover world-class tips that you can use to succeed on your test.**

To get your **FREE videos**, you can use the QR code below or email freevideos@studyguideteam.com with "Free Videos" in the subject line and the following information in the body of the email:

    a. The title of your product
    b. Your product rating on a scale of 1-5, with 5 being the highest
    c. Your feedback about the product

If you have any questions or concerns, please don't hesitate to contact us at info@studyguideteam.com.

Quick Overview

As you draw closer to taking your exam, effective preparation becomes more and more important. Thankfully, you have this study guide to help you get ready. Use this guide to help keep your studying on track and refer to it often.

This study guide contains several key sections that will help you be successful on your exam. The guide contains tips for what you should do the night before and the day of the test. Also included are test-taking tips. Knowing the right information is not always enough. Many well-prepared test takers struggle with exams. These tips will help equip you to accurately read, assess, and answer test questions.

A large part of the guide is devoted to showing you what content to expect on the exam and to helping you better understand that content. In this guide are practice test questions so that you can see how well you have grasped the content. Then, answer explanations are provided so that you can understand why you missed certain questions.

Don't try to cram the night before you take your exam. This is not a wise strategy for a few reasons. First, your retention of the information will be low. Your time would be better used by reviewing information you already know rather than trying to learn a lot of new information. Second, you will likely become stressed as you try to gain a large amount of knowledge in a short amount of time. Third, you will be depriving yourself of sleep. So be sure to go to bed at a reasonable time the night before. Being well-rested helps you focus and remain calm.

Be sure to eat a substantial breakfast the morning of the exam. If you are taking the exam in the afternoon, be sure to have a good lunch as well. Being hungry is distracting and can make it difficult to focus. You have hopefully spent lots of time preparing for the exam. Don't let an empty stomach get in the way of success!

When travelling to the testing center, leave earlier than needed. That way, you have a buffer in case you experience any delays. This will help you remain calm and will keep you from missing your appointment time at the testing center.

Be sure to pace yourself during the exam. Don't try to rush through the exam. There is no need to risk performing poorly on the exam just so you can leave the testing center early. Allow yourself to use all of the allotted time if needed.

Remain positive while taking the exam even if you feel like you are performing poorly. Thinking about the content you should have mastered will not help you perform better on the exam.

Once the exam is complete, take some time to relax. Even if you feel that you need to take the exam again, you will be well served by some down time before you begin studying again. It's often easier to convince yourself to study if you know that it will come with a reward!

Test-Taking Strategies

1. Predicting the Answer

When you feel confident in your preparation for a multiple-choice test, try predicting the answer before reading the answer choices. This is especially useful on questions that test objective factual knowledge. By predicting the answer before reading the available choices, you eliminate the possibility that you will be distracted or led astray by an incorrect answer choice. You will feel more confident in your selection if you read the question, predict the answer, and then find your prediction among the answer choices. After using this strategy, be sure to still read all of the answer choices carefully and completely. If you feel unprepared, you should not attempt to predict the answers. This would be a waste of time and an opportunity for your mind to wander in the wrong direction.

2. Reading the Whole Question

Too often, test takers scan a multiple-choice question, recognize a few familiar words, and immediately jump to the answer choices. Test authors are aware of this common impatience, and they will sometimes prey upon it. For instance, a test author might subtly turn the question into a negative, or he or she might redirect the focus of the question right at the end. The only way to avoid falling into these traps is to read the entirety of the question carefully before reading the answer choices.

3. Looking for Wrong Answers

Long and complicated multiple-choice questions can be intimidating. One way to simplify a difficult multiple-choice question is to eliminate all of the answer choices that are clearly wrong. In most sets of answers, there will be at least one selection that can be dismissed right away. If the test is administered on paper, the test taker could draw a line through it to indicate that it may be ignored; otherwise, the test taker will have to perform this operation mentally or on scratch paper. In either case, once the obviously incorrect answers have been eliminated, the remaining choices may be considered. Sometimes identifying the clearly wrong answers will give the test taker some information about the correct answer. For instance, if one of the remaining answer choices is a direct opposite of one of the eliminated answer choices, it may well be the correct answer. The opposite of obviously wrong is obviously right! Of course, this is not always the case. Some answers are obviously incorrect simply because they are irrelevant to the question being asked. Still, identifying and eliminating some incorrect answer choices is a good way to simplify a multiple-choice question.

4. Don't Overanalyze

Anxious test takers often overanalyze questions. When you are nervous, your brain will often run wild, causing you to make associations and discover clues that don't actually exist. If you feel that this may be a problem for you, do whatever you can to slow down during the test. Try taking a deep breath or counting to ten. As you read and consider the question, restrict yourself to the particular words used by the author. Avoid thought tangents about what the author *really* meant, or what he or she was *trying* to say. The only things that matter on a multiple-choice test are the words that are actually in the question. You must avoid reading too much into a multiple-choice question, or supposing that the writer meant something other than what he or she wrote.

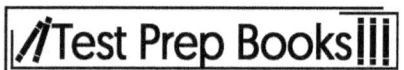

5. No Need for Panic

It is wise to learn as many strategies as possible before taking a multiple-choice test, but it is likely that you will come across a few questions for which you simply don't know the answer. In this situation, avoid panicking. Because most multiple-choice tests include dozens of questions, the relative value of a single wrong answer is small. As much as possible, you should compartmentalize each question on a multiple-choice test. In other words, you should not allow your feelings about one question to affect your success on the others. When you find a question that you either don't understand or don't know how to answer, just take a deep breath and do your best. Read the entire question slowly and carefully. Try rephrasing the question a couple of different ways. Then, read all of the answer choices carefully. After eliminating obviously wrong answers, make a selection and move on to the next question.

6. Confusing Answer Choices

When working on a difficult multiple-choice question, there may be a tendency to focus on the answer choices that are the easiest to understand. Many people, whether consciously or not, gravitate to the answer choices that require the least concentration, knowledge, and memory. This is a mistake. When you come across an answer choice that is confusing, you should give it extra attention. A question might be confusing because you do not know the subject matter to which it refers. If this is the case, don't

eliminate the answer before you have affirmatively settled on another. When you come across an answer choice of this type, set it aside as you look at the remaining choices. If you can confidently assert that one of the other choices is correct, you can leave the confusing answer aside. Otherwise, you will need to take a moment to try to better understand the confusing answer choice. Rephrasing is one way to tease out the sense of a confusing answer choice.

7. Your First Instinct

Many people struggle with multiple-choice tests because they overthink the questions. If you have studied sufficiently for the test, you should be prepared to trust your first instinct once you have carefully and completely read the question and all of the answer choices. There is a great deal of research suggesting that the mind can come to the correct conclusion very quickly once it has obtained all of the relevant information. At times, it may seem to you as if your intuition is working faster even than your reasoning mind. This may in fact be true. The knowledge you obtain while studying may be retrieved from your subconscious before you have a chance to work out the associations that support it. Verify your instinct by working out the reasons that it should be trusted.

8. Key Words

Many test takers struggle with multiple-choice questions because they have poor reading comprehension skills. Quickly reading and understanding a multiple-choice question requires a mixture of skill and experience. To help with this, try jotting down a few key words and phrases on a piece of scrap paper. Doing this concentrates the process of reading and forces the mind to weigh the relative importance of the question's parts. In selecting words and phrases to write down, the test taker thinks about the question more deeply and carefully. This is especially true for multiple-choice questions that are preceded by a long prompt.

9. Subtle Negatives

One of the oldest tricks in the multiple-choice test writer's book is to subtly reverse the meaning of a question with a word like *not* or *except*. If you are not paying attention to each word in the question, you can easily be led astray by this trick. For instance, a common question format is, "Which of the following is...?" Obviously, if the question instead is, "Which of the following is not...?," then the answer will be quite different. Even worse, the test makers are aware of the potential for this mistake and will include one answer choice that would be correct if the question were not negated or reversed. A test taker who misses the reversal will find what he or she believes to be a correct answer and will be so confident that he or she will fail to reread the question and discover the original error. The only way to avoid this is to practice a wide variety of multiple-choice questions and to pay close attention to each and every word.

10. Reading Every Answer Choice

It may seem obvious, but you should always read every one of the answer choices! Too many test takers fall into the habit of scanning the question and assuming that they understand the question because they recognize a few key words. From there, they pick the first answer choice that answers the question they believe they have read. Test takers who read all of the answer choices might discover that one of the latter answer choices is actually *more* correct. Moreover, reading all of the answer choices can remind you of facts related to the question that can help you arrive at the correct answer. Sometimes, a misstatement or incorrect detail in one of the latter answer choices will trigger your memory of the subject and will enable you to find the right answer. Failing to read all of the answer choices is like not reading all of the items on a restaurant menu: you might miss out on the perfect choice.

11. Spot the Hedges

One of the keys to success on multiple-choice tests is paying close attention to every word. This is never truer than with words like *almost*, *most*, *some*, and *sometimes*. These words are called "hedges" because they indicate that a statement is not totally true or not true in every place and time. An absolute statement will contain no hedges, but in many subjects, the answers are not always straightforward or absolute. There are always exceptions to the rules in these subjects. For this reason,

you should favor those multiple-choice questions that contain hedging language. The presence of qualifying words indicates that the author is taking special care with his or her words, which is certainly important when composing the right answer. After all, there are many ways to be wrong, but there is only one way to be right! For this reason, it is wise to avoid answers that are absolute when taking a multiple-choice test. An absolute answer is one that says things are either all one way or all another. They often include words like *every*, *always*, *best*, and *never*. If you are taking a multiple-choice test in a subject that doesn't lend itself to absolute answers, be on your guard if you see any of these words.

12. Long Answers

In many subject areas, the answers are not simple. As already mentioned, the right answer often requires hedges. Another common feature of the answers to a complex or subjective question are qualifying clauses, which are groups of words that subtly modify the meaning of the sentence. If the question or answer choice describes a rule to which there are exceptions or the subject matter is complicated, ambiguous, or confusing, the correct answer will require many words in order to be expressed clearly and accurately. In essence, you should not be deterred by answer choices that seem excessively long. Oftentimes, the author of the text will not be able to write the correct answer without offering some qualifications and modifications. Your job is to read the answer choices thoroughly and completely and to select the one that most accurately and precisely answers the question.

13. Restating to Understand

Sometimes, a question on a multiple-choice test is difficult not because of what it asks but because of how it is written. If this is the case, restate the question or answer choice in different words. This process serves a couple of important purposes. First, it forces you to concentrate on the core of the question. In order to rephrase the question accurately, you have to understand it well. Rephrasing the question will concentrate your mind on the key words and ideas. Second, it will present the information to your mind in a fresh way. This process may trigger your memory and render some useful scrap of information picked up while studying.

14. True Statements

Sometimes an answer choice will be true in itself, but it does not answer the question. This is one of the main reasons why it is essential to read the question carefully and completely before proceeding to the answer choices. Too often, test takers skip ahead to the answer choices and look for true statements. Having found one of these, they are content to select it without reference to the question above. The savvy test taker will always read the entire question before turning to the answer choices. Then, having settled on a correct answer choice, he or she will refer to the original question and ensure that the selected answer is relevant. The mistake of choosing a correct-but-irrelevant answer choice is especially common on questions related to specific pieces of objective knowledge.

15. No Patterns

One of the more dangerous ideas that circulates about multiple-choice tests is that the correct answers tend to fall into patterns. These erroneous ideas range from a belief that B and C are the most common right answers, to the idea that an unprepared test-taker should answer "A-B-A-C-A-D-A-B-A." It cannot be emphasized enough that pattern-seeking of this type is exactly the WRONG way to approach a multiple-choice test. To begin with, it is highly unlikely that the test maker will plot the correct answers according to some predetermined pattern. The questions are scrambled and delivered in a random order. Furthermore, even if the test maker was following a pattern in the assignation of correct answers, there is no reason why the test taker would know which pattern he or she was using. Any attempt to discern a pattern in the answer choices is a waste of time and a distraction from the real work of taking the test. A test taker would be much better served by extra preparation before the test than by reliance on a pattern in the answers.

Audiobook Access

We host multiple bonus items online, including this study guide in audiobook format. Scan the QR code or go to this link to access this content:

testprepbooks.com/bonus/nhaphleb

If you have any issues, please email support@testprepbooks.com.

Introduction to the CPT Exam

Function of the Test

The Certified Phlebotomy Technician (CPT) Exam is offered by the National Healthcareer Association (NHA). Individuals taking the CPT Exam must have a high school diploma or the equivalent. They must also meet the requirements for either the training program or work experience pathways to certification. More information on eligibility is available on the NHA website.

The exam is taken by individuals seeking certification as phlebotomists nationwide. In 2023, 52,571 individuals sought CPT Certification. Of that cohort, 40,128 test takers passed, yielding a 76.33% pass rate.

Test Administration

Individuals wishing to take the exam must apply through the NHA. In the application, the test taker will schedule their in-person exam with PSI or schedule the exam to be remote through Live Remote Proctoring (LRP). Candidates must bring the following manuals with them to the exam: Current Procedural Terminology (CPT) Edition, HCPCS Level II, and ICD-10-CM.

Whether taking the exam in-person or remote, the test taker must furnish the appropriate identification when requested.

Individuals who don't pass the exam can retake the CPT after a 30-day waiting period. Any individual who doesn't pass the CPT after three attempts will have to wait one year before retaking the exam. In accordance with the Americans with Disabilities Act, test takers with documented disabilities may request accommodations by submitting the NHA Request for Accommodations Form, which is available on their website.

Test Format

The CPT Exam consists of 120 questions, 100 of which are scored and 20 of which are pretest questions. The pretest questions are included for evaluation of potential questions for future exams and are not scored. However, the test taker is not informed as to which 20 questions are pretest questions, so each question should be completed to the best of their ability. The total examination time for all questions is 2 hours.

The content of the exam falls into five domains: Safety and Compliance, Patient Preparation, Routine Blood Collection, Special Collection, and Processing. Questions also require some core knowledge of phlebotomy including the role of phlebotomy technicians in patient care, blood group systems, basic

Introduction to the CPT Exam

anatomy, and more. The questions from the various categories are interspersed amongst each other throughout the exam.

Section	Category	# of Qs	Percent of Exam
1	Safety and Compliance	25	25%
2	Patient Preparation	23	23%
3	Routine Blood Collection	30	30%
4	Special Collection	7	7%
5	Processing	15	15%
Total		**100**	**100%**
Unscored		**20**	**NA**

Scoring

Scores are based on the total number of correct answers provided by the test taker, with no penalty for wrong answers beyond the missed opportunity to get another answer correct. This raw score is standardized and converted to a scaled score. The NHA sets the passing score at a level that indicates the minimum competency for a phlebotomy technician. Currently, the minimum passing score is 390.

The test taker receives an unofficial score report with a pass/fail notification within 48 hours of completing the exam. Score reports also contain detailed information about the test taker's score in each of the five domains. If the official score is determined as passing, the test taker will receive an email that their certification is be available to print online.

Study Prep Plan for the NHA Phlebotomy Exam

1 **Schedule** - Use one of our study schedules below or come up with one of your own.

2 **Relax** - Test anxiety can hurt even the best students. There are many ways to reduce stress. Find the one that works best for you.

3 **Execute** - Once you have a good plan in place, be sure to stick to it.

One Week Study Schedule

Day 1	Day 1: Core Knowledge & Safety and Compliance
Day 2	Day 2: Patient Preparation & Routine Blood Collection
Day 3	Day 3: Special Collection & Processing
Day 4	Day 4: Practice Test #1
Day 5	Day 5: Practice Test #2
Day 6	Day 6: Practice Test #3
Day 7	Take Your Exam!

Two Week Study Schedule

Day 1	Day 1: Core Knowledge	Day 8	Day 8: Practice Test #1
Day 2	Day 2: Safety and Compliance	Day 9	Day 9: Answer Explanations #1
Day 3	Day 3: Patient Preparation	Day 10	Day 10: Practice Test #2
Day 4	Day 4: Routine Blood Collection	Day 11	Day 11: Answer Explanations #2
Day 5	Day 5: Special Collection	Day 12	Day 12: Practice Test #3
Day 6	Day 6: Processing	Day 13	Day 13: Answer Explanations #3
Day 7	Day 7: Take a Break	Day 14	Take Your Exam!

Study Prep Plan for the NHA Phlebotomy Exam

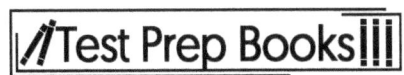

One Month Study Schedule							
Day 1	Day 1: Core Knowledge	Day 11	Day 11: Insert Venipuncture Device	Day 21	Day 21: Distribute Laboratory Results to Ordering Providers
Day 2	Day 2: Safety and Compliance	Day 12	Day 12: Blood Collection Devices	Day 22	Day 22: Chain of Custody Guidelines
Day 3	Day 3: Perform Quality Control for Laboratory Equipment	Day 13	Day 13: Palpation Techniques	Day 23	Day 23: Take a Break
Day 4	Day 4: HIPAA Regulations	Day 14	Day 14: Use of Needle Safety Devices	Day 24	Day 24: Practice Test #1
Day 5	Day 5: Standard Precautions	Day 15	Day 15: Take a Break	Day 25	Day 25: Answer Explanations #1
Day 6	Day 6: Patient Preparation	Day 16	Day 16: Special Collections	Day 26	Day 26: Practice Test #2
Day 7	Day 7: Take a Break	Day 17	Day 17: Perform Phlebotomy for Blood Donations	Day 27	Day 27: Answer Explanations #2
Day 8	Day 8: Patient Identifiers	Day 18	Day 18: Skin Preparation for Blood Culture Collections	Day 28	Day 28: Practice Test #3
Day 9	Day 9: Special Considerations	Day 19	Day 19: Pediatric Volume Calculations	Day 29	Day 29: Answer Explanations #3
Day 10	Day 10: Routine Blood Collections	Day 20	Day 20: Processing	Day 30	Take Your Exam!

Build your own prep plan by visiting:

testprepbooks.com/prep

As you study for your test, we'd like to take the opportunity to remind you that you are capable of great things! With the right tools and dedication, you truly can do anything you set your mind to. The fact that you are holding this book right now shows how committed you are. In case no one has told you lately, you've got this! Our intention behind including this coloring page is to give you the chance to take some time to engage your creative side when you need a little brain-break from studying. As a company, we want to encourage people like you to achieve their dreams by providing good quality study materials for the tests and certifications that improve careers and change lives. As individuals, many of us have taken such tests in our careers, and we know how challenging this process can be. While we can't come alongside you and cheer you on personally, we can offer you the space to recall your purpose, reconnect with your passion, and refresh your brain through an artistic practice. We wish you every success, and happy studying!

Core Knowledge

Role of Phlebotomy Technicians in Laboratory Testing

Clinical laboratory testing is the process by which patient specimens are examined, measured, and evaluated. Physicians use laboratory test results to make clinical decisions and provide appropriate medical care for their patients. Laboratory testing can be performed in a variety of settings. Inpatient hospitals and outpatient clinics are two types of clinical laboratories. These facilities typically limit their services to patients within the hospital or clinic. There are also reference laboratories that typically receive specimens from a larger service area. This may include patients within a specified city, state, or region.

Phlebotomy technicians assist with laboratory testing in various ways. Reliable laboratory test results begin with the collection of high-quality patient specimens. Phlebotomists support this by ensuring safe and effective specimen collection. They then use their knowledge and skills to carefully handle and efficiently deliver specimens to the clinical laboratory for testing.

Additionally, phlebotomy technicians may serve in the clinical laboratory setting as a laboratory assistant. Within this role, the phlebotomy technician assists various members of the laboratory team by performing tasks including basic laboratory testing and specimen processing. Lab assistants also engage in other administrative duties including maintaining quality controls, answering phones, maintaining cleanliness and organization of the lab environment, maintaining equipment, managing supplies, and performing general documentation.

Role of Phlebotomy Technicians in Patient Care

The core responsibilities phlebotomy technicians perform in the patient care setting are preparing patients for specimen collection, performing specimen collection, and properly preparing specimens for transport to the laboratory. In performing this role, it is necessary to have a thorough understanding of the legal, organizational, and professional guidelines for this work. Whether the technician is performing their duties in a clinic, a hospital, or a stand-alone laboratory draw site, the focus remains on providing safe and accurate care in a timely manner.

Phlebotomy technicians should maintain a safe environment for themselves, their colleagues, and patients. This includes being aware of trip hazards in their work areas, properly disposing of sharps and biohazardous materials (e.g., body fluids, chemicals), and being prepared for emergencies (e.g., inclement weather, fires, first aid, active shooters). Additionally, phlebotomy technicians must be aware of and always utilize infection control measures. This includes proper hand hygiene, decontamination of surfaces, and treating all body fluids as potentially infectious (universal precautions). Phlebotomy technicians must also be aware of laws and policies governing their work. This includes privacy laws (HIPAA), patient rights (i.e., informed consent), and practice guidelines for their organization.

The work that phlebotomists perform is vital, as the specimens collected are used to guide patient care decisions. It is critical for phlebotomy technicians to perform their work precisely and efficiently to ensure results are accurate and physicians can make timely patient care decisions. This requires phlebotomy technicians to have a deep understanding of proper techniques in collecting, preparing, and transporting patient specimens.

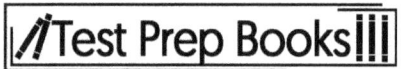

Core Knowledge

Lastly, phlebotomy technicians utilize professionalism and customer service skills to provide positive patient experiences. Phlebotomy technicians display professionalism through proper personal hygiene, work-appropriate dress, self-confidence, and appropriate behavior. They strive to maintain a calm, respectful tone in all communication. They demonstrate integrity, empathy, and reliability in their work and strive to provide patients with positive experiences.

Medical Terminology Related to Phlebotomy

Phlebotomy refers to the process where blood is withdrawn from a vein by piercing or cutting the skin. A *phlebotomist* or *phlebotomy technician* is someone who specializes in obtaining blood specimens via puncture of a vein (*venipuncture*). Blood can also be drawn from smaller blood vessels of the hands, feet, and ear lobe in a process called *capillary puncture*. Additionally, *arterial blood sampling* is a procedure performed by certain medical personnel where blood is drawn from an artery. The blood that is withdrawn from the vein is called a patient *specimen*, which is sent to a laboratory where various tests can be performed for diagnosis or management of patient health or health problems.

Many types of tests can be performed on blood specimens. Blood *chemistry* tests measure different chemicals in the blood and body, such as electrolytes (e.g., potassium, calcium, sodium, chloride), protein, glucose, or enzymes associated with the health of different organs in the body. *Toxicology* is concerned with identifying the presence and/or quantity of different toxins in the blood and body. *Therapeutic drug monitoring* tests the levels of medications in the body to ensure intended results. *Molecular diagnostics* involves identification of DNA and RNA changes that are associated with various diseases or risks for diseases. *Coagulation* studies help physicians understand how a patient's blood forms and breaks up clots.

Various medical specialties are involved in testing, evaluation, and management of blood and blood testing. *Hematology* is the study of the blood and disorders involving blood. *Serology* involves study of blood *serum* (the blood component that includes plasma and fibrinogen) and its involvement with the immune system's ability to appropriately respond to infection or substances. Serology looks specifically at different *antibodies* (proteins located in the blood that respond to things like pathogens, toxins, or foreign substances) and *antigens* (a substance that causes the body to have an immune response or production of an antibody when introduced into the bloodstream). *Immunohematology* is a specialty concerned with how antigen and antibody reactions relate to blood disorders. This field is involved with interactions associated with blood transfusions. *Microbiology* is another study which looks for the presence of microscopic organisms (e.g., bacteria, viruses, fungi) in blood and bodily tissues. *Histology* looks at and studies the structures of various tissues of the body. *Cytology* studies the various structures of individual cells.

Aseptic Techniques

Phlebotomy technicians promote safety by preventing the spread of infection. Healthcare facilities service a variety of rotating patients, visitors, and staff every day. Some may be very ill, while others may be physically well. Some may be carrying infection without realizing it, and others may be *immunocompromised* (their immune system is weak or cannot effectively fight infection). *Aseptic techniques*, or healthcare practices that reduce or eliminate the presence of microorganisms, dramatically reduce the chances of spreading infection.

Hand hygiene is one of the first aseptic techniques used to reduce the spread of infection. The World Health Organization (WHO) estimates that proper hand hygiene in the hospital setting reduces potential

Core Knowledge

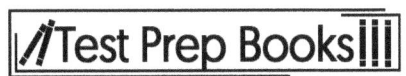

preventable infections by half. Hand hygiene should be performed prior to and after patient contact, when moving from one task to another unrelated task (e.g., helping a patient set up their meal tray and then performing a venipuncture), or prior to and following applying gloves. Alcohol-based cleansers are a convenient and effective method of performing hand hygiene in many situations and can be used in place of antimicrobial soap and water. However, if hands are visibly soiled or suspected to have come in contact with body fluids, it is advised to wash with soap and water as opposed to using an alcohol-based cleanser. Additionally, soap and water are required after contact with patients suspected or confirmed to have spore-forming infections such as *c. difficile*. Whether using alcohol-based cleanser or soap and water, care should be taken to scrub palms, fingers, underneath fingernails, tops of hands, wrists and the cuff of the forearms for at least twenty seconds.

Another aspect of infection control is management of supplies and equipment. When preparing a patient for a procedure like venipuncture, this begins with ensuring the surfaces and surrounding area are clear of any items that are not directly involved in the procedure. Surfaces should be disinfected with an antimicrobial cleanser or wipe using the instructions outlined on the manufacturer's packaging. Supplies should be gathered, keeping in mind that any unused disposable supplies should not be returned to general stock due to risk of package contamination. Supplies should be placed on a clean surface such as a bedside table or collection tray, and they should remain close enough to the technician that they are within easy reach. Packaged items should be inspected for sterility, verifying they are sealed and not expired. When opening the packaged items, it is also important to do so with clean, gloved hands and to avoid contamination by making sure they stay in the cleaned procedure area and do not get touched by uncleaned surfaces such as patient clothing or a hand or arm. Any needles should remain sheathed and can be left inside their opened sterile packaging until ready to use. If an item or surface is suspected of becoming contaminated (e.g., a patient coughs onto the procedure area or an item falls onto the bed or floor), these items should not be used. This may require the technician to restart the procedure or call for a colleague to assist with obtaining additional supplies as needed.

Proper handling and disposal of sharps and potentially infectious contaminants is yet another vital part of maintaining asepsis. After disinfecting the venipuncture site and allowing it to air dry, the needle should only ever puncture the skin once. If the needle is withdrawn from the skin for any reason prior to obtaining a blood sample, a new needle should always be used for the second attempt to avoid contamination. Using *universal precautions* (treating all body fluids as potentially infectious), phlebotomy technicians should handle any used needles with extreme care to avoid accidental needle stick injury to themselves or the patient. This includes maintaining awareness of the needle's position, using hand positioning that is safe and reduces risk of needle stick injuries, utilizing *needle safety devices* (NSD) such as needleless transfer systems or activating needle shields after use, and promptly disposing of any sharp into an appropriate sharps container. Additionally, body fluids should always be handled and disposed of properly per organizational and legal requirements. This means that any disposable items soiled with body fluids (i.e. blood, stool, urine) should be disposed of in appropriate biohazard waste. Contaminated surfaces should be disinfected, ensuring that patients and staff are utilizing the appropriate *personal protective equipment* (PPE) such as gloves, gowns, eyewear, and/or shoe covers as necessary to the situation.

Blood Components

Blood is a solution made from fluid and different types of specialized cells. This mixture travels through the circulatory system and functions to transport and supply the bodily organs and tissues with vital nutrients (e.g., sugars, oxygen, amino acids, minerals). It also serves as a waste disposal system, pulling things like carbon dioxide, lactic acid, and blood urea nitrogen (BUN) from the body. Lastly, blood also influences and assists in regulating body temperature through the expansion and contraction of the blood vessels, which impact the volume of blood sent to different areas of the body. The four major groups of cells that make up the blood are plasma, red blood cells (RBCs), white blood cells (WBCs), and platelets (PLTs).

Plasma makes up the largest percentage of blood volume at a little over 50%. This water-rich, pale-yellow substance is the "fluid" portion of the blood. Although plasma is over 90% water, it also contains many life-sustaining and vital substances needed for normal bodily function. This includes circulating oxygen as well as waste products containing carbon dioxide and nitrogen. Plasma also contains proteins (including albumin), fats (including triglycerides and cholesterol), carbohydrates (also called blood glucose), antibodies (which help with infection control), and fibrinogen (which assists with blood clotting). Additional substances contained in the plasma include electrolytes (e.g., sodium, potassium, magnesium, calcium).

Red blood cells (RBCs, or *erythrocytes*) are the next largest component of the blood with the average person having 4.5–5 million cells per cubic millimeter of total blood. These red, discoid cells containing *hemoglobin* (an iron-containing substance) circulate within the bloodstream and transfer oxygen from the lungs to the cells of the body. RBCs also collect carbon dioxide waste during circulation and return it to the lungs to be expelled during exhalation. The process of RBC formation, called *erythropoiesis*, is controlled by the hormone *erythropoietin*, which is produced by the kidneys. This hormone signals the bone marrow to begin producing RBCs. RBCs initially form with a nucleus but shed this prior to being circulated into the bloodstream. However, a small number of immature RBCs (called *reticulocytes* or *retic*) can be present in the circulation. RBCs have an approximate lifespan of about 120 days and then are efficiently metabolized by the liver and spleen, and any iron contained in the hemoglobin is sent back to the bone marrow to be used in the formation of new RBCs.

White blood cells (WBCs, or *leukocytes*) are another blood component and are present at approximately 5,000–10,000 per cubic millimeter of total blood. WBCs mainly function to recognize and respond to pathogens or foreign substances in the body. Unlike erythrocytes, WBCs are present within the bloodstream as well as outside of the bloodstream within the tissues. In fact, much of their work is performed in the tissues, with lifespans and function varying by the specific type of WBC. The types of WBCs are classified as *granulocytes* (cells with clear granule-like substances seen under microscope) or *agranulocytes* (cells with no visible granules seen under microscope).

The granulocytes are further classified into three types: Neutrophils, Eosinophils, and Basophils. *Neutrophils* make up the largest percentage of total WBCs at about 50–65%. They use the process of *phagocytosis* (enveloping and consuming) to destroy pathogens. Under a microscope, one can identify a segmented nucleus within the cell, and the granules stain lavender. Granulocytes live between 6 hours to a few days. *Eosinophils*, which make up approximately 3% of WBCs, respond to foreign proteins within the body. They stop immune responses and are particularly involved when there are allergies or parasites present. Under a microscope, these cells contain a two-lobed nucleus with beaded granules which stain orange-pink. Eosinophils live between 8–12 days on average. *Basophils* make up a very small percentage of total WBCs at less than 1%, and they initiate the inflammation response by releasing histamine and heparin. When viewed under a microscope, these cells contain a nucleus with an "S" shape and larger granules that stain a dark blue or black color. Basophils tend to live a few days.

Agranulocytes are further classified into two types: Lymphocytes and monocytes. *Lymphocytes* make up between 25–40% of all WBCs, making them the second-most prolific WBC. *T lymphocytes* (known as the "killer" cell) are a type of lymphocyte which directly attack damaged or sick cells. *B lymphocytes* operate more indirectly by helping with production of antibodies (immunoglobulins) that recognize and attack foreign cells in the body. Lymphocytes contain a very large, round nucleus that stains dark purple and is surrounded by a thin, pale blue cytoplasm. The life span of these cells varies widely, with some living a handful of hours to others living years. *Monocytes* are another type of agranulocyte that makes up between 3–7% of all WBCs. Monocytes are *phagocytes*—they consume cells through phagocytosis and scavenge for and clean up dead or damaged cells, pathogens, or other foreign substances. Under a microscope, monocytes are the largest of the WBC components and contain a large nucleus which stains dark and a gray-blue staining cytoplasm.

Platelets (also known as *thrombocytes*) are the final component of whole blood. These tiny cells are present in an average range of 150,000–400,000 platelets per cubic millimeter of blood. The main function of platelets is to assist with blood clotting (*coagulation*). Platelets are quickly mobilized when there is an injury in the body. The lifespan of these cells is approximately 10 days.

Blood Group Systems

Blood groups (or *blood types*) refer to different groups of inherited antigens (proteins) that can be present on the surface of an individual's red blood cells. This information is particularly important when preparing a patient to receive a donor blood transfusion. If blood containing a specific antigen is introduced into the bloodstream of a person who did not inherit that same antigen, the resulting immune response can result in serious or even fatal transfusion reactions. Blood banks minimize this risk by performing rigorous testing on donor and recipient blood (called *type and crossmatch*) to ensure patients receive compatible blood.

The most common blood group system a phlebotomist will encounter is the ABO blood group system. The four blood types represented by this group are A, B, AB, and O. There are two antigens involved with this system (*A and B*). Type A blood contains the A antigen. Type B blood contains the B antigen. Type AB, the least common blood type, contains both A and B antigens. Type O, the most common blood type, contains neither A nor B antigens. In addition to a person's inherited ABO blood type, they also carry innate antibodies that will respond to the opposite blood type. For an individual with type A blood, they carry an antibody against type B (called *anti-B*). Type B carries *anti-A* antibodies. AB blood types do not have antibodies against either A or B antigens. O type carries both anti-A and anti-B antibodies. Transfusion of an incompatible blood type results in a violent reaction between the antibody and antigen that causes clumping (*agglutination*) and disintegration (*hemolysis*) of the donor blood within the bloodstream. This is often fatal; therefore, ABO blood type matching is critical to safe blood transfusion.

Along with the ABO blood type, the Rh (Rhesus) blood group is another system that must be considered when matching a donor and recipient blood. The Rh system involves a single antigen (*D antigen* or *Rh Factor*). When the Rh Factor is present in an individual's blood, they are considered *Rh positive* (Rh+). When an individual's red blood cells do *not* contain the Rh factor, their blood is considered *Rh negative* (Rh-). Over three-quarters of the population is Rh+. When an Rh- individual is exposed to Rh+ blood, there is a delayed sensitization that occurs outside of the bloodstream. This means that initial exposure does not result in a reaction, but any future exposure could result in a reaction.

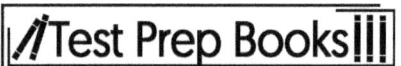

In addition to blood transfusion exposure, Rh factor incompatibility can also occur during pregnancy. If an Rh- mother is carrying an Rh+ fetus, they are at risk for being exposed to the fetal blood cells (often during childbirth) and becoming sensitized. Should this occur and the mother were to become pregnant with another Rh+ fetus, the mother's immune system can begin to attack the fetus' red blood cells due to the fact the Rh factor is able to cross the placental barrier. To minimize this risk, Rh- mothers are routinely given Rh immune globulin (RhIg; Rhogam) at specific times during the pregnancy as well as shortly after birth to rid the mother's body of any Rh+ cells that may have passed from the baby to the mother.

Phlebotomy-Related Vascular Anatomy

Safe and effective phlebotomy requires a deep understanding of phlebotomy-related vascular anatomy. This knowledge helps the phlebotomist differentiate between veins, arteries, and capillaries when selecting a site for blood sampling. Awareness of the anatomical structures that make up the vascular system and surrounding anatomy also helps phlebotomists choose an ideal and safe location to perform a blood draw. Lastly, recognition of external landmarks guide phlebotomists when they are identifying the most appropriate location for their draws.

All veins (except for the pulmonary vein) carry lower pressured, unoxygenated blood toward the heart. This means they tend to have thinner walls, are a darker bluish color, and are easier to pierce with a needle during venipuncture. This also means that veins can be easily compressed (occluded) with the fingers or a tourniquet. Arteries, on the other hand, carry higher pressured, oxygenated blood that is being pumped away from the heart. These vessels must have thicker walls to withstand the higher pressure from the pumping heart, and this pumping action also creates the pulse that can be felt when one gently presses against (palpates) an artery. Capillaries are much tinier vascular structures that carry blood from the arteries and away to the veins, and they contain a mixture of unoxygenated and oxygenated blood that facilitates exchange of nutrients and waste within the body's tissues and cells.

In adult patients, veins are the most common blood vessel used for obtaining blood specimens for testing. The ideal venipuncture site to start with is the area known as the *antecubital fossa*. This area is located on the inside (anterior) bend of the elbow. There are several larger veins, known as the *AC veins*, that run close to the surface of the skin and are easier to identify and access. The *cephalic vein* is located in the *lateral* forearm, which is the outside portion that aligns with the thumb when the palm is facing up. The *median cubital vein* is the vein that tends to be located near the middle toward the portion of the forearm that aligns with the pinky finger when the palm is turned up. The *basilic vein* is a vein that is situated on the most medial portion of the antecubital fossa.

The positioning of the AC veins varies from person to person, but phlebotomists most often encounter two general patterns: The *H*-shaped pattern and *M*-shaped pattern. The *H*-shaped pattern is present in almost three-quarters of the population. Individuals with this anatomical pattern have a median cubital vein that runs across from the cephalic vein (lateral side) up to the basilic vein (medial side) just below the crease of the elbow. For this presentation, the median cubital vein tends to be the preferred choice for venipuncture as it is stable, larger, and more superficial (close to the skin). The cephalic vein is the next best choice for venipuncture with this pattern but can be more difficult to palpate than the median cubital vein. Lastly, though the basilic vein can be more easily palpated, this is the least recommended choice as it is more likely to move and is near the medial cutaneous nerve and brachial artery.

For the quarter of individuals with an *M*-shaped pattern, the median antebrachial vein runs up the center of the forearm and branches out to the median cephalic and the median basilic veins just below

Core Knowledge

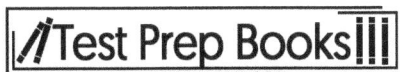

the elbow crease. The median cephalic vein branches out to connect with the lateral cephalic vein near the crease of the elbow, and the median basilic vein branches out to connect with the basilic vein just above the elbow. For this arrangement, the antebrachial vein at the center of the forearm tends to be the best choice because it is more anchored and farther from the brachial artery or nerves. This makes this site safer and typically less painful. The median cephalic vein is the second-best choice as it is still farther from nerves and the brachial artery but can be less successful due to its length and proximity to valves. The median basilic vein is the last option for this pattern due to its proximity to the major nerve branches and the brachial artery.

The veins of the forearms tend to be less superficial and become smaller as they approach the hands. The forearms are not an ideal first choice for venipuncture due to these factors. The veins of the hands are more superficial, which can make them an alternative only if the AC veins are not accessible. This location must be used cautiously because the veins of the hands are much smaller, and this area tends to be much more painful for venipuncture. Also, the veins of the hands tend to be less anchored, making them more susceptible to rolling. Ideal hand veins for venipuncture should be straight and should bounce back when palpated. The wrist should be avoided due to its proximity to major nerves and risk for injury and pain to the patient.

Cardiovascular System

The *cardiovascular system* uses the heart and blood vessels to circulate blood to the tissues and organs of the body. Proper function of the cardiovascular system is necessary for adequate supply and flow of blood throughout the body. Blood circulation facilitates oxygen and carbon dioxide exchange, nutrient delivery, and waste disposal. It also assists with temperature regulation, coagulation, and infection control.

The heart is the pump of the cardiovascular system. This muscular organ is situated slightly left of center in the thoracic cavity, and it contains four cavities (*chambers*) which synchronously expand and contract to facilitate movement of blood throughout the cardiovascular system. The upper two chambers of the heart are called the *atria* and receive blood from the peripheral circulation. The lower chambers are called the *ventricles* and deliver blood back into circulation. The upper and lower chambers are separated by one-way valves called the left atrioventricular valve (left AV; also called *bicuspid* or *mitral valve*) and the right atrioventricular valve (right AV; also called *tricuspid valve*) that ensure blood continues to pump in the right direction. The left and right chambers of the heart are also divided by a *septum* that prevents blood from passing from left to right. Additionally, the *right semilunar valve* (or pulmonic valve) is positioned between the right ventricle and pulmonary artery and prevents blood from returning to the ventricle when it relaxes. The left *semilunar valve* (or *aortic valve*) is positioned between the aorta and the left ventricle to prevent blood from returning to the left ventricle when it relaxes.

Specialized electrical nodes send timed impulses to the highly conductive cardiac cells and bring the cardiac pump to life. The *sinoatrial (SA) node,* positioned above the right atrium, sends the initial signal through both atria and causes them both to contract and squeeze blood through the AV valves and into the ventricles. This signal sets the pace of the heart pump, which is why the SA node is often referred to as the "pacemaker" of the heart. The electrical impulse then travels through the *internodal pathway* (located within the wall of the right atrium) and into the *AV node* within the bottom of the right atrial septum. The AV node serves to slow the electrical impulse long enough to allow the atria to fully contract before sending the signal through the *AV bundle* (*bundle of His*). The bundle of His, located in the septum at the top of the ventricles, sends the impulse through the ventricles and causes them to contract, which pushes blood through the semilunar valves and into circulation. The atria and ventricles relax briefly before the cycle begins again. Each cycle represents a single heartbeat and occurs an average of 60–100 times per minute for most individuals. This electrical pathway is also what is recorded during an electrocardiogram (EKG or ECG) procedure.

Hemostasis and Coagulation Process

Hemostasis is a term that refers to the body's ability to stop bleeding after injury. The body must achieve this without disrupting the rest of the circulatory system in the process. One of the main ways it accomplishes this is through the process of coagulation. *Coagulation* is the process by which the body converts liquid blood to a semisolid *clot*.

Coagulation occurs with the assistance of a collection of proteins known as *coagulation factors*. Coagulation factors can be further categorized as enzyme precursors, cofactors, and substrates. *Enzyme precursors* are proteins that activate to become *enzymes* (proteins that can cause chemical reactions with other substances). *Cofactors* are a type of protein that further speed the chemical reactions caused by enzymes involved in the coagulation process. *Substrates* are the substances that interact with and change in response to exposure to enzymes. *Fibrinogen* (factor I) is the main coagulation substrate and interacts with *thrombin* (IIa), which is the main coagulation enzyme. The result of this interaction is *fibrin*, which is the protein fiber that creates a mesh-like reinforcement for blood clots.

Within the human body (*in vivo*), coagulation cascades occur as a complex interaction between various processes. The *extrinsic pathway*, which occurs in the tissues rather than the vascular system, initiates the coagulation cascade when tissues are damaged. There is a release of *tissue factor* (TF, factor III) from the site of injury that results in the conversion of fibrinogen to fibrin (a fibrous protein that provides a mesh-like structural support to clots). Within the bloodstream, there is also an *intrinsic pathway* that occurs in response to injury. Initial intrinsic response is constriction of the blood vessel (called *vasoconstriction*) to limit blood loss. A sticky coagulation factor (von Willebrand factor or vWF) is released from damaged endothelial cells and causes platelets to begin sticking to the damaged tissue. This causes platelets to partially activate to signal for fibrin delivery. Thrombin produced by the extrinsic pathway leads to more platelet clumping (aggregation) and a *platelet plug* forms on the damaged tissue. This process takes approximately 30 seconds, and if this is a very minor injury the endothelial cells will secrete *inhibitor proteins* that stop the coagulation cascade.

If an injury is more severe, these cascades will receive much stronger stimulus to continue. The delivery of fibrin and thrombin will persist until a stable blood clot forms. Natural inhibitors circulating within the blood help to keep these coagulation factors from migrating to other areas of the body. Additionally, the process of *fibrinolysis* (breakdown of fibrin) occurs to dissolve clots within the vessels and remove blood clots once they are no longer needed by the body. In a healthy system, the body maintains a balance between thrombosis (clot formation) and fibrinolysis (clot breakdown).

In the lab setting, *in vitro* (test tube) coagulation is observed in the preparation and handling of blood specimens. If a blood sample is placed into a test tube that does not contain anticoagulant, the specimen will clot via the intrinsic pathway as the blood cells contact clot activating substances or the tube itself. Extrinsic coagulation of blood specimens can also occur if tissue injury from venipuncture results in tissue factor being drawn into the needle.

Impact of Pre-Analytical Errors on Test Results

The *pre-analytical* phase of testing involves all activities from the time an order is placed to the time the specimen begins being tested. This interval is impactful to the testing process because there are so many variables and opportunities for error that can impact the validity of test results. This is particularly concerning because physicians rely on test results to make decisions regarding patient diagnoses and treatment decisions. Prevention of pre-analytical errors is, therefore, critical to patient safety.

One area where errors can occur is with patient identification. Proper identification is required for every patient and during each interaction. This includes initial verification of identity, validating that medical records and paper forms match, verifying (and correcting, if necessary) any errors within the medical record, and properly labeling all specimens. Errors in this area can mean that results are added to the wrong patient's medical record or that specimens are delayed or not processed at all. This can result in delays in care or medical errors.

It is also critically important to consider patient preparation factors that can impact test results. Hydration levels, for example, can impact certain test results. Dehydration reduces serum plasma levels, which impacts the concentration of certain blood components (e.g., RBC, electrolytes, enzymes, iron, coagulation factors). Too much hydration right before a lab draw can lead to decreased hemoglobin and can alter electrolyte levels. Food intake can also impact certain tests (e.g., cholesterol, triglycerides, glucose levels, liver enzymes, ammonia, urea, uric acid). For this reason, tests that can be impacted by food consumption will typically require patients to fast between 8–12 hours prior to specimen collection.

Some blood components (i.e., hormone levels) are susceptible to cyclical changes occurring daily (*diurnal*) or in 24-hour (*circadian*) cycles. These tests will be ordered for a specified time, so it is important for the phlebotomist to complete these as close to the ordered time as possible to ensure test accuracy.

Patient medications can also alter lab results. Aside from expected and unexpected changes in lab results that can occur when taking medications, there are also cases where medications can interfere with certain lab tests. This can result in false increases or decreases. Drugs that can interfere with blood test results should be stopped between 4 and 24 hours before collection. Drugs that have the potential to impact urine test results should be held for 48–72 hours prior to collection.

Changes in patient position just prior to a blood draw can also result in inaccurate results for certain tests (e.g., protein-containing components, potassium, cholesterol, triglycerides, red blood cells). This occurs due to shifts in fluid in response to position change. A good practice is to have patients sit in the drawing chair while the phlebotomist reviews paperwork and orders prior to a draw to avoid any position-related errors. Additionally, advise patients not to pump their fist prior to venipuncture, as this can falsely increase potassium levels.

Improper draw techniques are a major area of concern for phlebotomists. Choosing the correct tube is critical to ensuring tests are valid and can be processed. Drawing labs in the correct order is also very important, because incorrect order of draw can result in specimen contamination from lab tube additives. This can result in hemolysis, invalid specimens, or inaccurate results. Underfilling or overfilling tubes can also lead to invalid specimens or inaccurate results. Leaving the tourniquet in place for too long can result in hemolysis, which occurs when red blood cell membranes rupture and release hemoglobin. Other potential causes of hemolysis include shaking tubes too hard when mixing,

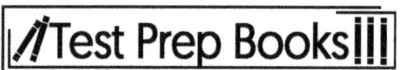

Core Knowledge

continuing to draw through a vein with a *hematoma* (blood that has leaked from the blood vessel and collected in the surrounding area), using excessive suction to collect blood specimen, or using a needle that is too small.

Preparation, storage, and transportation are additional factors to consider. For example, temperature and humidity extremes can impact the stability of specimens and can also impact the efficacy of lab equipment. Additionally, specimens travelling off-site need to be packaged and protected from extremes of temperature. This includes accounting for time delays and different climates, depending on how far the specimen will be travelling. Specimens must also be protected from physical damage during transportation.

Needlestick Safety and Prevention Act

Phlebotomy technicians and other healthcare staff work in environments where there is increased risk of exposure to bloodborne pathogens. The Occupational Safety and Health Administration (OSHA) recognized that in addition to general standards to protect workers against exposure, special consideration was needed to protect healthcare workers from needlestick injuries. In 2000, OSHA addressed this need by issuing the *Needlestick Safety and Prevention Act* as an amendment to their *Bloodborne Pathogens Standards* of 1991.

This amendment provided an expanded definition of *engineering controls* (safety practices and policies) related to sharps. Sharps safety controls include items such as sharps disposal systems, sharps equipped with safety mechanisms, needles that use internal or external sheathing mechanisms, and needleless devices. Within each of these categories of control are many different types of mechanisms and devices. They vary depending on type (e.g., scalpel, prefilled syringe, needle) as well as manufacturer.

The Needlestick Safety and Prevention Act also required employers to specifically address sharps safety within their bloodborne pathogen exposure plans. Employers are required to identify job categories that are at risk for exposure to bloodborne pathogens and sharps injuries. Once identified, employers must involve these at-risk groups to identify and implement additional sharps safety controls. Employers must specify protocols for handling sharps injuries, provide and track staff education related to sharps safety, and document all sharps injuries.

Documentation and Reporting Requirements

Any activity performed within the healthcare setting must be well-documented. Documentation is used as a tool to promote continuity (consistency in care) and to further communication within the interdisciplinary team. It is also used to create an ongoing timeline of care for each patient. Documentation is used by organizations to monitor and improve business and healthcare practices, and administrators will use documentation to evaluate performance of individuals and teams. Healthcare documentation can also be used for legal and regulatory purposes.

The patient medical record is one of the main sources of documentation performed by a phlebotomist. This record contains a chronological account of a patient's health and healthcare. This information is confidential and is federally protected by the Health Insurance Portability and Accountability Act of 1996 (HIPAA). This means that there are limitations to who can view and document within a patient's medical record. This also means that phlebotomists are legally required to take action to protect the privacy of protected patient information (PPI). The Health Information Technology for Economic and Clinical Health Act of 2009 is another law that impacted medical care by pushing healthcare organizations to

Core Knowledge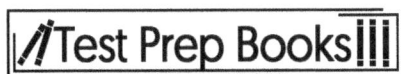

utilize electronic systems to document patient care. The goal of this law was to enhance healthcare outcomes by increasing continuity and communication between providers.

Any entry made into a patient's medical record must be complete, factual, and clear. The type of record-keeping system differs between organizations, and there can be specific documentation requirements per facility. Patient care documentation, at a minimum, should always include items such as specimen(s) collected, test(s) performed, anatomical site used for collection (if applicable), the date and time of collection, and how the patient looked when they arrived and left. Additional documentation of communications and unusual occurrences or adverse events (e.g., fainting, reporting nausea) is also required to maintain a complete and accurate medical record.

Other examples of documentation and reporting occur within the healthcare and lab settings. For example, any medical or diagnostic equipment used for storage and processing of specimens (e.g., centrifuge, refrigerators, freezers, heat block) require detailed logs of maintenance, temperatures, and incidents involving those items. Organizations also use data and reporting to track quality control issues and form quality improvement plans for labs or areas within a hospital setting.

Organizations utilize internal, confidential forms such as incident reports or performance improvement plans. Incident reports are used to document occurrences that are considered a potential risk for an organization (e.g., falls, workplace violence, hospital-acquired infection, injury, medical errors). These are not part of the medical record but are used internally to track, manage, and respond to these types of events. Performance improvement plans are a tool that managers and administrators use to track and address performance issues with employees.

Verbal and Non-Verbal Communication

Spoken dialog is a common form of communication that phlebotomists encounter. Spoken conversations can occur with providers, colleagues, patients, family, or administration. This type of encounter involves both verbal and non-verbal communication. Effective spoken communication involves taking turns sending (speaking) and receiving (listening). Part of ensuring accurate information exchange is through the *feedback loop* where both parties clarify or confirm their understanding of what the other party has said. When engaging in spoken dialog with others, it is important to use language that is easy to understand for the individual, be considerate of cultural differences, and speak clearly and concisely. Additionally, being aware of one's own body language as well as paying attention to the body language of the other party can help with accurate exchanges of information.

A critical part of spoken dialog is active listening. This means that the listener is using their energy to try to understand what the speaker is saying, and they are also communicating to the speaker that they are interested in understanding what the speaker has to say. Use of non-verbal body language (e.g., facing the speaker, making eye contact, leaning toward the speaker, displaying an engaged facial expression, keeping arms uncrossed) can help to communicate ongoing interest and engagement in the conversation. Additionally, using feedback by summarizing what the speaker said or asking clarifying questions is another way to demonstrate active listening.

Written communication is another form of communication that a phlebotomist can encounter. Unlike verbal dialog, this form of communication is asynchronous, meaning that it may not be sent and received at the same time. Another major difference with written communication is the lack of non-verbal input. This can result in potential conflict and misunderstanding if the receiver misinterprets the intent of the sender's words. It is critical for phlebotomists to utilize professional written communication that avoids biased, emotional, casual, or offensive language. Written communications should be grammatically correct. It is also recommended that written communication be used cautiously when introducing sensitive topics such as complaints or criticisms, as there is higher risk for misinterpretation and misunderstanding. Lastly, it is important to remember that written communication can be permanently retrievable.

Patient Characteristics Impacting Communication

As a phlebotomist develops skills to effectively communicate with patients, it is important to consider patient characteristics that impact communication. Various social, cultural, financial, and educational factors can influence patient-phlebotomist interactions. For example, a patient may speak a different language than the phlebotomist. An effective strategy for managing this communication barrier is to obtain a medical interpreter. Also, cultural differences can influence things like eye contact, who communicates with the phlebotomist, the environmental setup (such as maintaining modesty and privacy), or even who is permitted to care for the patient. Limited education levels and financial history can influence a patient's communication because they impact childhood brain development, language and communication development, and access to information. For this reason, it is recommended that phlebotomists speak simply and clearly to patients, taking care to avoid the use of medical terms (jargon) during interactions.

Patient-specific circumstances can also impact communication with the phlebotomist. Stress from life circumstances can have a dramatic impact on emotions, focus, comprehension, and rationality. Therefore, when a phlebotomist cares for a patient who is showing signs of potential stress or anxiety (e.g., irritability, impatience, difficulty focusing, erratic behaviors), they can show compassion and take steps to assist the patient by remaining calm and reassuring them. Another patient-specific circumstance that can impact communication would be a relational issue (personality difference, conflict, patient preference) with the phlebotomist or another caregiver.

Health-related factors have a major impact on communication as well. Comprehension is highly influenced by the patient's emotional state. Stress, fear, anxiety, grief, and anger are all examples of emotional states that change the way a person interacts with others. Patients being seen in the healthcare setting are susceptible to these states, as they are often going through difficult medical and life situations. Fear of medical professionals or fear related to procedures (e.g., fear of needles) are common. Symptoms such as pain and fatigue can also make it challenging for patients to communicate effectively. Treatment medications or the use of illicit substances can influence a patient's level of consciousness and make communication more challenging. Visual impairment, hearing impairment, and speech impairment are additional factors to consider. Medical diagnoses such as neurological disorders (e.g., stroke, brain injury), mental health disorders (e.g., anxiety, depression, schizophrenia), and intellectual disabilities can also significantly impact comprehension and communication. For individuals who are unable to make their own medical decisions, whether this be due to age or incapacitation, there should always be a caregiver or medical power of attorney present to consent on their behalf and participate in communication with the healthcare team.

Professionalism

Phlebotomists are individuals trusted to perform skilled procedures for patients within the healthcare system. As a recognized healthcare professional, phlebotomists have a responsibility to maintain that trust. This is achieved through the embodiment of the ethical and technical standards held by the phlebotomy profession.

Appearance is the first opportunity for phlebotomists to communicate professionalism. This begins with maintaining proper personal hygiene and grooming practices. Be mindful of any strong or potentially offensive odors (e.g., perfume/cologne, body odor). Clothing or uniforms should be conservative and follow any policies imposed by the employer. Generally, uniforms should be clean and free from wrinkles or stains.

Attitudes and behaviors are another dimension of professionalism. Some of these qualities include confidence, honesty, dependability, and consistency. It is also important for phlebotomists to approach their work and patients with compassion. Compassion helps the phlebotomist remain sensitive to the needs and feelings of others while performing their work. Another trait associated with professionalism is self-motivation, which refers to an individual's ability to complete their work with minimal or no prompting from others. Self-motivated individuals will also ask questions and seek resources and additional information if they are unsure or need clarification on a task.

Ethical Standards Applicable to the Practice of Phlebotomy

Ethics are principles that guide behaviors and decisions. Due to the relative unpredictability of daily life, ethical standards provide a foundation for individuals to make consistent choices based on moral principles. Within phlebotomy, there are several overarching ethical standards that govern practice.

Confidentiality is an ethical principle that is concerned with maintaining patient privacy. Protection of confidential patient information is one significant area where this principle comes into play. This involves keeping the electronic medical record system safe and secure by not sharing passwords and logging off before walking away from a computer. It also includes not providing patient information to unauthorized personnel and being discreet with patient specimens. Physical privacy can be protected by knocking before entering a room and closing doors or pulling privacy curtains prior to performing procedures.

Informed consent is another ethical principle that governs phlebotomy practice. Informed consent is a requirement that patients must be informed about and provide consent *prior* to any medical procedure (including the obtaining of patient information). Phlebotomists must receive permission via implied, verbal, or written consent prior to performing any procedure. For individuals who cannot consent for themselves (e.g., children, individuals with intellectual disability) an authorized medical representative must consent on the patient's behalf. Additionally, patients or medical representatives have the explicit right to refuse medical procedures at *any* time prior to or during the procedure. If a patient has consented to a procedure and then revokes their consent, the phlebotomist must immediately stop the procedure and complete any necessary documentation of the events.

Integrity is yet another ethical standard that guides phlebotomists in their work. *Integrity* is a broad term that involves maintaining honesty, competency, and professionalism. Examples of integrity include being truthful during interactions, maintaining knowledge and skills level, reporting any errors (and taking action to correct and prevent them in future), and acting with respect for oneself as well as their organization and profession. This principle also involves maintaining the highest standards of handling and processing of specimens to prevent errors.

Nonmaleficence (seeking to do no harm) is an additional ethical standard that phlebotomists should seek to uphold. This standard is concerned with the promotion of health and safety of others. In phlebotomy, this includes using Universal Precautions, maintaining proper hand hygiene, and using safe practices when performing procedures. This also involves protecting the safety of self and others

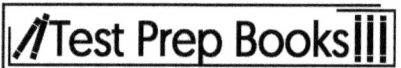

through maintaining clear pathways, promptly containing and cleaning spills, and adhering to all safety and health guidelines within the workplace. Additionally, it involves taking care of one's health and taking measures to prevent the spread of infection (e.g., using personal protective equipment, staying home when sick).

Safety and Compliance

Adhere to Regulations Regarding Workplace Safety

Phlebotomist technicians are required to understand, use best practices of, and follow guidelines on workplace safety. Biological hazards are determined, regulated, and enforced by the Occupational Safety and Health Administration (OSHA). Their guidelines are published under Title 29 of the Federal Code of Regulations. Occupational safety in healthcare that affects laboratory and phlebotomy staff is published as Standard 1910.

OSHA regulations and standards require employers to provide their staff with education and instruction on real and potential hazards in the workplace. There are over 500,000 workers employed within laboratories across the United States who are exposed to risks from physical, radioactive, chemical, biological, and occupational stress. Phlebotomist technicians' job duties include working in direct patient care; drawing blood and other potentially infectious body fluids and tissues; and storing, transporting, and using equipment to perform testing. The goal is to maintain safety for both patients and staff and to perform the work in a manner that protects specimens against compromise that could alter results.

The responsibility for ensuring that laboratory workers, including phlebotomists, are provided appropriate and sufficient training falls on the management and supervision of these departments. Competencies are used to test the effectiveness of the education and provide evidence that the employee was held accountable for complying with the regulations. Employees who do not follow the standards that are set by OSHA may face consequences that affect their careers. This may include requiring additional training, disciplinary action, and, depending on the severity of the insubordination, possible loss of employment.

Phlebotomy technicians' actions and care techniques are paramount to success in providing safety for patients, themselves, and staff.

Employers have an obligation to provide their employees with an environment, tools, and protective equipment that keep the employee free from exposure to hazards that may cause harm or death. Healthcare facilities are encouraged by regulating bodies to develop standardized policies and procedures based on the guidelines and laws for employees to refer to and follow. Clearly defining and setting policies of practices such as organizational operations, methods of sterilization, safe handling and disposal, biohazard decontamination and disposal, and testing procedures create strong safety protocols. These protocols must be updated on a regular basis to align with research, best practices, and any new guidance; be accessible for staff to use for reference; and be widely educated on. Failure to adhere to regulations set by OSHA and other regulatory entities can result in fines, loss of licensure, and a decrease in safe patient and employee outcomes.

Safe practices and commitment to a culture of safety are necessary to provide an environment that mitigates risk and controls operations involving biohazardous work. OSHA enforces this within their Standards by requiring a Chemical Hygiene Officer position to be assigned as well as keeping a current Chemical Hygiene Plan. Other Standards cover the safe handling of, exposure response to, and protection from bloodborne pathogens; personal protective equipment use; hand protection; eye and face protection; and control of hazardous energy.

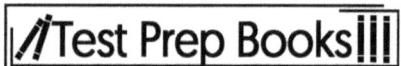

Adhere to Regulations Regarding Operational Standards

(e.g., the Joint Commission, Clinical and Laboratory Standards Institute, Center for Disease Control)

Laboratories are regulated and must meet the minimum standards set by multiple industry leaders such as the Joint Commission (TJC), Centers for Disease Control (CDC), and the Clinical and Laboratory Standards Institute (CLSI). These entities provide guidance for national and international laboratory standards. These are aimed at improving patient safety and care, developing requirements for laboratory accreditation, and setting proficiency benchmarks.

TJC alone accredits 1500 organizations across the United States including hospital ambulatory laboratories, point-of-care testing sites, physician offices, toxicology labs, and histology and pathology sites. The standards for accreditation are published and distributed as the *Comprehensive Accreditation Manual for Laboratory and Point-of-Care Testing*. Laboratories must be inspected and accredited by TJC every two years.

The Joint Commission also partners with the American Society for Clinical Pathology (ASCP) to improve quality outcomes, support laboratory transparency, and elevate the profession in development and leadership. The program Leading Laboratories is their joint effort to set gold standards and recognize laboratories that meet and exceed the standards.

The CDC has established several programs that support the operations of the labs that perform over one billion laboratory tests every year in the United States. The CDC provides information about proficiency testing, reference materials, training, and guidelines and may provide consultation at request. All of these resources are voluntary for the facility or laboratory to participate in or use, and the majority are offered free of charge.

Strategic frameworks established by the CDC are aimed at developing clinical laboratories that have strong operational foundations. The Division of Laboratory Systems' goal is to prepare labs to be technically capable via training, quality analysis, reporting, and best practices of safety. Patient-centered care is at the forefront of the mission to reduce diagnostic errors through connections with other facilities, subject matter experts, and multidisciplinary teams. Innovation is encouraged through the use of support tools, mobile apps, and training delivered via virtual reality settings.

The first complete and comprehensive set of competencies unique to laboratory employees was established by the Association of Public Health Laboratories (APHL). Competencies are observable and measurable assessments of the knowledge, abilities, and skills that are required for individuals to perform work safely, accurately, and effectively. The CDC/APHL Competency Guidelines include fifteen competencies that cover a wide range of topics. These are rated by skill level: beginner, competent, proficient, and expert. These competencies are also categorized with general domains covering the largest amount of information. Quality management, ethics, leadership, security, communication, emergency management and response, and workforce development are covered by the base domain. The next domain is cross-cutting technical that encompasses safety, surveillance, informatics, and general laboratory practices. The last domain narrows in scope to areas of specialization such as microbiology, chemistry, research, and bioinformatics.

The Clinical and Laboratory Standards Institute (CLSI) is a not-for-profit organization that sets global standards for laboratory quality, safety, and efficiency in specimen testing processes. Clinical laboratory technologists, scientists, and volunteer subject matter experts have contributed to the development of these standards through collaboration and consensus of their knowledge, regulatory mandates, and specialized skill sets. Membership, services, and trainings are available on a fee basis. There are a limited number of webinars that are available for free on the website. Free webinars such as *Quality Management: Approaches to Reducing Errors at the Point of Care*, *Planning for Laboratory Operations During a Disaster*, and *Protection of Laboratory Workers from Occupationally Acquired Infections* are a few of the selections that can be found on the CLSI website.

Adhere to HIPAA Regulations Regarding Protected Health Information

In 1996, the Health Insurance Portability and Accountability Act (HIPAA) put safeguards into place that protect the rights of a patient's health information that is accessed by certain types of organizations, entities, and individuals. These Covered Entities (CEs) and Business Entities (BEs) include health care providers, health plans, and employees or contracted individuals that work for CEs.

The type of information that is protected by HIPAA may be defined as any and all health information that may relate to an individual's current, past, or future physical health, mental health, health condition, or the payment for the provision of healthcare for such. The regulation is also expanded to any uniquely identifiable patient information that is contained within the health information record. Health information that must be protected is referred to as Protected Health Information (PHI). PHI is not limited to that obtained from the Electronic Health Record but may be any patient health information that is on a computer, paper, or other media.

There are three rules that are the center of the regulations formed within HIPAA: the Privacy Rule, the Security Rule, and the Breach Notification Rule. The Privacy Rule protects the privacy of health information that is individual and identifiable. The Security Rule is the set of regulations and laws that provide the national standard for securing PHI. The Breach Notification Rule sets the requirements for reporting noncompliance. The responsibilities and requirements for training related to the HIPAA Privacy Rule and the HIPAA Security Rule are set forth in 45 CFR § 164.530(b)(1) and 45 CFR § 164.308(a)(5) respectively. The compliance has been loosely left to be determined by the CEs and states that each member of the workforce must have initial training in a reasonable amount of time from the start date of employment with the training being documented.

Patients must be informed of how a healthcare entity and their staff intend to use and disclose their health information. The patient must be provided with a Notice of Privacy Practices (NPP) upon their initial visit, and this document must be updated. The notice must state the duties to protect privacy, provide the NPP, and abide by the terms contained within. The notice must describe patients' legal rights, including the right to complain to the healthcare organization or provider as well as to the US Department of Health and Human Services (HHS). Points of contact for complaints are to be clearly stated in the notice.

Adhere to Scope of Practice and Comply with Ethical Standards

Scope of practice defines the role limitations and responsibilities that a professional in that field must adhere to. These are set in place to facilitate safe practices, prevent medical malpractice, and guide practice based on profession, education, training, and experience. Adhering to the scope legally and ethically protects the phlebotomist from overstepping professional boundaries and mitigates the risk of harm to self, patients, and coworkers. The patient, above all, must have their best interests protected.

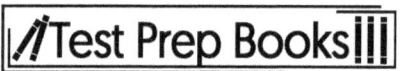

Safety and Compliance

Scope of practice may vary depending on the state that the phlebotomist is in and should be reviewed along with healthcare facility policy and procedure.

Phlebotomists may be exposed to patient, family, and healthcare situations that are ethically challenging. The patient must always be respected as a human and their dignity maintained. The patient's dignity and privacy can be protected by ensuring that HIPAA regulations are followed, sensitive tests and results are kept confidential and are not discussed except by the responsible healthcare provider, and that any ethical concern is escalated through the chain of command and/or referred to an ethics committee for review.

Perform Quality Control for Laboratory Equipment

Laboratory quality controls are aimed at preventing errors and delays, limiting the need for repeat tests, and promoting safe equipment and material usage and storage. These controls must be completed timely and regularly to ensure that equipment and tests are able to run accurately and as expected.

A system is beneficial to monitor and collect the data for the quality control test results. Phlebotomists trained to use equipment, collect samples, and run tests must learn and maintain competency in quality monitoring. Aspects that must be standardized, adhered to, and validated regularly include collection, handling, methods, and processes of following policy. Staff must document the results and report any deviations from the expected normal control test results. The Clinical Laboratory Improvement Amendments of 1988 (CLIA) developed stringent quality testing standards which include maintaining a process for performing a test and reporting the results, performing calibration checks at least every six months, and assaying at minimum two levels of control materials each day.

Quality control measures that are standard to ensure consistent reproducibility of results for laboratory equipment include checks for testing equipment such as analyzers (particle and moisture) and spectrophotometers. Microscopy and imaging equipment such as optical and electronic microscopes are assessed for proper function. Temperature controls must be run on incubators, autoclaves, freezers, and refrigeration systems to prevent contamination, ensure there is no hazardous material exposure to patients, and affirm the integrity of reagents, samples, and cultures.

Perform Quality Control for CLIA-Waived Tests

Certain tests have been deemed safe and low-risk for home use, including tests that are not utilized for medical decision-making and some point-of-care tests. Tests that are considered CLIA-waived meet the criteria that they have a small window of error and that any erroneous results do not carry high risks. Any QC requirements are not specifically identified by CLIA and are left to the discretion of best practice or the manufacturer's directions.

Some tests that are included in this category include dipstick or tablet reagent analysis, urine pregnancy tests, blood glucose monitoring devices, certain hemoglobin and hematocrit tests, all qualitative color comparing pH monitoring of fluid other than blood, and cholesterol monitoring.

Identify and Dispose of Sharps and Biohazards

Safety measures are necessary to prevent exposure to biohazards when working with blood and other biohazardous materials. Phlebotomists are exposed to and actively use sharp instruments including needles, scalpels, auto-injectors, lancets, and pipettes. Phlebotomists are also at risk for contact with broken glass. Sharps waste and needle disposal procedure is a requirement for employers to establish. Policy must provide safe practice standards that include safety engineered devices. Lack of adherence to infection prevention and bloodborne safety measures result in poor patient outcomes, staff disengagement, and loss of trust.

Phlebotomy and laboratory staff require sufficient training and competencies to ensure that training includes best practices in safe disposal methods and preventing sharp injuries. This should be done at the start of employment and revisited at least annually.

Topics that must be covered include blood spillage clean up, use of personal protective equipment (PPE), and appropriate sharps waste disposal. Sharps containers must be plentiful and accessible in areas where blood and specimens are obtained. FDA approved containers are recommended as these have safeguards to prevent punctures, leaks, and overfilling. Any container should be easily identifiable with a clear, legible label.

Any container that has been filled must be removed from the healthcare facility for transport and disposal at a medical waste disposal facility. State regulations dictate disposal rules, but facilities are typically required to remove waste within thirty days.

Follow Exposure Control Plans in the Event of Occupational Exposure

Exposure control plans provide employees with a protocol to follow should an adverse event occur. These events are typically bloodborne pathogen related, but may include radioactive, chemical, or inhalation hazards.

Material Safety Data Sheets (MSDS) must be readily available for employees and have unrestricted access, regardless of digital or paper form. An MSDS contains information regarding the use, safety precautions, and emergency response for materials that may be hazardous. When exposure to a chemical occurs, these must be referred to for appropriate steps to prevent harm or an adverse effect. Exposure to bloodborne pathogens may be through direct contact, indirect contact, or respiratory droplet transmission.

Exposure to bloodborne pathogens requires following specific steps for immediate action to protect oneself. Whenever a sharps injury occurs, the area should be flushed with water and any wound cleaned with soap and water or a skin disinfectant, when available. Any concern of or actual exposure must be reported immediately to the supervisor. Treatment protocols for injuries that may involve exposure to HBV, HCV, or HIV are available from CDC at the Clinicians' Post Exposure Prophylaxis Hotline (PEPline) at 888-448-4911.

Post-exposure prophylactic treatment is recommended to start immediately and should never be postponed.

Follow Transmission-Based Precautions

Transmission-based precautions are dictated by the method of spread of the identified microorganism. For microbes spread through touch, contact precautions require gloves and gowns.

A surgical mask is required for droplet precautions.

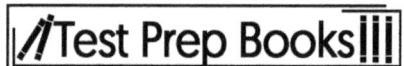

Airborne precautions are utilized for pathogens such as COVID-19 and tuberculosis infections. In addition to gloves and a gown, an N-95 respirator mask with fit testing is essential to prevent exposure. Facilities are advised to provide negative pressure rooms that have the filtering capability to exchange air six to twelve times per hour.

It is important to note that these are the minimal recommendations; PPE should be chosen based on critical thinking and identified risk via assessment of the environment, task to be completed, and patient presentation. Anytime the phlebotomist expects to contact bodily secretions, eye protection and a mask are necessary.

Follow Standard Precautions Regarding Personal Protective Equipment

Standard precautions provide the minimal standards set for protecting patients, providers, and visitors against the spread of pathogenic organisms. Covering the mouth and nose with a tissue when sneezing or coughing and performing proper hand hygiene is critical to prevent the spread of respiratory disease.

Personal protective equipment (PPE) provides a barrier between the phlebotomist and patient from disease-causing microorganisms. Gloves, lab coats/gowns/scrubs, masks, eye protection, and face shields protect from direct contact and any splash exposure to blood or other bodily fluids. Each day, the laboratory tech should inspect their hands for any abrasion or cuts and cover them with a waterproof adhesive dressing.

Needles, lancets, and sharps must be used only once and disposed of correctly. Follow healthcare facility policy and manufacturer guidelines for the use of built-in safety features, such as retractable needles or sheaths.

Use Aseptic and Infection Control Techniques Throughout the Phlebotomy Process

Aseptic technique is an infection control process that must be adhered to in order to prevent nosocomial spread within the healthcare system. This set of practices includes the use of sterile supplies, equipment, and protective barriers and following strict guidelines for environmental controls and contact with patients.

When preparing the patient, special attention must be given to the following: hand hygiene, patient skin preparation with appropriate antiseptic, drying time prior to skin puncture, and ensuring that a sterile field is always maintained during invasive and high infection risk procedures, such as venipuncture.

Follow Hand Hygiene Guidelines to Prevent the Spread of Infections

Hand hygiene has been proven to be one of the most effective methods of controlling infection spread through limiting the routes of transmission.

When performing hand hygiene, antibacterial soap coverage of all surfaces of the hands, between the fingers, and under the nails is followed with scrubbing that lasts for at least twenty seconds. Hands are then rinsed with running water and patted dry with a paper towel. Avoid touching the faucet directly to turn it off; instead, use the paper towel to turn off the faucet. Soap and water must be used in the presence of *C. difficile*.

When hand sanitizer is utilized, a dime-sized amount should be rubbed over the surface of hands and fingers before being air dried. Any medical-grade hand sanitizer must be at least 60 percent alcohol-

Safety and Compliance

based to be effective in eliminating microbial pathogens. Hand sanitizer is not effective when hands are visibly soiled.

It is advised that healthcare providers and staff with direct patient contact avoid wearing false nails or jewelry as the risk of colonization is higher. Crevices may harbor bacteria that are not easily washed away. Appropriate nail length is less than one quarter of an inch long. If rings are worn, care should be taken that there are no sharp edges that may cause tears or holes in gloves. It is highly recommended that phlebotomists avoid wearing rings or other hand jewelry.

Initiate First Aid and CPR When Necessary

Adverse effects that may occur related to phlebotomy include hematoma, unstopped bleeding, nerve injury, vasovagal response, and pain. First aid interventions that phlebotomists should be prepared for include using compression to stop bleeding, using proper site selection to prevent pain or nerve damage, and comforting and talking with a patient to prevent breath holding or bearing down which may cause dizziness or fainting. Nausea is another side effect that can occur; the phlebotomist should stop the procedure and provide the patient with an emesis bag in the case of nausea. The patient's nurse should be notified immediately of any complications.

In the hospital setting, when a patient has an emergent health crisis, such as cardiac or respiratory arrest, the phlebotomy technologist should first initiate a call for help. This may be via calling for assistance, pressing an emergency response button, or utilizing a mobile device. The patient should be quickly assessed for a Do Not Resuscitate (DNR) bracelet prior to initiating cardiopulmonary resuscitation (CPR). Phlebotomists may also be called to rapid response events to draw blood for vital labs to guide treatment.

Comply With Documentation and Reporting Requirements

With any documentation, the first step is to verify the correct patient. Documentation may vary according to facility but may include type of test, site of draw, amount of blood taken, number of attempts to access, patient's response, and type of dressing placed. In addition to this, the date, time, initials of the phlebotomist, and type of specimen should be noted in the chart and on the specimen container.

As a healthcare worker, phlebotomists must report any suspicion or witness of patient abuse. This should be reported to their immediate supervisor or the assigned nurse immediately. Occupational exposures must be reported as soon as safely possible. This includes any sharps injury, needlestick, or bodily fluid splash. Any other issues, such as drawing blood specimens from the incorrect patient or lab tube, utilizing unclean equipment, or patient injury must be reported as well.

Resources and Regulations Regarding Workplace Safety

OSHA standards and information directly related to hazards within the laboratory environment may be found on the OSHA website. Up-to-date publications on the standards and workplace safety information are available at the website, including guidance booklets, fact sheets, and videos that may be used for governance, education, and training purposes. It is important to note that not all states follow the federally set OSHA guidelines. There are twenty-eight state plans that are OSHA approved. These are separate entities from federally controlled OSHA that operate health and occupational safety agendas

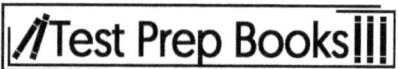

Safety and Compliance

that are required to meet or exceed the standards set forth by OSHA. Health care organizations and staff must have knowledge of the state in which they are practicing particular laws.

Operational Standards

As outlined previously, operational standards are set by organizations such as TJC, CDC, and CLSI. Healthcare facilities must align their standard operating procedures (SOPs) to encompass published minimum requirements and recommendations. SOPs are written to the unique challenges and qualities the specific lab encounters based on a risk assessment of the environment.

Employees must be knowledgeable and compliant with following the standards outlined in an SOP. Topics that are typically included are:

- **Engineering controls:** Employees must know how to operate and use safety features such as specialized ventilation including fume hoods and HEPA-filtered vacuum lines. For any equipment, emergent use of pressure relief devices, temperature control, and other preventative measures against hazards should be educated on. Other protective devices may include safe sharps devices, signage and knowledge of symbols, non-reactive containers and their use with certain chemicals, and protective coverings for surfaces such as plastic-lined cloths, pads, or bench paper.

- **Work practice controls:** Laboratory workers should be aware of their designated areas, maintenance and cleaning standards within those areas, and the lockout procedures in place during maintenance to prevent accidental function or power of equipment with servicing. Down-time and after-hour processes must be outlined with forms readily available. All preventative maintenance must be scheduled, completed, and tracked with logs to monitor compliance.

- **Emergency response:** Drills should be conducted to ensure continuous readiness is in place for emergencies. Emergent telephone numbers should be posted for ease of reference with education on who the emergency responders are. All staff must be able to identify location and use of fire alarms, fire extinguishers, eye wash stations, and decontamination showers. The drill should include all steps of the procedure for requesting assistance for different types of emergencies and how to respond if one does occur.

- **Accident procedures:** The majority of accidents within a lab are related to spills or exposure. Spill kits must be readily available with staff knowledge of how to use them. The emergency shutdown procedures should be recognized by all lab staff with emergency manuals available that detail the process to shut down and persons to notify when this does occur.

- **Monitoring:** All employees who are exposed to certain chemicals or radiation must be compliant with wearing sensors that detect unsafe levels over time. Other standard monitoring includes gas release, spills, temperature and pressure of machinery, and functioning and activation of alarms.

HIPAA Regulations

It is the responsibility of all healthcare professionals, including laboratory staff, to protect PHI. The phlebotomist and laboratory staff should have access to rules and regulations that are set at the federal

Safety and Compliance

and state levels and be sure to employ diligence in adhering to protecting patient health information. Failure to comply with HIPAA can result in civil and criminal penalties for individuals and companies, including fines of up to $1.5 million per violation category per year, personal fines of up to $250,000, and jail sentences of up to ten years.

Phlebotomists and laboratory staff frequently access the medical record, identify patients with unique patient identifiers, and have access to personal and private patient information records. At all times when accessing patient information, it should be on a secure electronic device with encryption and password protection. Staff must always use their own login information when accessing the patient health record and be sure to log out or secure their computer prior to exiting the area. Any paper information should be kept in a secure location that is locked when not in use. Patient information must be kept private; any conversations are on a need-to-know basis, and discussion of patient information should be limited to private areas where individuals who are not a part of the patient's care cannot overhear. It is important that a patient's consent is obtained prior to sharing with any other individual. Due to the nature of the laboratory processes, labels are a failure point for protecting patient information, as these can easily be dropped or left unattended. Proper storage and disposal of private patient information will assist with unintended breaches.

A significant vulnerability for a security breach of patient information comes from cybercrime. When accessing computers, only access the patient records that are part of assigned job duties. Be wary when opening any file or email that may be suspicious or from an outside source.

Manufacturer Recommendations for Laboratory Equipment

Laboratory equipment is sensitive and requires frequent safety checks and inspections. Laboratory equipment comes with hazards involving electricity, compressed gasses, high and low pressures, and extreme temperatures. Other hazards may involve mechanical risks from rotating, drilling, or cutting equipment. Strict adherence to the recommendations from the manufacturer should be followed to avoid accidents related to misuse or lack of maintenance. All manuals included with equipment should be accessible to staff and updated frequently. The recommendations for cleaning, calibration, inspection, maintenance, and monitoring must be used to create scheduled checks.

Quality Control and Assurance Procedures

Laboratory staff, including phlebotomists, that utilize equipment and devices to analyze specimens must be aware of the requirements for quality control testing and how to perform quality and assurance diagnostics. Manual testing and automated testing are both important parts of this process. Laboratory testing devices may require self-checks to be initiated at certain times of the day or week. Other tests may involve controls that require the laboratory staff to run a quality control test with aqueous controls, optical filters, or other devices. Always follow facility policy and the manufacturer's recommendations.

Guidelines Related to CLIA-Waived Tests

CLIA-waived tests are not strictly regulated as the probability of erroneous results is low, and these are used primarily for assessing and awareness rather than guiding medical treatment. Although quality and control measures are not regulated, care should be taken to follow the manufacturer's recommendations for storing, preparing, and performing the test, and the test should be discarded if it is expired.

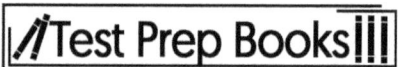

Safety and Compliance

If test results must be confirmed due to results being outside of parameters or if there is any question as to the validity of the test, follow facility policy for recollection and testing requirements. Any deviation or irregularity in the collection or testing process should be noted.

Ensure that the test has not expired prior to opening. Staff must follow hand hygiene, PPE usage, biohazard disposal, and cleaning procedures for these types of tests as with any other laboratory test.

Records should be maintained of types of CLIA-waived tests performed, the CLIA-waiver certificate, manufacturers' recommendations and specifications for each type of test performed at the facility, training log of employee competencies, and test storage area temperature log.

Bloodborne Pathogens Standard

There are over twenty bloodborne pathogens that are known to cause disease in humans, including hepatitis B, hepatitis C, and human immunodeficiency virus (HIV). These three are identified as being the biggest risk for healthcare workers who have a risk for exposure. Hepatitis B has the highest risk for transmission, ranging from 6 to 30 percent. Vaccinations are mandated to be made available for any healthcare worker with a high risk for occupational exposure to this bloodborne pathogen.

Employees may protect themselves from contracting this disease if exposure should occur by receiving the three-dose vaccination at the appropriate time intervals. Active participation in mandatory and refresher training, use of proper PPE, proper handling and disposal of sharps with care, usage of built-in safety devices, and following protocol should an exposure occur are standards that all phlebotomists should follow to keep safe.

Requirements Related to Biohazards

The phlebotomist must understand the requirements for safe handling and disposal of biohazards. All potentially biohazardous waste must be handled carefully to avoid cross-contamination between biohazardous waste and other materials. Biohazard signs must be placed with appropriate biosafety levels at all laboratory entrances that have potentially infectious material or human tissues.

Appropriate PPE is imperative to avoid the risk of exposure. This includes gloves, a gown, a face shield or goggles, and a mask. A full protective suit may be appropriate based on the exposure risk and the pathogen involved. Always follow facility guidelines for the type of PPE.

Separate containers that are specific to biohazardous waste must be utilized by the phlebotomist to prevent the spread of pathogens. Plastic bags with biohazard symbols may be used for solid waste. Caution should be used to fill bags only three-fourths of the way full.

All work surfaces must be cleansed with approved disinfectant at the end of each day. For biohazardous spills, immediate decontamination must be completed with the following steps:

1. Don PPE, including double gloves
2. If sharps or broken glass, use tongs and broom to remove
3. Use absorbent material to contain spill and remove once saturated
4. Use approved EPA registered disinfectant on and around edges of spill
5. Allow to sit for manufacturer's recommended time
6. Utilize paper towel to remove disinfectant
7. Dispose of paper towel and remove outer layer of gloves

Safety and Compliance

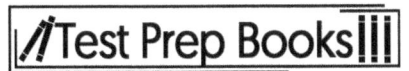

8. Place in biohazard bag, remove inner gloves, remove other PPE, then dispose
9. Wash hands with soap and water

Facility policy and manufacturers' recommendations must be followed for handling, cleaning, sanitizing, and sterilization of all equipment.

Strict adherence to no eating, drinking, chewing tobacco use, or applying cosmetics within the laboratory is required. Any use of such products must be outside of the laboratory setting, such as a breakroom.

Requirements for Sharps Disposal

Sharps disposal containers must be used to dispose of any used needles, blades, scalpels, lancets, or other objects that can puncture or slice. Any sharps must be placed into the disposal container immediately after use. Care should be taken not to compromise a used needle by breaking, removing, recapping, or bending prior to placing it into the container. A contaminated syringe with an attached needle may be placed in a container as one unit. Other contaminated materials, such as gauze, gloves, dressing, or other biohazardous waste, should be disposed of in appropriate bags.

Sharps disposal containers must be replaced once three-fourths full. Filling higher than this level increases the risk of exposure to a bloodborne pathogen and sharps injury.

Exposure Control Protocols

Protocols to limit exposure must be supported by evidence-based best practices. These include infection control practices. The phlebotomist must be informed and educated on the risk to self and patient. Control practices include engineering controls, work practice controls, PPE use, and following universal precautions. Policies should include who is responsible for determining and updating the plan, risk based on job classification, vaccination requirements and recommendations, training standards, PEP guidelines, root cause analysis of laboratory incidents related to exposure, and requirements for record keeping.

Standard Precautions

Standard precautions are the minimal infection control and prevention practices that should be used by all healthcare providers to avoid pathogen exposure and spread. PPE use should be based on the risk of activity and exposure. Hand hygiene and PPE use are utilized with the care of any patient regardless of health status.

Transmission Based Precautions

Transmission based precautions are initiated when a known pathogen is present. The phlebotomist must adhere to the required PPE and guidelines based on the known disease. This can include contact, droplet, or airborne spread.

Personal Protective Equipment

Personal protective equipment is the technical term for the supplies worn to protect employees from workplace injury or illness. Gloves, gowns, masks, and eye shields are the most common types of PPE in the healthcare environment. Employers are required to provide PPE and to ensure that proper training

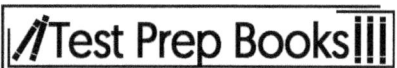

Safety and Compliance

is available. Training for this equipment should include how to put it on, where equipment is located, when it should be used, how it is removed, and proper disposal. PPE should be put on in the following order, depending on how much protection in needed:

- Gown
- Mask
- Eye wear
- Gloves

When wearing a gown, the opening is in the back, and it secures at the back of the neck and around the person's waist. The gown should be worn on top of the uniform or clothes and must cover all clothing from the neck down to the knees. A new gown should be worn every time the patient's room is entered and must be thrown away when leaving the room. This prevents contamination from spreading into hallways or other patients' rooms.

Masks are placed over the nose, mouth, and chin. First, pull apart the mask from top to bottom so that it will fit the face, and then place the top ridge on the bridge of the nose. This ridge is meant to conform over the nose, and it must be bent and squeezed to ensure a tight fit. Next, pull the lower edge of the mask under the chin. Tie the top ties on top of the head so that the ties go above the ears. Tie the lower ties behind the neck. As with any PPE, use a new mask when entering a room, and remove it when exiting. Fit-tested respirators, or N-95 masks, are placed in a similar way to regular masks, but the seal must be tighter. Education on the N-95 mask will occur during the fit-testing process.

Eye shields or goggles should cover the eyes, and they should not slip off when bending down. Some eyewear, such as glasses or goggles, are attached to a mask like a shield. When putting on gloves, make sure to pull them above the wrists and above the cuffs of the gown if one is worn.

Removing PPE occurs in this order:

- Gloves
- Goggles
- Gown
- Mask or respirator

Peel off one glove by pulling on the outside of the glove and folding it down. Hold the removed glove in the hand that is still gloved and use the exposed hand to slide the fingers under the cuff, peeling it off. Throw the gloves away in the proper trash. To remove eye protection, grab the sides of the eyewear and throw them away. Avoid touching the front of the eyewear, which is considered contaminated. When removing a gown, reach back and untie the ties. Pull the gown off inside out from behind the neck or back so that exposed hands are kept off of the outside and front of the gown. Once the gown is off, keep the clean, inside part of the gown on the outside and roll it up. Then dispose of the gown in the proper bin. Remove the mask last by untying the ties and not touching the front of the mask. When removing a respirator, or exiting a room in airborne precaution, it is important to close the door before taking the mask off. Handwashing must always be performed after disposing of PPE.

Hand Hygiene Guidelines

Phlebotomists are advised to follow strict hand hygiene policies from expert sources, as outlined previously. This includes washing or sanitizing hands before and after contact with a patient, prior to

Safety and Compliance

eating, and when visibly dirty. Hands should always be cleansed at the start of a shift. While wearing gloves, exposure to blood, after performing micro-puncture, or the use of a non-vacuum-based blood collection device warrants doffing gloves and performing hand hygiene. At any deviation from the standard phlebotomy process, hand hygiene should occur.

First Aid and CPR

First aid is aimed at addressing immediate bleeding, pain, and infection prevention strategies. The phlebotomist should be skilled at initiating pressure over puncture sites to prevent or staunch any bleeding. Cautious watching post venipuncture to identify post-access bleeding is important to prevent hematoma formation. Any profuse or continued bleeding should be reported to the immediate supervisor, attending nurse, or healthcare provider.

If the patient loses consciousness during or after venipuncture, the phlebotomist may need to perform CPR. In an inpatient setting, the phlebotomist can call for assistance by pressing an emergency response button or utilizing a mobile device. In the outpatient setting, the phlebotomist should begin CPR immediately if the patient is not breathing and call 911. If the patient is breathing, the phlebotomist must call 911 if the patient has lost consciousness for over two minutes.

In the inpatient setting the patient should be quickly assessed for a Do Not Resuscitate (DNR) bracelet prior to initiating cardiopulmonary resuscitation (CPR).

Patient Preparation

Introduce Yourself to the Patient

The first thing to do when meeting a patient is to identify oneself as the phlebotomist. The phlebotomist should identify their name and role as well. It is important for the patient to feel comfortable and be aware of what will happen during their venipuncture. Next, the phlebotomist should explain the procedure for attaining their specimen. The phlebotomist should also explain what the patient should expect before, during, and after the procedure. An example of an appropriate introduction may sound like, "Good morning, my name is _____. I am a phlebotomist, and I will be drawing your labs today." The introduction and conversation should help the patient to feel at ease with both the phlebotomist and the process.

Positively Identify the Patient Based on Specific Identifiers

Identifying the patient appropriately is a critical task and should not be taken lightly. Identifying the patient correctly will eliminate errors that could cause the patient harm. Two identifiers are required according to laboratory standards. The phlebotomist should ask the patient to state their name and date of birth. This information should be compared to the information on the requisition form. If this is in an inpatient hospital setting, the information should also be compared to the patient's identification wristband. If the patient is unable to state their own name and date of birth, the information can be obtained from their caregiver. Again, properly identifying the patient and comparing the information to the requisition form is vital to safe practice and preventing harm.

The Health Insurance Portability and Accountability Act (HIPAA) has specific rules about identifying a patient. This includes asking the patient verification questions when face-to-face. According to HIPAA rules, healthcare providers can also ask for valid government-issued identification cards, although this is not required when performing a venipuncture.

Receive Implied, Informed, or Expressed Consent from the Patient

The phlebotomist should ask for the patient's consent. This can be done verbally or through a written consent form. At times, even nonverbal consent can be used. For example, the patient may take off their jacket and expose their arm or possibly lift their sleeve. This implies consent as they are allowing the phlebotomist access to the venipuncture site. Another example of implied consent is that the patient willingly sits in the chair provided after being informed about the venipuncture. If at any time the patient declines venipuncture or says stop, the phlebotomist must stop immediately. A patient always has the right to refuse care at any time.

In order to gain consent, it is the phlebotomist's responsibility to explain the procedure. This explanation should include the benefits and risks of the venipuncture. To appropriately give consent, the patient must have a thorough understanding of what will happen during the venipuncture and any possible complications that may arise from the procedure.

Review and Clarify the Requisition Form

A phlebotomist should review the requisition form to ensure that it has all the required information. Without this information the phlebotomist's job will be impossible. If there are any areas on the

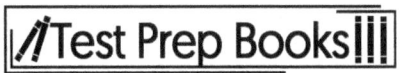

requisition form that are unclear or not filled completely, the ordering provider should be contacted for clarification. Failure to clarify the requisition form can cause the patient to submit to another venipuncture.

Reviewing the information also gives the phlebotomist an idea of what tests are needed and in what order and speed they should be processed. This is useful when preparing the necessary equipment for the venipuncture. This will ensure a timely appointment and venipuncture. In addition, if the phlebotomist knows the information, they will be able to obtain all the tests with only one venipuncture. This prevents the patient from being stuck multiple times during the appointment or having to return on a different day.

Verify Patient Compliance with Testing Requirements and Proceed Accordingly

Many laboratory tests require different actions on the part of the patient. For example, some tests require a patient to fast before testing. This would mean that the patient should not have had any food or drink after the midnight before the test. It is important that this type of information is given to the patient before their test day or appointment. It is the responsibility of the phlebotomist to verify that the patient has followed the directions given by the provider's office before acquiring the specimens used for testing. The following are instructions that may be given to the patient:

- Fasting specimen:
  - No food or drink after the midnight before the blood is drawn
- Basal state:
  - No food or drink—besides water—for twelve hours before blood is drawn
  - Patient should be well rested
  - Venipuncture should ideally be in the morning
  - No exercise for twenty-four hours prior to testing
- Dietary requirements:
  - The patient should fast before a test for triglycerides or glucose is taken
  - The patient should avoid alcohol as this will cause blood sugar to elevate for a period
  - The patient should avoid caffeine as this can elevate levels of many different levels that may be tested
- Exercise:
  - Exercise can increase many different lab levels and should be avoided for up to twenty-four hours before testing

The phlebotomist should discuss the provider's instructions with the patient and any requirements listed on the requisition form with the patient. If the patient has not been compliant with the instructions, it may be best to reschedule the patient or contact the provider for further instructions.

Interview Patients to Identify Special Considerations

Just as there are testing requirements such as fasting and basal state, there are other special considerations to be taken when a phlebotomist is preparing the patient for testing. These special considerations include stress, fever, nicotine use, nutritional status, mastectomy, medications, and more.

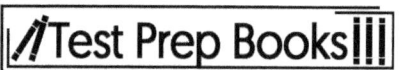

Patient Preparation

These special considerations can cause changes in lab values that may alter the course of a patient's treatment from their provider. Patient harm may occur if the phlebotomist does not consider these issues. For these reasons, the following special considerations should be addressed:

- Stress
  - Elevation of platelets, neutrophils, cortisol, and cholesterol
  - Decrease in eosinophils, basophils, lymphocytes, and monocytes
- Fever
  - Elevation of glucose and glucagon
  - Nicotine (all forms—chewing, smoking, vaping, patches, lozenges, gum, etc.)
  - Elevation in lipids, glucose, cortisol, and more
- Malnutrition
  - Increases in ketones, lactic acid, bilirubin, and triglycerides
  - Decreases in glucose, albumin, and protein
- Newborns
  - Antecubital is not well developed—use vessels of the hands or a heel stick
  - 70 percent isopropyl alcohol should be used; chlorhexidine should not be used on newborns less than two months old
- Neonates (Birth–28 days old)
  - Blood volume is very small (95 mL of blood per 1 kilogram of body weight)
  - Maximum volume of blood that can be drawn is 2.5 percent of total blood volume
  - Must be kept warm
  - Work quickly to avoid too much stimulation
  - For pain/comfort, provide sucrose nipples to suck on during venipuncture
- Pediatrics
  - May be scared, stressed, and not be able to hold still
  - Provide distraction and comfort
- Older Adults
  - Fragile skin—use caution with a tourniquet. A blood pressure cuff inflated to no more than 40 mmHg will be better. Deflate before needle insertion to avoid bleeding or hematoma. Skin should be stabilized before needle insertion.
  - Fragile veins—less elastic; vessels may move, making them less stable; vessels walls are stiff, making them harder to access
  - Dehydration is more common
- Obesity
  - Vessels are deeper and more difficult to compress with a tourniquet
  - Use of a blood pressure cuff may work in lieu of a tourniquet
  - Limit use of blood pressure cuff or tourniquet for two minutes or less
  - Fatty tissue may feel like blood vessels—use caution
  - The cephalic vein is more accessible than other veins in those with obesity
- Mastectomy
  - Women and transgender men who have had a mastectomy with lymph node removal are at risk for lymphedema. Using a tourniquet further increases this risk. Venipuncture on the side of a mastectomy is also at increased risk for infection because of lymph node removal.
  - Use the side opposite a mastectomy for venipuncture

- In the case where a mastectomy has been done bilaterally, consult the ordering provider
- Needle phobia (belonephobia)
    - Occurs in up to 10 percent of the adult population
    - May appear mildly anxious to obviously anxious, diaphoretic, and pale
    - Some patients may have a vasovagal response to this stress and faint
    - Ask the patient what will help them the most; consider different positions such as laying down, using topical anesthesia, and using distraction. If possible, do not let the patient see the needle.
- Medication
    - Follow the provider's recommendations on when or if to take medications before labs are drawn
    - Some tests are to determine if a medication is at a therapeutic level for the patient
    - Some tests can be used to see if a medication is causing harm

Explain the Phlebotomy Procedure to be Performed to the Patient

Explaining the phlebotomy procedure is important for the patient, especially patients who have needle phobia or are anxious. The procedure should be explained in a way that is easy to understand for the patient, using language that is understandable and uncomplicated.

The language used to explain the procedure should be at a fifth-grade level. This ensures that the patient understands the procedure. This information should be discussed after the phlebotomist introduces themselves to the patient and prior to consent and testing.

The phlebotomist should explain that they will use a small needle to draw blood for the tests ordered by the patient's provider. The phlebotomist will then tell the patient that they will label the tests in front of the patient, having them verify their information on the lab label. The phlebotomist will then inform the patient that their results will then be sent to the patient's provider.

After this information has been explained to the patient, the patient will be asked if they consent to the tests. At this point the venipuncture can proceed if consent is provided either verbally or implicitly.

Position the Patient

The most typical positions used for phlebotomy are supine or sitting. Other positions can influence test results. In most cases, a lab will be set up with specific chairs for patients to sit in with armrests that can be used as a table.

As a patient is having blood drawn in a sitting position, there should be a back to the chair, armrests, and an extended armrest that comes to the front of the patient. This provides safety in the event the patient becomes dizzy or loses consciousness. The goal of these protections is to prevent injury from falls. Patients sitting in a chair or on a hospital bed without these protections are contrary to national guidelines.

For patients who have needle phobia, anxiety, or a history of fainting while having blood drawn, the supine position is best. Supine position is when the patient is laying on their back. This position keeps the patient from falling and getting injured if they do faint or get lightheaded.

It is important to ask the patient what position will help them to be comfortable. Keeping the patient comfortable using blankets or pillow support will help them to remain still and calm throughout the procedure. The positioning of the patient must not only be comfortable but also safe for the patient.

Determine Site for Specimen Collection

Site selection is very important when performing a venipuncture. This decision should be based on the patient's vasculature and their age. This decision can make the venipuncture easier or more difficult and, if done poorly, can cause nerve damage or hematoma.

For neonates and infants up to six months old and between three to ten kilograms, a heel prick is the appropriate choice. The heel prick should be on the medial or lateral plantar surface. The stick should not be any deeper than 2.4 millimeters.

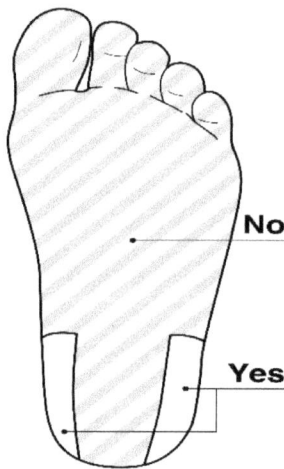

For patients six months through adolescents, a venipuncture in the arms is appropriate following the same information for adults. The key for this population is ensuring that they can hold still. This can be accomplished through the help of parents, coworkers, or using restraint devices.

A patient greater than six months old should have their arm extended. The phlebotomist should examine the antecubital fossa and the forearm, looking for an appropriate vein. Veins that should be considered are of good size, visible without a tourniquet, and straight. The venipuncture should not be done at a junction of two vessels and valves should be avoided. The vein should also be straight and the skin clear.

The median cubital vein is a good choice for the phlebotomist. This vein tends to be larger and is positioned between muscles, making it easier to find. The basilic vein is above a nerve and an artery, and, as a result, this vein is a risk for complications including nerve damage, bleeding, and hematoma.

Locations that can be used other than the antecubital fossa:

- Dorsal side of hand (veins on the top of the hand when palm is down)
    - Use butterfly needle
    - More fragile, often roll, smaller and shorter, more painful
- Ankle and foot veins
    - Last choice for venipuncture

Patient Preparation

- Use a butterfly needle
- Never use the ankle or foot in a patient who has diabetes mellitus or peripheral vascular disease
- Difficult to access, easy to injure, painful

Locations to avoid:

- Above any intravenous site
- Peripheral and central venous access device
- Mastectomy side or fistula containing arm
- Areas with edema
- Scarring
- Hematomas

For hospitalized patients, the phlebotomist can access the veins above or others that they find appropriate; however, the phlebotomist should avoid accessing an existing intravenous site or areas in an existing access site. Accessing these areas or sites has the potential to give erroneous results due to contamination, uncleared intravenous fluids, or medications. This can also result in hemolysis which will cause a sample to be unusable.

In the hospital setting, nurses, advanced practice providers, and physicians can access central venous lines. These lines should be accessed following hospital policy or protocol. Phlebotomists should not access these sites. These lines also have the potential for hemolysis, contamination, uncleared intravenous fluids, and uncleared medications. This, again, can cause inaccurate results.

Instruct Patients on Collection of Specimens

It is important to give easy to understand, thorough explanations of the collection of non-blood specimens such as stool samples, urine samples, semen, and sputum. The patient should verbalize understanding the instructions. Improper collection of these types of specimens can result in erroneous results and could possibly cause patient harm.

Urine:
- Regular voided
  - Instruct the patient to urinate in the sterile specimen container
- Midstream
  - Instruct patient to void into the toilet then place the sterile container under the urine stream
- Midstream clean catch
  - Instruct the patient to clean the urethral opening and groin prior to urinating in the sterile container. Cleaning for this test is very important because it is used to detect urinary tract infections.
- Urinary catheter
  - Sample is taken after the insertion of a sterile catheter into the bladder
- Pediatric
  - For patients who are not yet bathroom trained, a collection bag can be used
- 24-hour urine

Patient Preparation

- Patient will urinate into the toilet first thing in the morning. The patient will have a large container to collect urine, and they will write the date and time that they voided. This will be the start of the 24-hour urine.
- For the next twenty-four hours, the patient should collect all urine. This urine should be kept cold in the refrigerator.
- If the patient needs to have a bowel movement, they should take care to urinate before passing stool. A bowel movement can contaminate the sample, and the patient would need to start over.
- At the 24-hour mark that the patient wrote down, the patient should urinate and collect this last sample.
- The patient should seal the container, keep it cool using ice or a cooler, and transport it to the lab.

Stool:
- The patient should place their name and label on the collection container
- The patient should use a toilet hat or loosely draped plastic wrap that is wrapped over the sides of the toilet to catch the stool
- Do not use stool that has mixed with urine or anything else
- A sample can be picked up with a plastic spoon or a tongue depressor
- The sample only needs to be dime sized
- Take the labeled collection container to the laboratory as soon as possible
- The sample can be stored in the refrigerator or freezer depending on timeline of sample return and/or specific tests

Semen:
- The patient should place their name or the provided label on the specimen container
- The patient should wash and dry their hands and penis
- The patient should ejaculate directly into the provided container
- The sample should be kept at room temperature and delivered to the laboratory within one hour

Sputum:
- Sputum is the mucous that is in the respiratory tract. It is the material that is coughed up from people with a possible respiratory illness.
- Patient should produce specimen first thing in the morning
- Wait for one hour after eating if not producing the sputum first thing in the morning
- Patient should remove dentures before producing sputum

Patient Identifiers

Patient identification must include (at least) one verification from the first section and one verification from the second section. Patient identification is a critical part of the testing process. Failure to identify the patient appropriately can cause harm to the patient and others.

- **Identification Verification Section 1:**
  - Stated name and date of birth
  - Caregiver stating patient's name and date of birth

- Government issued identification card
- **Identification Verification Section 2:**
  - Requisition form
  - Hospital/facility armband
  - Medical record number

Informed, Expressed, or Implied Consent Requirements

Informed Consent/Expressed Consent: The patient is informed of the risks, benefits, and process of the procedure. What the patient should expect is clear, and the patient verbalizes understanding. After this information is conveyed, the patient will sign a consent form acknowledging they have been fully informed. This type of consent is not typically done for phlebotomy.

Verbal Consent: The patient is informed just as in the informed consent, but in this case the patient does not need to sign a consent form. Instead, the patient acknowledges the information and agrees verbally to have the procedure done.

Implied Consent: In this case, the patient understands the procedure and indicates through their actions that they consent to the procedure. For example, a patient may follow the phlebotomist into the exam room, sit down, and roll up their sleeve. The patient's actions indicate that they know what is happening and are agreeable to it.

Requirements of Requisition Forms

Requisition forms are a critical component of the venipuncture process. These forms can be brought by the patient from their doctor's office or sent electronically. Requisition forms provide the information necessary for the phlebotomist to determine their course of action. The following information should be provided on a requisition form:

- Patient demographics:
  - Full name, age, gender, and birthdate
  - Patient identification number
- Ordering physician information:
  - Physician name and signature/electronic signature
  - Diagnosis code (this is a billing code, also known as an ICD code)
- Tests ordered:
  - List of requested tests
  - Priority of tests
  - Timed, routine, or stat
  - Date and time of requested tests

Requisition forms allow the phlebotomist to understand the who, what, and when of each venipuncture. This further allows the phlebotomist to appropriately prepare for each patient. This can prevent the phlebotomist from having to perform multiple venipunctures on the same patient.

Timing Requirements of Draws

- **Peak**: A peak draw is blood that is usually drawn one hour after medication administration. This will tell the provider how much medication is circulating in the blood after the patient receives medication.

- **Trough**: A trough draw is blood that is drawn thirty minutes to one hour before the next administration of a medication. This will tell the provider what the lowest amount of medication circulating in the blood is. This will allow the provider to adjust dosage.

- **Stat**: This lab is of the utmost importance and should be drawn and processed as fast as possible.

- **Routine**: This type of lab is usually to monitor patients; there is no need to draw or process these tests quicker than others.

- **Time of day**: The test should be drawn as ordered, whether first thing in the morning or any other time.

- **Timed**: This type of draw can be done based on frequency, such as every four or six hours.

Testing Requirements

Before testing, ensure the patient has complied with the testing requirements (if required for test):

- **Fasting**: No food or drink, except water, for eight to twelve hours.

- **Medication**: If the test is finding the level of a medication in patient's blood, instruct the patient to take the medication at a specific time and note the time.

- **Basal State**: This test should be done first thing in the morning, and the patient should not eat or drink for twelve hours prior to test, the patient also shouldn't exercise for twenty-four hours prior to the test.

Patient Interviewing Techniques

When communicating with patients, phlebotomists will work with all different types of communicators. It's important to recognize the type of communication that a patient expects and to provide them with that information in the way that is most effective. There are four main types of communicators:

- Analytical Communicators
    - Like exact information, facts, direct communication
    - Explain the procedure to these type of communicators in a direct and matter-of-fact style
- Intuitive Communicators
    - Generally like a broad approach but may have a lot of questions
    - Explain the procedure to this type of communicator very broadly and answer questions as they ask them
- Functional Communicators
    - Information should be given in a logical and organized manner, step-by-step

Patient Preparation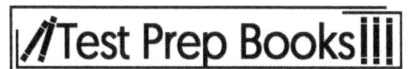

- Explain the procedure to this type of patient very directly, using a specific order that they can follow; they may like to hear step-by-step directives
- Personal Communicators
    - Use connection and have a more emotional approach to communication, good listeners
    - The phlebotomist should try to make a connection with the patient while building rapport
    - Explain the procedure simply and answer any questions

Variables That May Impact Collections

There are variables that are important to discuss with the patient before performing venipuncture to protect the patient from harm.

- Allergies
    - Ensure that the patient doesn't have any allergies to the equipment that will be used. The phlebotomist should pay particular attention to latex and adhesive allergies. Some facilities only use latex-free equipment.
- Medications
    - Some medication levels are tested with phlebotomy; in that case, the patient should take the medication at the instructed time. Ensure that the patient is compliant in taking the medication at the appropriate time and that they have the tests done at the correct time. Failure to do so could cause patient harm through erroneous results.
- Recent surgeries
    - Recent surgeries can impact test results.
- History of Fainting
    - If the patient has a history of fainting, ensure that the arm of the phlebotomy chair is locked. Observe the patient for at least fifteen minutes after the venipuncture.
    - Interventions for fainting include distraction, lowering the patient's head, instructing the patient to take deep breaths, and loosening any clothing, especially around the neck.
    - If the patient loses consciousness and doesn't wake immediately, call a rapid response or dial 911.
    - Document the fainting incident.

Special Considerations

In the case of patients with special needs who need phlebotomy, the phlebotomist should assess the patient's needs to properly care for the patient.

- Physical Conditions
    - Blindness: Ensure that the patient is comfortable, assist them if requested to the exam room, and thoroughly explain the procedure to the patient's comfort
    - Deafness: Ensure that the patient understands and can communicate with the phlebotomist, either through a caregiver or the use of word charts and written words
- Physical disabilities

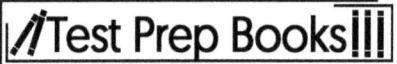

- - o Modify the environment to accommodate the patient's needs
  - Mental Conditions
    - o Inability to understand: Use terms that patient can understand or give the information to the caregiver
    - o Phlebotomist should be as non-threatening as possible

Non-Blood Specimen Collection Procedures

- Urine
  - o Ensure that the patient performs hygiene if necessary for the test
  - o Sample should be collected at the laboratory
- Stool
  - o Instruct patient how to collect sample, specific refrigeration/freezer temperatures and times, and when to return sample
- Sputum
  - o Instruct the patient to produce a sample first thing in the morning after brushing their teeth/dentures and rinsing mouth with water
- Semen
  - o Ensure that the patient performs genital cleaning before providing sample
  - o Sample should be delivered to laboratory within one hour

Minimum and Maximum Blood Volume Requirements

Older patients, underweight patients, and pediatrics patients may be susceptible to phlebotomy-induced iatrogenic anemia. Iatrogenic anemia is a type of anemia that is caused by phlebotomy, medical treatment, and/or examination including labs.

- Older adults — Risks include:
  - o Medications taken by the patient that suppress the bone marrow
  - o Decreased nutritional intake
  - o A blood draw of less than 100 milliliters can cause decrease in hemoglobin and hematocrit
- Cancer patients — Risks include:
  - o Medications with bone marrow suppression
  - o Cancer itself can cause anemia
- Pediatrics/Infants — Risks include:
  - o Premature or low birth weight are at higher risk of iatrogenic anemia
  - o No more than 10 percent of blood volume should be taken over eight-week period
  - o No more than 1–5 percent of blood volume within twenty-four-hour time frame

Patient Positioning

Patients should be positioned in a sitting position. A supine position is also acceptable. The phlebotomist should position the patient for easy access to the antecubital fossa area.

Site Selection Criteria

- Ask the patient which arm they prefer or which arm is successful for them
  - o Some patients have a preference on which arm is used for personal reasons.

Patient Preparation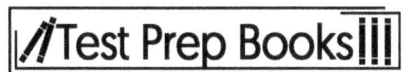

- Some patients may be difficult sticks; these patients are often able to tell the phlebotomist which sites work well and which sites don't. This is valuable information.
- Avoid the side if a patient has had a mastectomy
    - Risks to venipuncture on the side of mastectomy include lymphedema and infection.
- Avoid the side if a dialysis fistula is present
    - Venipuncture to a fistula can permanently damage the site, making it useless for dialysis. This would cause harm to the patient. They would have to have a temporary dialysis catheter placed. A new fistula could be placed, but these take time to mature and become usable.

Routine Blood Collections

Select and Assemble Equipment Needed for Blood Collection(s)

Equipment selection can vary widely depending on the facility, tests ordered, and patient. Phlebotomy supplies are usually available nearby in both inpatient and outpatient venues. Equipment should be assembled and ready before a tourniquet is placed on the patient. The requisition form should also be verified, ensuring that it has all the necessary information. The equipment and supplies should be arranged in a way that is easy to access. Be sure to keep needles capped until it is time to use them; this ensures the safety of both the phlebotomist and the patient. Place a barrier between the phlebotomy supplies and any possible contaminated materials/surfaces.

Outpatient Setting: Doctor's Office or Lab Collection Location

- Supplies are likely to be in a specific area where a phlebotomy chair is available.

Inpatient Setting: Medical Facility or Hospital

- Supplies may be available in each unit or in a centralized location.
- Clean the bedside table before use or put a barrier between the supplies and the tray.

Equipment to assemble:

- Needle system
    - Evacuated tube system
    - Syringe system
    - Butterfly needle
    - Hub, adapter, or transfer device
- Gloves
- Isopropyl alcohol swabs
- Gauze pads
- Tape, adhesive bandage, bandage, or wrap
- Tourniquet
- Blood collection tubes

Verify Quality of Equipment

Verify and inspect all supplies, including needles, cleaning pads, tubes, and any other sterile items, before use for each draw. Verify that all equipment is within its use by date—do NOT use expired equipment. Ensure that proper storage has been maintained.

Do not remove the rubber stopper, which is used to puncture during blood transfer.

Look for any defects in the manufacturer's packaging that may indicate compromised sterility, including:

- Tears, rips, or holes in packaging
- Moisture within packaging

Routine Blood Collections

If any irregularity or defect is identified, dispose of the equipment appropriately. Ensure needles are disposed of in sharps containers.

Tubes with no vacuum should not be used. Causes of loss of vacuum include:

- Expired product
- Opened rubber stopper
- Manufacturer error
- Dropped tubes
- Incorrect storage practice
- Failed or incorrectly performed blood draw

Tubes should be labeled by the manufacturer with additives, the expiration date, and the volume.

Follow Standard Tourniquet Application and Removal Procedures

Tourniquets are used to locate and assess appropriate veins for venipuncture. A tourniquet can help by slowing venous blood return, causing the veins to swell and making it easier to find and draw blood. The Clinical and Laboratory Standards Institute (CLSI) has guidelines that should be followed for tourniquet use during venipuncture.

CLSI recommends the following:

- Single-use tourniquet (reusable tourniquets for multiple patients are not acceptable)
- Reusable tourniquet for a single patient only, provided that the tourniquet is inspected for any defects, such as tears, rips, or being overly worn
- Latex-free tourniquet
- Blood pressure cuff inflated to less than the diastolic blood pressure

Tourniquets should be applied in such a way that they are easily removed with one hand. The method shown below is a slipknot. It is the preferred method.

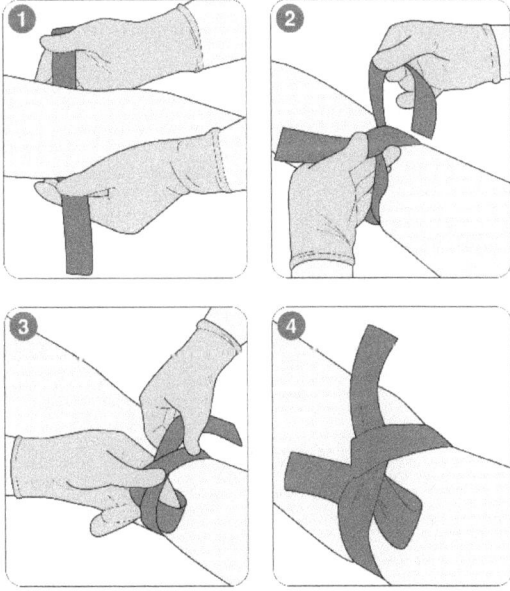

The tourniquet is initially applied to find an appropriate vein. During this time, the tourniquet should not be left on longer than 1 minute. When the tourniquet is left on longer than 1 minute, it can cause hemoconcentration, leading to erroneous results. If the tourniquet is left on for longer than 2 minutes, it can cause damage to the veins. Once the vein of choice is located, the tourniquet should be removed for assembly of the equipment used for the venipuncture.

When the equipment is assembled and ready, the tourniquet can be reapplied, and the blood drawn. The tourniquet may be left in place until the last tube has blood in it, and then the tourniquet should be released while the last tube is filled. The time for which the tourniquet is on the patient for the venipuncture should also remain under 1 minute.

Select Final Site Through Observation and Palpation, for Specimen Collection

Ensure that the side used for the blood draw does not have any restrictions, such as a dialysis fistula or the side of a mastectomy. Other factors that can make palpating or seeing a vein more difficult are tattoos, edema, hematoma, an existing intravenous (IV) line, scarring, or sclerosed veins. Avoid drawing blood while an infusion is running through an IV.

- **Edema**: Extra fluid can alter test results and cause increased pain.
- **Hematoma**: Blood can alter test results and cause increased pain.
- **Scarring**: Tissue can be difficult to penetrate and can lead to increased pain.
- **Tattoos**: These can cause decreased visibility.
- **IV infusion**: This can alter results; use the arm opposite the running IV line or go below the IV. IV infusions include fluids, medications, and blood transfusion—all should be avoided.

Ask the patient which side they prefer. Apply the tourniquet and palpate for a vein; if none is located, ask the patient to use the other arm (if appropriate—not in the case of dialysis fistula or mastectomy).

Veins of the antecubital area should be assessed first. The first choice for a location is the median cubital vein. This vein is typically easy to find and is less painful to access. The second choice should be the cephalic vein on the outside surface of the arm. The cephalic vein will likely be the best choice for patients with obesity. The third choice may be a vein in the hand. The final choice, if all other options are exhausted, may be the basilic vein. The basilic vein is bundled next to a nerve and artery, increasing the risk of bleeding, pain, and nerve damage.

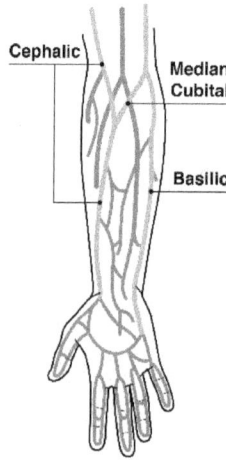

When palpating a vein, observe for one that feels bouncy, is straight, with no bulges, and is close to the surface of the skin. Visualization may also make it easier to access.

For infants through 12 months of age, the first choice is the heel. Do not stick through previous sticks, hematomas, or any other defects in the skin.

For dermal puncture, the middle and ring fingers are preferred. Use the nondominant hand and puncture to the side of the finger pad. Avoid calluses, any cuts or other defects, bone, or the nail bed.

Apply Antiseptic Agent to Blood Collection Site

The phlebotomist should wear gloves when starting the process of venipuncture. They must be worn before cleansing the skin. An individually wrapped single-use alcohol wipe or swab should be used. The alcohol wipe or swab should be at least 70% isopropyl alcohol for proper cleaning.

Before cleaning, try not to handle the alcohol wipe excessively.

Place the alcohol wipe or swab directly on the location of the vein. CLSI has changed its recommendation for cleansing the site of venipuncture. Previously, it was believed that cleaning in concentric circles was the best method; however, that is not the case. The phlebotomist should instead place an alcohol pad with 70% isopropyl alcohol over the venipuncture site and cleanse the area in a back-and-forth motion.

Allow the alcohol to air-dry. Do not blow on it, as this may also cause cross-contamination from the phlebotomist. Allowing the alcohol to dry can also prevent a stinging sensation when the needle stick occurs. If necessary, a sterile gauze can be used to dry the area if it becomes oversaturated with alcohol.

When testing for alcohol levels, do not use an alcohol-based cleaner before venipuncture. Refer to facility policy. Using an alcohol wipe in this case can cause erroneous results. This also applies in the case of a forensic draw when the sample will be used in a legal case. Certain rules should be followed in legal cases to follow the chain of custody and other requirements from law enforcement.

For dermal punctures, on the fingers or heel, a 70% isopropyl alcohol wipe or swab should be used. Rub the area vigorously to remove bacteria and microbes. Do not use povidone-iodine for dermal punctures, as this can cause erroneous results.

There are a few things that can be done to assist in locating hard-to-find veins:

- Apply a warm cloth or a heel warmer for an infant
- Let the arm hang down to the side to help the veins swell
- Lightly rub the area
- Do NOT smack the patient's skin; this can cause damage to the veins and be painful

Anchor Below Venipuncture Site

Anchoring the skin will help the phlebotomist have a smooth venipuncture. Doing this keeps the vein from rolling and keeps the needle from moving while in the skin. It also reduces the pain associated with the puncture. Anchoring the skin and inserting the needle quickly can help prevent losing the vein and having to do extra venipunctures on the patient.

Routine Blood Collections

To anchor the vein after it has been found, the skin cleaned, and the tourniquet applied:

1. Place the thumb of the nondominant hand at least 2 inches from the insertion site.
2. Pull the skin taut, distal from the insertion.
3. Do not push down into the arm—just pull the skin taut to prevent pain to the patient.
4. Insert the needle into the planned vein.

It is important to only pull the skin distally. The phlebotomist should NOT place any part of their hand or fingers above where the needle will enter the skin (proximal). Some refer to this as the "C" method, "C-hold," or two-finger stretch. This places the phlebotomist at risk of inadvertent needle stick and harm.

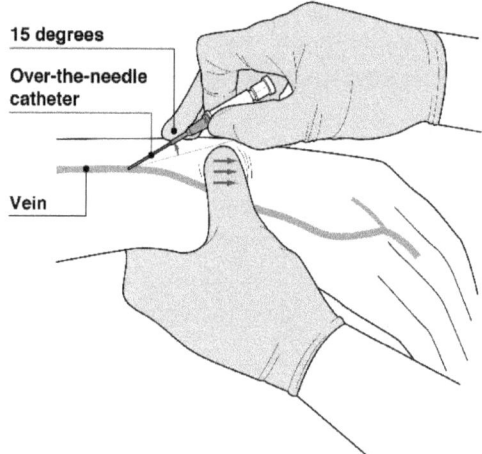

After the needle has been inserted, the dominant hand that is holding the needle will become the anchor so that the needle and skin can be held in place while the evacuated tubes are inserted into the transfer device.

Insert Venipuncture Device

When inserting a needle into the patient, ensure that the bevel is always facing UP.

In the antecubital region, the angle of the needle should be between 15° and 30°.

- Shallow vein: Less than 15° is too shallow, and the vacuum from the evacuated tube can adhere to the vein and stop any blood flow from happening.
- Deep vein: More than 30° is too steep an angle, which can cause the needle to pass through the vein, leading to a failed puncture. It can also cause the needle to pass into the tendon and nerve, possibly resulting in pain and damage to the patient.

In the dorsum of the hand, the angle should be approximately 10°.

- At less than 10°, the bevel of the needle can adhere to the vein and prevent blood return.
- At more than 10°, the needle can go through the vein and cause pain and damage to the patient.

Follow Order of Draw When Performing Venipuncture

CLSI has standardized the order of draw, or the order in which tube colors should be drawn. This is done to provide the most accurate results possible. When using a transfer device, some of the additive can be taken up by the needle and end up in the following evacuated tubes. This can cause erroneous results in some cases. The order of draw is as follows:

1. Light yellow tube or blood culture bottles (Additive: Sodium Polyanethole Sulfonate [SPS])

- These usually come in sets of aerobic and anaerobic bottles and/or tubes.
- If using bottles, it is best to use the syringe method.
- If using tubes, the anaerobic tube should be used first with a syringe allowing the blood to be transferred to the tube; the aerobic tube can be used next with a transfer device attached to a butterfly needle.

2. Light blue tube (Additive: Sodium Citrate)

- This tube should be the first to be drawn after culture tubes.
- If this is the first tube to be filled, it is important to first attach a tube without any additive (not for testing) to the transfer device when using a butterfly. This is because the butterfly tube contains air that will be pulled into the blue tube, causing a short draw—which means that there will not be enough blood in the tube to get accurate results. This type of tube must be completely filled to the fill line.

3. Serum tube—red, gold, speckled red and gray, red and black, orange (Some have no additive, some have a clot activator)

- Serum tubes should be allowed to clot completely before processing.

4. Orange tube (Additive: Rapid Serum Tube [RST])

- Used for rapid or STAT blood collections.
- Serum tubes only need to be allowed to clot for 5 minutes before processing.

5. Green tube (Additive: Lithium, Sodium, or Ammonium Heparin)

- Used in emergency/STAT testing for whole blood chemistry tests or plasma testing.

6. Lavender/Purple tube (Additive: EDTA)

- Used for hematological tests including CBC and A1c.

7. Pink tube (Additive: EDTA)

- Used for blood bank testing including blood typing and antibody screening.

8. Gray tube (Additives: Sodium Fluoride and Potassium Oxalate)

- Used for testing glucose or blood alcohol levels.

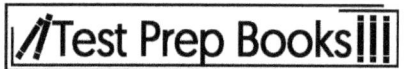

9. **Light yellow tube** (Additive: Acid Citrate Dextrose [ACD])

- Typically used for DNA testing, HLA phenotyping, and blood bank studies.

10. **Royal blue tube** (Additives: EDTA, or empty)

- Used for trace element testing and toxicology.

Again, it is extremely important to follow the order of the draw to maintain the accuracy of test results.

Ensure Patient Safety Throughout the Collection

Environment
Ensure that there are no trip hazards or anything that could cause harm.

Patient safety should be a priority. Ensure that the patient is seated in the phlebotomy chair correctly, and if they have a history of fainting, ensure that all safety measures are taken.

If using a non-phlebotomy chair, ensure that the chair has no wheels and is stable.

Patient
Monitor the patient's emotional state, including anxiety, and observe their body language.

If the patient is showing any concerning signs of anxiety, nervousness, or irritation, proceed with caution. The patient may need special care.

If the patient has a history of fainting, follow safety precautions. Make sure that the arm of the phlebotomy chair is locked. If the patient needs to lie down, provide a space to lie down for the procedure.

When a patient verbalizes that they have a needle phobia, ensure that they do not see the needle. The phlebotomist can direct them to focus their attention on something else.

Explain the procedure to the patient and tell them that they may feel a small pinch.

It is a good idea to let the patient know when the phlebotomist is ready to puncture the skin. This will help cue the patient to hold still during the venipuncture. The phlebotomist can verbally state that they are about to begin or offer a verbal countdown to venipuncture. However, it's always best to ask the patient if they want a warning because it may actually increase their anxiety instead.

Use therapeutic communication. The phlebotomist should always speak confidently with compassion and understanding for patients experiencing anxiety and nervousness. The phlebotomist should listen attentively and address all concerns that the patient vocalizes.

Patient Physical Assessment
The area of venipuncture and surrounding tissues should be observed. Ensure that the skin is intact and that there are no wounds, rashes, or other irregularities. The phlebotomist should be aware of any intravenous line that may be in place if the patient is in the hospital setting.

Most patients will not have any issues with having labs drawn. While the process moves forward, continue assessing to ensure the patient is tolerating the procedure well. Observe for changes in breathing, sweating, or other signs of anxiety. If the patient stops talking suddenly, ask them how they are doing to be sure they are still tolerating the procedure.

Recognize and Respond to Potential Complications Resulting from Procedure

A patient can lose consciousness at any time during the process, from checking in for the lab to leaving the clinic. If at any time a patient experiences a loss of consciousness, immediately stop what you are doing and check for breathing. Note the time when the loss of consciousness occurred.

If the patient is not breathing, the phlebotomist must immediately call 911 and then begin CPR.

If the patient is breathing, they have likely fainted. If the patient faints, safety must be the top priority. Make sure the patient's airway is clear. Ensure the patient cannot fall from where they are. Fainting is usually very short. A cold compress can be applied to the forehead or neck. Never give an unconscious patient anything in their mouth, including water. If the patient is still unconscious after 2 minutes, 911 must be called. When in an inpatient facility, follow the protocol for getting immediate assistance. Do NOT leave the patient.

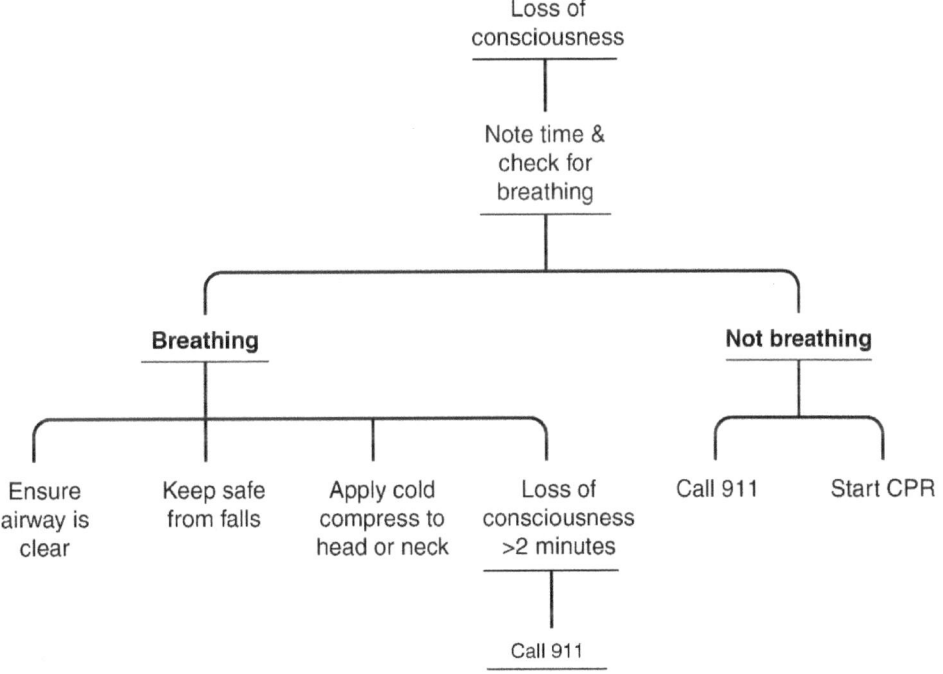

Inpatient settings can include patients who are combative or cannot hold still. A second person is needed in these cases. Ask for help from another phlebotomist or the patient's nurse or certified nursing assistant.

Remove Venipuncture Device

Remove the needle at the same angle as the angle of insertion. The bevel of the needle should be facing up. Do not hold pressure on the site of insertion until the needle is out of the skin. The removal should be quick, and a cotton ball or gauze should immediately be pushed onto the exit site. Pressure should be held until a wrap is placed over the cotton ball/gauze to hold that pressure.

1. Remove the needle at the same angle as entry with the bevel up.
2. After the needle has left the skin, immediately engage the safety to cover the needle.
3. Hold pressure with a cotton ball/gauze.
4. Place tape or wrap over the cotton ball/gauze for continued pressure.
5. Ensure bleeding has stopped before allowing the patient to leave.

Invert Evacuated Tubes with Additives According to Procedural Guidelines

After filling the evacuated tubes, they should be inverted 3–10 times to properly mix the blood with the additives within the tubes. If this is not done properly, the specimen may clot and be unusable.

Being overly aggressive while tubes are inverted, such as shaking, can cause hemolysis, which would also render the sample unusable.

When tube inversion is not done properly, samples are made unusable; this can cause the patient to have the lab drawn again.

Invert the tubes according to their colors and additives:

- Light yellow: 8–10 inversions
- Light blue: 3–4 inversions
- Red, SST: 5 inversions
- Green: 8–10 inversions
- Lavender: 8–10 inversions
- Gray: 8–10 inversions

Perform Dermal Puncture for Capillary Collection

Infants through the age of 12 months will have a heel stick capillary collection. The outside and inside of the plantar portion of the heel are acceptable. The middle of the heel should be avoided to prevent pain and patient harm due to the proximity of the heel bone.

Children and adults should have capillary collection on their fingers. The middle and ring fingers are the best locations. It is also best to use the patient's nondominant hand. The capillary stick should not be done on the pad of the finger or anywhere near the nail.

Capillary collections can be performed when the patient is at risk for iatrogenic anemia or even when a patient's veins are difficult to find or access. They can also be used when a smaller amount is needed in the case of a microtube.

The phlebotomist should specify that the collection was capillary in nature on the label of the specimen.

Follow Order of Draw When Performing Capillary Collection

Capillary order of draw is different than regular order of draw because capillary blood starts to clot immediately. This can impact draws that are not intended to have any clotted blood. It is also used to prevent cross-contamination of additives. Just as in venipuncture, capillary collection transfers can cause additive from one tube to contaminate the following tube.

Routine Blood Collections

Order of Draw for Capillary Collection

1. (For Infants): Blood gas collection tubes (typically purple/green)

    - Infants tend to cry during venipuncture; the crying can alter the results of the blood gases. Collecting this lab first helps ensure blood gases are as close to baseline as possible before crying begins.

2. EDTA—pearl, purple, lavender, pink tubes

    - This is done next because the clotting of the specimen can alter the results of these tubes.

3. Green

4. All other tubes

5. Serum—red or gold

    - These have no additives, so blood will clot, making these last in order since there is no concern about the blood clotting.

Label All Specimens

Before performing the venipuncture, the identity of the patient should be verified. This should be done again when labeling the specimens. Label the specimens before the patient leaves the room. The phlebotomist should hold the label to the patient and ask them it their information is correct. Only put labels on specimens that you have collected. Never label for another phlebotomist or for a patient who has already left. Errors in labeling can cause severe harm to the patient.

Labels should be applied in such a way that barcodes can be easily scanned and do not hang off the bottom or cover the rubber stoppers.

Occasionally, an extra specimen is needed, and there is no label available. Should the phlebotomist encounter this, they should create a label. To create a label:

1. Use pen only, no pencil.

2. Writing should be clear and easily legible.

3. Record patient information, including:

    - Full name
    - Date of birth
    - Medical identification number
    - Date and time of draw
    - Initials of phlebotomist

Another option with inpatients is to use a regular patient label. Patient labels or any created label should be verified with the patient to ensure accuracy and appropriate patient identification.

Perform Post-Procedural Patient Care

Hemostasis is the bodily process that stops bleeding and bruising. The goal after the procedure is to achieve hemostasis without any complications. To do this, the phlebotomist should use adequate pressure to stop any bleeding and use a dressing to maintain the pressure and hemostasis.

After the venipuncture and after the needle has been removed, quickly place a dressing over the insertion site. The dressing can be a bandage, cotton ball, or gauze with self-adhering wrap.

Special circumstances:

- For patients with significant amounts of hair, use self-adhering bandages.
- For patients with thin or fragile skin, usually found in older adults, use self-adhering bandages.

Observe the patient for any post-procedure complications, including shortness of breath, lightheadedness, new confusion, or changes in responsiveness.

Once the patient is doing well and has achieved hemostasis, they may leave the facility. If inpatient, ensure that all equipment and supplies have been removed from the area and that none have been left on the bed. A needle cap or other plastic could cause a pressure injury in an older adult or be a choking hazard for a child. Ensure the room is as safe as, if not safer than, when the phlebotomist first entered it.

Blood Collection Devices

Evacuated Tube System (ETS)

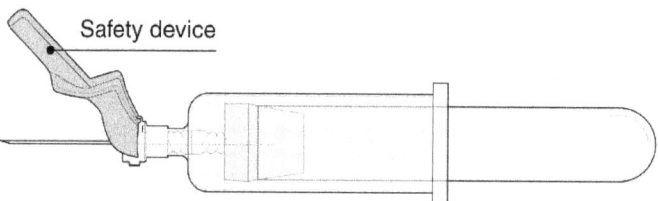

- Best use: good for general use on most people
- Double-sided needle with a tube holder
- The tube has a vacuum that draws blood through the needle into the tube.

Syringe Method

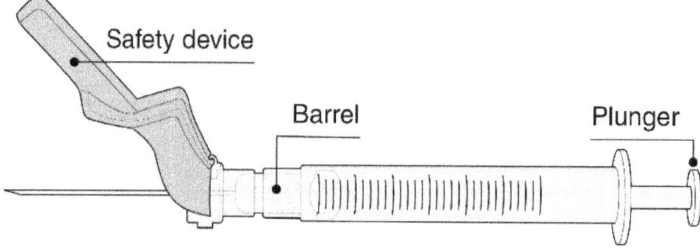

- Best use: fragile veins, veins that easily collapse
- Single-sided needle attached to a syringe

Routine Blood Collections

- Allows for better control of the suction so that a smaller amount of suction can be used to allow the vein to stay open while drawing blood. Blood is drawn more slowly with less pressure.
- The blood is first collected in the syringes, and then a transfer device is used to move the blood into the evacuated tubes.

Butterfly Needle Method (Winged Needle)

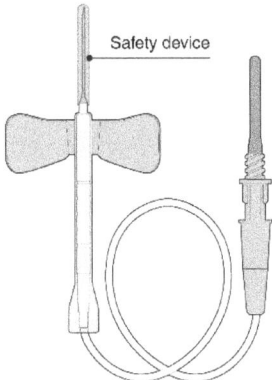

- Best use: small veins, difficult-to-access veins
- The largest different between this method and the others is that there is a small tube between the needle and the adapter. The adapter can go either directly into a transfer device attached to an evacuated tube or to a syringe. The syringe would then be attached to a transfer device to move the blood into the evacuated tubes.
- All adapters and needles are single-use and should never be reused.

Considerations for Device Selection

There are some factors to consider when deciding which method is best to draw blood. Each drawing method has advantages and disadvantages. Much of the equipment in each drawing method is the same. What differs is the needle type, the way the blood is pulled from the vein, and the way the blood is drawn into the evacuated tubes.

Different facilities may have preferences on what they use and what equipment is available to phlebotomists, but generally:

Evacuated tube systems (ETS) are well suited for the majority of patients.

The syringe method is best suited for patients who have fragile veins that collapse easily.

The butterfly (winged) method is best suited for small veins or veins that are difficult to access. The butterfly needle can fit into places the larger options cannot.

Needle Gauge Sizes and Lengths

The needle gauge should be between 21 and 23. The standard needle size is 21-gauge. The larger the gauge, the smaller the needle. The length of the needle should be 1 to 1.5 inches. The needle should also be hollow and beveled. NEVER reuse needles, not even on the same patient. ETS needles are double-sided. One side goes into the patient, and the other side is for the evacuated tubes. This side of

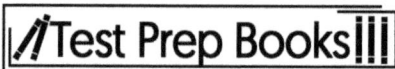

the needle is covered with a sheath and surrounded by a protector. The plastic protector keeps the phlebotomist from accidentally being stuck with the needle. The sheath also keeps blood from dripping while the phlebotomist switches tubes.

- Needle: 1 to 1.5 inches long, 21 to 23 gauge, hollow and beveled
- NEVER reuse a needle, NEVER recap a needle. Use the built-in safety to cover the sharp.
- Attached to the needle is a hub/adapter that also has a needle to fill the tubes.

Evacuated Tubes Required for Laboratory Testing

- Serum Separator Tube (SST)
  - Contains a gel that doesn't affect the sample but helps with processing in the lab
- Serum Tube—Red, Gold, or Orange
  - Used for whole blood collection, hematology, and donor screening
  - Glass may have no additives (not typically used due to possible breakage and safety hazard) or may have tripotassium ethylenediaminetetraacetic acid (EDTA)
  - Plastic tubes contain dipotassium EDTA
  - Plastic red and gold tubes also contain a clot activator
  - Plastic orange tubes contain a thrombin-based clot activator for STAT collection
- Light Yellow Tube—Blood Culture Bottle
  - Used for bacterial studies
  - Contains SPS
- Pink Tube
  - Used for blood bank, crossmatching
  - Contains dipotassium EDTA
- Light Blue Tube
  - Used for coagulation blood tests
  - Contains sodium citrate
- Royal Blue Tube
  - Used for trace element testing
  - Contains a clot activator or EDTA
- Yellow Tube
  - Used for blood bank and DNA testing
  - Contains acid citrate dextrose (ACD)
- Green Tube
  - Used for chemical levels
  - Contains sodium, lithium, or ammonium heparin
- Purple/Lavender Tube
  - Used for hematology and whole blood testing
  - Contains EDTA
- Gray Tube
  - Used for glucose and lactic acid
  - Contains potassium oxalate/sodium fluoride
- Serum Tube
  - Used for blood tests that require blood to be clotted

Order of Draw, Number of Tube Inversions, Angle of Tube Insertion, Fill Level/Ratios

Order of Draw	Tube Color	Inversions	Additives	Fill Level
1	Light Yellow	8–10	Sterile	10 mL
2	Light Blue	3–4	Sodium citrate	4.5 mL, must be filled completely
3	SST/Serum: Red, Red and Gray Gold, Orange, Royal Blue	5	Gel separator tube, clot activator, no additive, or gel separator with thrombin	Red 7 mL Gold 6 mL Royal Blue 7 mL
4	Green, Royal Blue Dark Green	8–10	Gel separator with heparin, heparin	7.0 mL Dark Green 5 mL
5	Lavender, Pink, Tan, Royal Blue, Pearl	8–10	EDTA, gel separator with EDTA	Pearl 4 mL Lavender 3 mL Pink 4–6 mL Tan 5 mL
6	Gray	8–10	Potassium oxalate, sodium fluoride	Minimum 2 mL to 4 mL
7	Dark Yellow	8–10	ACD	8.5 mL

Tubes will be guided to the transfer needle by a plastic protector that surrounds the transfer needle or transfer device.

Equipment Quality Control Checks

All equipment should be verified and inspected for the following:

- Equipment:
    - Is within the use-by date and NOT expired.
    - Package is intact—no moisture, rips, or tears.
    - Storage is appropriate and well maintained.
    - If any irregularity is found, the item should be disposed of properly.
- Alcohol wipes and swabs should be moist; if they are dry, do not use them.
- Tourniquets are single use; inspect new tourniquets for any damage.

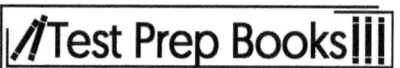

- ETS tubes:
  - If there is no vacuum when drawing blood, dispose of the tube and use a new one.
  - Do not remove the rubber stopper; if done, the tube should not be used.
  - Other reasons for loss of suction include expired tubes, manufacturer error, dropped tubes, bad storage, and failed or incorrect blood draw.
  - Tubes should be labeled by the manufacturer with the additives, expiration date, and volume. If the label is missing, the tube should be thrown out.

Standard Tourniquet Application and Removal Procedures

An alternative to a tourniquet is a blood pressure cuff inflated to less than diastolic blood pressure.

Tourniquet application procedures:

1. Apply the tourniquet in an easy-to-remove way (must be able to remove it one-handed). It should be placed at least 4 inches above the target vein.
2. Within 1 minute, locate and palpate an appropriate vein.
3. Release the tourniquet within 1 minute.
4. Assemble supplies.
5. Reapply the tourniquet when ready in the same easy-release way.
6. Perform venipuncture.
7. Leave the tourniquet in place until the last tube to be filled has blood in it.
8. Release the tourniquet (again, within 1 minute).

Tourniquets should be latex-free, single-use.

Tourniquets left on longer than 2 minutes can cause hemoconcentration, erroneous results, and damage to the vein.

Palpation Techniques

Palpation should be done with the pad of the finger; the pad is the most sensitive part of the finger.

Palpation for the vein should begin lightly with very little pressure; the finger should bounce up and down on the vein without lifting off the patient's skin.

Tendons should be avoided. Tendons feel hard and stiff like a bone.

Veins that are hard should be avoided, as they are likely sclerosed (abnormally hardened) or scarred.

A vein that can be seen but cannot be felt should not be used, as it is likely superficial. Superficial veins are not large enough to accommodate the needle. No blood will be returned.

Once a vein is found, the direction of the vein should be identified. The phlebotomist should palpate up and down the vein to locate the direction.

In case of difficulty finding a vein:

- A warm blanket or warm pack can be placed on the antecubital space.
- Do not use heating pads or hot water bottles. These can be too hot and burn the patient.
- Instruct patient to hang the arm down so that gravity can help fill the veins.

- Rubbing the arm is okay, but slapping or aggressive rubbing can cause damage to the veins and pain to the patient.

The ideal vein should be:

- Bouncy, spongy to palpation
- Straight with no bulges
- Easy to access

Ideally, ask the patient which arm they prefer.

- First choice: median cubital vein
- Second choice: cephalic vain
- Third choice: dorsal side of the hand
- Final choice: basilic vein (risk for pain, bleeding, and nerve damage)

Skin Integrity, Venous Sufficiency, Contraindications

Skin that should be avoided if possible include:

- Edema: The extra fluid can alter test results and cause pain.
- Hematoma: The blood can alter test results and cause pain.
- Scarring: The scarring and tough tissue may make it difficult for the needle to penetrate and cause pain.
- Tattoos: Causes decreased visibility for the phlebotomist.
- IV: Avoid the side an IV is on; if not possible, draw blood distal to the IV site.
- Dialysis Fistulas/Mastectomies: Avoid arms with dialysis fistulas or the side of a mastectomy.
- Obesity: For patients with obesity, the first-choice site is the cephalic vein.
- Sclerosed veins (scarred or hardened veins):
  - These veins are not appropriate for venipuncture and should be avoided.
  - Sclerosed veins are too tough to penetrate with the needle and can be painful.

Contraindications to venipuncture:

- Observe for skin issues; avoid sclerosed or hardened veins, superficial veins, scars, and hematomas or bruising. For best visualization, avoid tattooed areas. Do NOT perform venipuncture on the side of an IV line or above an IV. Do not perform venipuncture on the side with a dialysis fistula or mastectomy.

Types of Antiseptic Agents and Methods of Application

Antiseptic agents:

- 70% isopropyl alcohol—swab, wipe, gauze soaked in alcohol
- Chlorhexidine gluconate (CHG)

Method of application:

1. Wear gloves.
2. Use a single-use cleansing device.

- 70% isopropyl alcohol swab or wipe (do NOT use for alcohol levels)
- CHG (use for cultures)
- Do NOT use povidone-iodine
3. Open the cleansing agent, but do not handle it excessively.
4. Place the cleanser directly on top of the site chosen for venipuncture.
5. The area should be cleaned in a back-and-forth motion.
    - For CHG used for cultures, this step should last at least 30 seconds. In addition, it should be scrubbed up and down as well as back and forth.
6. Allow the cleansing agent to dry thoroughly before performing the venipuncture.
    - Do not touch the area after it is cleansed, or it must be cleansed again.
    - Do not blow on or fan the area; it will need to be cleansed again.
    - Allowing the alcohol to dry also saves the patient pain during the venipuncture.

Techniques for Anchoring the Vein

Anchoring the vein helps to hold it still and straight. In addition, it keeps the vein from "rolling" or moving away. Other benefits of anchoring the vein include less pain for the patient and an easier time keeping the needle still.

To anchor the vein after the vein has been found, skin cleaned, and the tourniquet applied:

1. Place the thumb of the nondominant hand at least 2 inches below the insertion site.

Tip: Always use the nondominant hand to leave the dominant hand free for managing the needle.

2. Pull the skin taut, below the insertion. Do not push down on the vein.

3. Insert the needle into the planned location.

4. After insertion, the dominant hand will become the anchor and hold the needle in place. Not changing hands will prevent the needle from being moved while in the middle of the venipuncture. While doing this, the nondominant hand will fill the evacuated tubes.

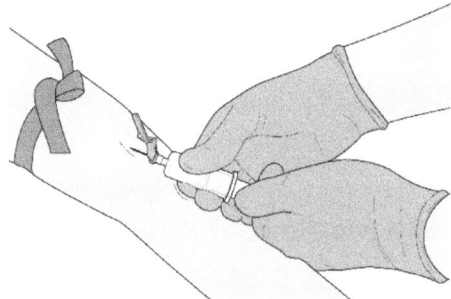

In this picture, the phlebotomist is holding the needle with their dominant right hand and filling the tubes with their nondominant left hand.

Tip: Do NOT use the "C method" while anchoring the vein. This is when the phlebotomist has their thumb below the site and the fingers of the same hand above the site. This is a risk for the phlebotomist that can result in a needle stick.

Angle of Needle Insertion and Withdrawal

When inserting a needle into the patient, ensure that the bevel is always facing UP. Do not turn or rotate the needle while it is in the skin.

For needle insertion:

- Antecubital region: The angle of needle insertion should be between 15° and 30°.
    - Shallow vein: 15°
    - Deep vein: 30°
    - Any angle outside this range can cause problems with the venipuncture or can cause the patient pain and possible harm.
- Dorsum of the hand: The angle should be approximately 10°.
    - Any angle more or less than this can cause a failed venipuncture or cause pain and possible harm.

For withdrawal/removal of the needle:

- Ensure the needle is pulled out the same way it went in, bevel up.
- Pull the needle completely out of the vein before putting pressure on the venipuncture site.
- Holding pressure while removing the needle will cause pain and possibly damage the vein.
- Hold pressure until hemostasis is achieved, then cover with a bandage, clean cotton ball, or gauze and tape or self-adhering dressing. Ensure bleeding has stopped before leaving the patient.

Problematic Patient Signs and Symptoms During Collection

The phlebotomist should always be aware of the patient and how they are responding to the whole process of phlebotomy.

Signs/symptoms of patient complications:

- Verbalized anxiety
- Verbalized needle phobia
- Diaphoresis/sweating
- Sudden stop of interaction
- Nausea/vomiting
- Lightheadedness, dizziness
- Fainting
- Seizure
- Shock

Signs/symptoms of complication with the venipuncture:

- Pain
- Numbness or "pins and needles"
- Bruising
- Hematoma formation
- Swelling

- Redness of the vein (phlebitis)

It is very important for the phlebotomist to be aware of the patient and their behavior as well as how the skin and vein are also responding to the venipuncture. Interventions for these complications are listed in the following section.

Potential Complications Resulting from Procedure

Hematoma— the most common complication:

- Signs/symptoms: Pain, bruising
- Cause: Needle progressing through the vein, causing bleeding under the skin
- Action: Stop the venipuncture immediately if it appears during collection; hold pressure after the needle is out and apply a wrap that will maintain the pressure. If a hematoma occurs after the venipuncture, apply pressure and again wrap with pressure.
- Hematoma should disappear within a few days of venipuncture.

Nerve damage:

- Signs/symptoms: Pain, numbness, pins and needles feeling
- Cause: Hitting a nerve with the needle
- Action: Stop the venipuncture immediately
- If symptoms persist after needle has been withdrawn, the patient may need to see a provider.

Thrombosis:

- Signs/symptoms: Hard ball (blood clot) felt under the skin; if deeper, the arm will be swollen
- Cause: A blood clot partially or completely blocking a vein or artery
- Action: Do not use the affected area or arm for venipuncture.

Petechiae:

- Signs/symptoms: Small red dots on the skin below the tourniquet
- Cause: Tourniquet applied too tightly or for too long; occasionally, it can happen from appropriate use of a tourniquet
- Action: Continue and finish the venipuncture; apply appropriate pressure to site afterward.

Phlebitis:

- Signs/symptoms: Inflammation of a vein, redness, sometimes swelling
- Cause: Repeated use of the same blood vessel
- Action: Find a new location for venipuncture.

Syncope:

- Signs/symptoms: Lightheadedness, fainting
- Cause: Anxiety, physical reaction to venipuncture
- Action: See complications section above.

Seizure:

- Signs/symptoms: Rhythmic movements, "spacing out," loss of consciousness
- Action: Stop venipuncture immediately, note the time.
    - Outpatient: Call 911.
    - Inpatient: Get immediate assistance.
- Ensure patient safety:
    - Do not restrain the patient.
    - Do not place anything in the patient's mouth.
    - Keep the area clear around the patient.
    - Stay with the patient until help arrives.

Shock:

- Signs/symptoms: Patient becoming pale, cool or cold, or clammy, staring off, increased heart rate, shallow breathing
- Action: Ensure the airway is clear. Call for help if available or call 911. If possible, lower the patient's head below the body (if lying down); stay with the patient until help arrives.

Physical reactions:

- Signs/symptoms: Anxiety, sweating, dizziness, nausea, and more
- Action: Stay with the patient; ensure a safe environment and keep the patient safe from falls. Recovery will usually be quick.

Nausea:

- Signs/symptoms: Verbalized nausea, sweating, turning pale or "green"
- Action: Wait until nausea passes before venipuncture, provide an emesis (vomit) bag or trash can, provide a cold compress, provide water to sip on, stay with the patient.

Diaphoresis (sweating):

- Signs/symptoms: Excessive sweating
- Action: Observe for other signs as to what is causing the sweating. Do not perform venipuncture until the diaphoresis stops to prevent complications.

Collection/processing errors:

- Consequences: Patient harm, misdiagnosis, even death
- Examples: Patient misidentification, wrong tube, not following order of draw, not inverting tubes, failing to invert tubes enough times or doing it roughly, lack of documentation, hemoconcentration
- Action: Follow appropriate guidelines.

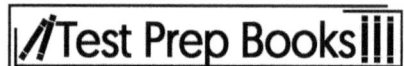

Adjustments for Establishing Blood Flow

When a flash is not seen in a butterfly needle:

1. Pull the needle back, very slowly and very little. If you have gone through the vein (transfixed), this will bring the needle back into the vein.
2. Do NOT push or dig blindly into the patient's arm. This can cause pain and damage to the vein or surrounding tissues.
3. Palpate the site again with the needle still in the skin, feeling for the vein location in relation to the needle.
4. If the vein can be felt and is close to the needle, anchor the vein again and use your dominant hand to push the needle toward the vein.
5. If blood is returned, continue the draw.
6. If no blood is returned or the patient experiences pain, the venipuncture must be stopped. The venipuncture will need to be repeated.

When blood stops flowing or will not proceed into the evacuated tubes using the evacuated tube system:

1. Do not move the needle under the skin.
2. The needle may be moved a small bit further into the patient. If no blood is returned, the needle may be pulled back out slightly.
3. If blood is returned, continue the draw.
4. If no blood is returned, the venipuncture must be stopped. The draw will need to be repeated.

Procedural Steps When Removing Tourniquet, Tubes, and Needle

Filling/removing the evacuated tubes:

1. Insert the tube into the plastic guide, where it will be pierced by the covered needle. When the tube is filled based on the suction, the phlebotomist should remove the tube. The next tube should be inserted and so on until all the evacuated tubes are filled.
2. When the venipuncture is complete, the tubes should be inverted gently the required number of times to properly mix the blood with the additives.

Tourniquet removal:

1. The tourniquet should not be kept on for more than 1 minute for locating a vein.
2. The tourniquet should not be kept on for longer than 1 minute for the venipuncture.
3. The tourniquet should be wrapped in a way that it is easy to release and can be done with one hand (do not tie it in a knot). A slipknot is the best choice.
4. The tourniquet should stay in place until the last evacuated tube has blood in it. After blood is seen in the tube, the tourniquet can safely be removed.
5. To release the tourniquet, pull one end of the tourniquet that should be hanging from the top. This should completely release the tourniquet.

Removing the needle:

1. Do not rotate the needle; the bevel should be facing up.
2. Remove the needle at the same angle at which it went into the skin.
3. Remove the needle quickly without placing pressure on it.
4. After the needle is completely out of the skin, quickly place a bandage, gauze, or cotton ball on the site and hold pressure until hemostasis is achieved.

Use of Needle Safety Devices

1. Locate the safety device before using the needle to prevent accidental sticks. (Safety features can vary depending on the device and manufacturer.)
2. As soon as the needle has left the skin, engage the safety device for the needle.
3. Dispose of the needle with the safety engaged in the sharps container.

Type of safety devices:

- Plastic covers for transfer device needles
- Self-sheathing: a shield slides over the needle and locks in place
- Retractable: the needle retracts into a plastic part
- Add-on device: hinged or sliding piece that is attached to the needle and snaps over the needle
- There are other types of safety devices; the phlebotomist should always be aware of the safety device's function before performing a venipuncture using that device.

Dermal Puncture Procedures for Capillary Collection

For infants through 12 months of age, the first choice is the heel. The sides of the heel should be used. Avoid the middle of the heel to prevent pain and damage. Do not stick through previous sticks, hematomas, or any other defects in the skin.

For dermal punctures of children and adults, the middle and ring fingers are preferred. Use the nondominant hand and puncture to the side of the finger pad. Avoid calluses, any cuts or other defects, bone, or nail bed.

1. Cleanse the area appropriately and allow to dry thoroughly.
2. Perform the dermal puncture according to the patient's age following the guidelines above.
3. Ensure the safety is engaged after the stick if not automatic.
4. Hold pressure until hemostasis is achieved.

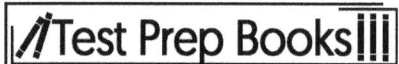

Order of Draw for Capillary Collection

Capillary Order of Draw	Tube Color	Inversions	Additives
1	Venous Blood Gas (Infants)—typically Green/Purple	8–10	Without gel Sodium heparin or lithium heparin
2	Pearl, Purple, Pink, Lavender	8–10	EDTA
3	Green	8–10	Sodium heparin or lithium heparin
4	All Other Tubes	8–10	Various
5	Serum (Red/Gold)	5	No additive

Bandaging Procedures and Considerations

After the needle is removed in venipuncture, the safety of the needle must be engaged, and the phlebotomist should immediately hold pressure on the site using a bandage, gauze, or cotton ball. Hemostasis should be achieved before pressure is released or the patient left alone.

On older adults with thin skin or patients with a lot of hair, a self-adhering dressing should be used to hold pressure after hemostasis has been achieved. Tape can be used on other appropriate patients.

The final dressing should be applied with slight pressure—not excessive—before the patient is allowed to leave.

1. Apply the bandage, gauze, or cotton ball immediately after removing the needle.
2. Hold pressure until hemostasis is achieved.
3. If bloody, change the dressing for a clean one.
4. Use tape or self-adhering wrap to hold the dressing in place.

Labeling Procedures and Requirements

Do NOT ever label a specimen that you did not collect.

Do NOT ever label a specimen after a patient has left.

1. Verify the identity of the patient before venipuncture.
2. After venipuncture, label the specimens in front of the patient.
3. Have the patient verify that their information is correct.
4. Place the label on the tube.
5. Ensure that the barcode can be read and does not hang off the bottom of the tube or cover the rubber stopper.

6. For extra labels, if unable to print a label, the phlebotomist may create one. The label should be created in pen, not pencil. This label should include:
    a. Full name
    b. Date of birth
    c. Medical identification number
    d. Date and time of draw
    e. Initials of phlebotomist

7. (If using extra/created label): Verify the label with the patient and ensure that all information is correct.

Post-Procedural Complications and Precautions

1. Ensure hemostasis to prevent bleeding and bruising.
2. Use appropriate bandaging including self-adhering wraps on older adults with fragile skin and on those with a lot of hair.
3. Observe the patient for signs/symptoms of complications: nausea, shortness of breath, confusion, excessive talking, change in speech patterns or talking less, blank stare.
4. Ensure that all equipment is cleaned up and removed from the patient area for safety.
5. In an outpatient setting: Clean up for the next patient, ensure the environment is safe and that there are no fall/trip hazards.
6. In an inpatient setting: Ensure no supplies are left in the bed to prevent patient harm.
7. Assist the patient as needed with moving and exiting the area.

Special Collections

Prepare Peripheral Blood Smear

To prepare a peripheral blood smear, the phlebotomist reviews the physician's order and determines whether they will collect the sample via capillary or venous puncture. For venous sampling, the phlebotomist confirms the patient's identity and prepares the specimen, using all appropriate measures to ensure safe and accurate specimen collection. The phlebotomist ensures the labeled specimen tube is mixed for at least two minutes to allow anticoagulant additives to be evenly and thoroughly distributed throughout the sample. Next, the phlebotomist gathers supplies to perform the peripheral smear.

The phlebotomist performs hand hygiene and applies clean gloves. They begin to visually inspect the two frosted slides and the third pusher slide for any defects, damage, and contaminants. A lens paper is used to remove lint and fingerprints from the slides. The two frosted slides are labelled with a pencil.

After removing the cap from the EDTA tube, the phlebotomist uses a capillary tube to collect a small amount of blood and deposit a single drop just above the frosted edge of one of the labelled specimen slides. Care is taken to ensure the droplet is placed in the center of the slide. Once this is done, the phlebotomist places the specimen slide into the non-dominant hand, grasping the edges securely with their thumb and index/middle fingers. They pick up the pusher slide by pinching one end with their fingertips.

The opposite end of the pusher slide is placed perpendicularly across the specimen slide, just above the blood drop. The phlebotomist ensures the pusher slide is held at an approximate 30-degree angle before pulling it back until it just touches the blood droplet. They watch the blood sample spread along the edge of the spreader slide before smoothly and swiftly sliding it across the length of the specimen slide. The phlebotomist ensures they are not pressing against the slide, and they also do not lift the pusher slide while performing the smear. A second smear is performed using the same steps, with the edge of the first specimen slide being used as the pusher slide for the second smear. The phlebotomist allows the two blood smears to air dry before packaging them for transport. They also dispose of biohazards appropriately before removing gloves and performing hand hygiene.

Perform Blood Culture Collections

To perform blood culture collection, the phlebotomist should first identify their patient, provide an explanation of the procedure, and then obtain consent to proceed. After performing hand hygiene, the phlebotomist dons clean gloves before placing a tourniquet and locating an appropriate venipuncture site. Equipment is gathered and prepared, avoiding potential contamination by aseptically handling and assembling items.

Using the appropriate cleanser, the phlebotomist cleanses the venipuncture site using friction rub for 30-60 seconds. The site is allowed to air dry while the phlebotomist inspects the blood culture bottles for defects and confirms their expiration date. The flip tops are removed from blood culture bottles. Cleanse the top of each bottle with an alcohol prep pad and use a pen to mark the minimum and maximum fill lines for each bottle.

The tourniquet is reapplied, and venipuncture is performed. The phlebotomist does this without touching the skin. If directly filling culture bottles, connect the butterfly set to the bottle using the

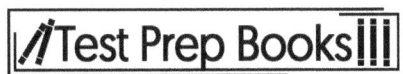

Routine Blood Collections

6. For extra labels, if unable to print a label, the phlebotomist may create one. The label should be created in pen, not pencil. This label should include:
    a. Full name
    b. Date of birth
    c. Medical identification number
    d. Date and time of draw
    e. Initials of phlebotomist

7. (If using extra/created label): Verify the label with the patient and ensure that all information is correct.

Post-Procedural Complications and Precautions

1. Ensure hemostasis to prevent bleeding and bruising.
2. Use appropriate bandaging including self-adhering wraps on older adults with fragile skin and on those with a lot of hair.
3. Observe the patient for signs/symptoms of complications: nausea, shortness of breath, confusion, excessive talking, change in speech patterns or talking less, blank stare.
4. Ensure that all equipment is cleaned up and removed from the patient area for safety.
5. In an outpatient setting: Clean up for the next patient, ensure the environment is safe and that there are no fall/trip hazards.
6. In an inpatient setting: Ensure no supplies are left in the bed to prevent patient harm.
7. Assist the patient as needed with moving and exiting the area.

Special Collections

Prepare Peripheral Blood Smear

To prepare a peripheral blood smear, the phlebotomist reviews the physician's order and determines whether they will collect the sample via capillary or venous puncture. For venous sampling, the phlebotomist confirms the patient's identity and prepares the specimen, using all appropriate measures to ensure safe and accurate specimen collection. The phlebotomist ensures the labeled specimen tube is mixed for at least two minutes to allow anticoagulant additives to be evenly and thoroughly distributed throughout the sample. Next, the phlebotomist gathers supplies to perform the peripheral smear.

The phlebotomist performs hand hygiene and applies clean gloves. They begin to visually inspect the two frosted slides and the third pusher slide for any defects, damage, and contaminants. A lens paper is used to remove lint and fingerprints from the slides. The two frosted slides are labelled with a pencil.

After removing the cap from the EDTA tube, the phlebotomist uses a capillary tube to collect a small amount of blood and deposit a single drop just above the frosted edge of one of the labelled specimen slides. Care is taken to ensure the droplet is placed in the center of the slide. Once this is done, the phlebotomist places the specimen slide into the non-dominant hand, grasping the edges securely with their thumb and index/middle fingers. They pick up the pusher slide by pinching one end with their fingertips.

The opposite end of the pusher slide is placed perpendicularly across the specimen slide, just above the blood drop. The phlebotomist ensures the pusher slide is held at an approximate 30-degree angle before pulling it back until it just touches the blood droplet. They watch the blood sample spread along the edge of the spreader slide before smoothly and swiftly sliding it across the length of the specimen slide. The phlebotomist ensures they are not pressing against the slide, and they also do not lift the pusher slide while performing the smear. A second smear is performed using the same steps, with the edge of the first specimen slide being used as the pusher slide for the second smear. The phlebotomist allows the two blood smears to air dry before packaging them for transport. They also dispose of biohazards appropriately before removing gloves and performing hand hygiene.

Perform Blood Culture Collections

To perform blood culture collection, the phlebotomist should first identify their patient, provide an explanation of the procedure, and then obtain consent to proceed. After performing hand hygiene, the phlebotomist dons clean gloves before placing a tourniquet and locating an appropriate venipuncture site. Equipment is gathered and prepared, avoiding potential contamination by aseptically handling and assembling items.

Using the appropriate cleanser, the phlebotomist cleanses the venipuncture site using friction rub for 30-60 seconds. The site is allowed to air dry while the phlebotomist inspects the blood culture bottles for defects and confirms their expiration date. The flip tops are removed from blood culture bottles. Cleanse the top of each bottle with an alcohol prep pad and use a pen to mark the minimum and maximum fill lines for each bottle.

The tourniquet is reapplied, and venipuncture is performed. The phlebotomist does this without touching the skin. If directly filling culture bottles, connect the butterfly set to the bottle using the

Special Collections

appropriate needle housing. While filling each bottle, keep the tubing and bottle below the venipuncture site. Additionally, ensure the blood culture medium does not splash onto the rubber stopper or needle during filling. Remove each bottle prior to inverting to mix. After removing the second bottle before inverting, withdraw the needle, place gauze on the puncture site, and activate the safety mechanism. Apply pressure at the venipuncture site, then discard the butterfly set. If using a syringe to transfer specimens to blood culture bottles, remove the needle before attaching the transfer device and filling each blood culture bottle. Ensure the patient's skin is cleaned if an iodine tincture was used to prepare the skin.

Proper labeling of bottles includes patient identification and blood collection location, time, and date. Any used equipment should be disposed of in the appropriate receptacle. Thank the patient before doffing gloves and performing hand hygiene. Document the procedure per facility guidelines and ensure the specimen is transferred to the lab as quickly as possible.

Assist Other Healthcare Professionals with Specimen Collection

In some circumstances, phlebotomists may be tasked with assisting other healthcare professionals with specimen collection. This typically occurs in situations where blood is being collected from a vascular access device (VAD). Examples of VADs include peripheral intravenous catheters (PIV), peripherally inserted central catheters (PICC), arterial lines (A-line), implanted ports, arteriovenous (AV) shunts, or central vascular access devices (CVAD). While phlebotomists may not be able to assist with blood sampling in these scenarios, they can assist in other meaningful ways.

Phlebotomists can support healthcare professionals by retrieving necessary equipment for specimen collection, including tubes and transfer devices. Additionally, the phlebotomist may assist with order of draw or methods to prevent pre-analytical error during the sampling process. This may include providing feedback to prevent issues related to improper dilution from flushing of access devices prior to draw. Other areas of expertise include prevention of hemolysis, fill volumes, and post-draw handling and storage. Phlebotomists may assist with transferring the blood sample from syringes to the appropriate tubes. Lastly, phlebotomists may be tasked with transporting specimens collected by another healthcare professional. Phlebotomists must always confirm proper patient identification and labeling if transporting a specimen they did not personally collect.

Collect Blood Samples for Inborn Errors of Metabolism

Newborn screening (NBS) is a process of blood sampling that aims to identify certain serious health conditions that babies can be born with but may not show signs of right away. Each state has its own legislature that dictates which conditions it includes in this mandatory screening, but all states screen for at least twenty-six conditions. Many of these involve *inborn errors of metabolism* (genetic disorders that cause issues with the body's ability to convert food to energy). One example of a genetic metabolic disorder is *phenylketonuria* (PKU), which results in a dangerous buildup of the amino acid phenylalanine. It is important to identify this disorder very early, as management of this disorder involves strict avoidance of foods containing phenylalanine.

After reviewing the order, introducing oneself, identifying the patient (and guardian), reviewing the procedure, obtaining consent, and identifying any considerations impacting testing (e.g., allergies, test requirements, positioning challenges, age-related considerations), the phlebotomist performs hand hygiene and gathers supplies. The phlebotomist dons clean gloves and positions the patient. An appropriate site is selected, and the skin is warmed as necessary. The phlebotomist firmly grasps the heel with the non-dominant hand and places the lancet flat against the site with their dominant hand. After activating the lancet, the heel is lowered, and gentle pressure is applied to produce the first blood drop.

The phlebotomist wipes away the first blood drop and then carefully picks up the NBS card, bringing the card close to the heel. Each circle is filled appropriately by touching the filter paper carefully to the drop of free-flowing blood. Gauze is applied, and the heel is elevated while pressure is applied to the site. The phlebotomist examines the site to ensure bleeding has stopped. A bandage is avoided due to risks of injury to the skin. Used supplies are disposed of appropriately, the patient and guardian are thanked, and the phlebotomist performs hand hygiene before leaving.

Perform Phlebotomy for Blood Donations

Blood donations are collected by venipuncture using a special (sterile) closed-system collection bag. These units feature a large gauge needle (16-18 gauge) and tubing that are connected to a collection bag. Within the collection bag is an anticoagulant preservative solution (citrate-phosphate-dextrose or CDP) that ensures blood does not clot and the cells remain viable.

Donors go through health screening, are informed about what to expect, and provide consent for the procedure. Donors are encouraged and offered fluids to reduce the risk of fainting during or following donation. Patient identification is confirmed, and the collection bag is properly labeled. Whenever possible, the patient should be reclined with feet up (supine) during the procedure.

A site is selected (preferably a large antecubital vein that is visible without a tourniquet), and the skin is prepared in a similar manner to blood culture collection and following strict aseptic technique. Needle size is determined by the size of the vein to be used for blood collection. A piece of tape is applied under the venipuncture site to anchor the needle and tubing during collection. The tourniquet can be removed for comfort once blood flow is established. Advise the patient to slowly open and close their fist approximately every 10–12 seconds while the unit is filling.

The collection bag is placed below the patient's arm to allow gravity to assist with filling the bag. As the bag fills, it should be gently agitated to mix the blood with the preservative solution within the collection bag. Careful site selection and accurate placement of the needle are especially important, because the needle attached to the collection set can only be used once. If the flow of blood stops prior to complete filling of a bag, a new set will need to be used. Once the bag has filled, the needle is withdrawn, and the needle safety mechanism can be engaged. Gauze and pressure are applied to the venipuncture site, and the patient is advised to elevate their arm. A bandage may be applied once bleeding has stopped. The phlebotomist confirms the patient's identity again and confirms with the patient that the unit is accurately labeled.

Throughout blood collection, the phlebotomist continuously monitors the patient and the venipuncture site for any signs of distress or adverse effects. This includes monitoring the patient for pallor, sweating, or reports of feeling lightheaded or dizzy, which could indicate the patient is at risk of fainting. Monitor the venipuncture site for swelling and pain that could indicate the formation of a hematoma. Monitor the tubing and collection bag to ensure proper and ongoing flow. After donation, the patient should be instructed to rest for a few moments prior to slowly getting up. Before leaving, the donor should be able to stand up without becoming dizzy, and their venipuncture site should be free from bleeding.

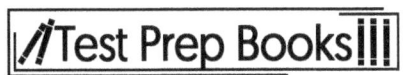

Special Collections

Calculate Volume Requirements

Certain patient populations are at a higher risk of developing iatrogenic anemia. *Iatrogenic anemia* is a lowering of hemoglobin and hematocrit that results from medical intervention such as repeated blood draws. Since patients can have multiple providers, it can be challenging for providers to recognize this as a potential source of anemia (particularly in outpatient care settings). For this reason, many organizations will limit daily blood draw volumes to 3% of a patient's total blood volume and will limit monthly blood draw volumes to 10%. At risk populations may have even stricter limits.

Infants and children pose the highest risk for development of iatrogenic anemia. Removal of more than 10% of an infant's total blood volume in a single draw can result in shock or cardiac arrest. Therefore, it is critical to document and track blood draw volumes during blood collection.

Adult patients at increased risk for developing iatrogenic anemia include ICU patients, patients undergoing treatment for cancer, and geriatric patients. In these populations, iatrogenic anemia can be a significant factor contributing to patients requiring blood transfusion. It is important for providers to consider reducing unnecessary routine testing as well as grouping orders into fewer draws, when possible.

Perform Non-Blood Specimen Collection

Urine is the most common non-blood specimen that phlebotomists encounter, and this is typically encountered in the outpatient setting. Phlebotomists will most often provide instructions for the patient to self-collect. When providing instructions, patients should always be given written instructions even if verbal instructions are provided. There are different types of urine tests, including *random* urine, *first morning* (or 8-hour urine), *fasting*, *timed*, and *2-hour postprandial* (after meal) specimen collection. There are also *24-hour urine* collections where patients collect all urine over a 24-hour period. Urine specimens may be collected without any special preparation (regular void specimen), *midstream* collection (patient voids a small amount before placing collection container to urine stream), or as a *clean catch* (midstream process with added cleaning of genital area prior to specimen collection).

When instructing a female patient to collect a clean-catch urine specimen, the phlebotomist explains that the patient should wash hands well before removing the lid to the container. Take care to avoid touching the inside of the lid or container. While standing in a squatting position over the toilet, spread the folds of the labia. Use a fresh wipe on the left side, a second wipe on the right side, and a third wipe to cleanse the urinary opening. Always wipe from front to back. Used wipes can be discarded in the trash. While continuing to keep the folds of the labia separated, void into the toilet for a few seconds. Pick up the urine container, touching only the outside, and bring the container under the urine stream. Ensure the lip of the container does not touch the skin. Fill the container between 30 to 100 mL. Finish voiding and then cover the specimen with the lid without touching the inside of the container. Use an antiseptic wipe to remove any urine from the outside of the container before washing hands and delivering the specimen to the phlebotomist.

For a male patient, the instructions are similar except they should be instructed to use a wipe to cleanse the end of the penis, using circular motions from the urinary opening and back. Repeat with another clean wipe. If uncircumcised, foreskin should be retracted prior to cleaning. Void into the toilet for a few seconds, continuing to hold back the foreskin (if applicable).

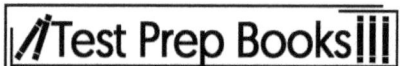

Special Collections

Confirm patient identification and label the specimen, taking care to include the time and date. The location and the type of specimen collected may also be required to distinguish the type of specimen or site of specimen collection. Additionally, be aware of storage and handling requirements associated with different specimen types.

Equipment Needed for Peripheral Blood Smears

Peripheral blood smears are performed by smearing a droplet of blood into a thin layer across a microscope slide. Specimen slides may be clear or frosted. A frosted edge makes labelling of the specimen slide easier. It is important to note that pencil is recommended for labelling, as pen ink may dissolve when the specimen is fixed. Care should be taken to ensure that slides are free from defects or damage, and lens paper may be used to clean any debris, fingerprints, or contaminants off the surface of each slide.

A third slide, called the *spreader* or *pusher* slide, is used to push the droplet along the specimen slide, which creates the smear. This may simply be another microscope slide or it could also be a specialized spreader slide with beveled edges. As with the specimen slides, it is important to inspect the slide to ensure the slide is clean with edges free from damage. This is because any irregularities or contaminants on these slides will impact the shape and quality of the smear.

Blood samples may be collected using capillary puncture or via collection in an EDTA tube. If collecting a specimen via capillary puncture, a small droplet of blood may be directly applied to a specimen slide or may be collected into a capillary tube. If a specimen is collected via venipuncture using an EDTA tube, the droplet may be collected by removing the cap and using a capillary tube (for thin smear), a pipette (for thick smear), or a blood drop delivery adapter (such as a "DIFF-SAFE" device) to ensure correct sample size.

Techniques to Perform Peripheral Blood Smears

Although techniques may differ between professionals, the steps and general techniques used to perform peripheral blood smear are generally the same. After labelling the specimen slide, the preparer applies the small droplet of blood just above the frosted edge (or 0.5–1 inch from one edge), centering the droplet on the slide.

The preparer picks up the specimen slide and uses the thumb and the index/middle fingers to grasp it at the ends. Next, the preparer uses the dominant hand to pick up the pusher slide by grasping the edge with the fingertips. Then, the opposite edge of the pusher slide is held against the specimen slide, just in front of the droplet of blood. The thickness of the smear will be determined largely by the angle of the spreader slide and the size of the droplet of blood. A 30-degree angle is appropriate for a thin blood smear using a typical sample.

The spreader slide is pulled back until it just touches the edge of the blood droplet. The preparer pauses briefly to allow the blood to spread across the edge of the pusher slide. Then, the spreader slide is swiftly pushed across the specimen slide to the opposite edge using smooth, even movement. A second specimen slide is prepared in the same way. When preparing the second slide, the first specimen slide can be used as the spreader slide for the second specimen slide to conserve supplies. Specimen slides should be allowed to air dry before packaging them for transport. The preparer should never blow on the specimen to aid in the drying process, as this can compromise the sample.

Special Collections

An acceptable blood smear covers approximately half to three-quarters of the specimen slide. The smear should be free from spots, lines, or jagged edges. When held to the light, the smear should show a smooth gradient that goes from the thicker edge to a thin, rounded *feather* edge.

An inappropriate angle used to perform a smear or inappropriate droplet size can create issues with the length or the thickness of a smear. Uneven smears or horizontal lines across the smear are typically associated with too much pressure when pushing the spreader slide. Spots on the smear can be caused by contaminants, and streaks along the smear are typically due to defects or contaminants along the edge of the spreader slide. Lifting of the spreader slide during smear can result in the absence of the feather. Not allowing the blood droplet to spread across the spreader slide before performing the smear will result in a narrow, bullet-shaped smear.

Type of Sample for Blood Smears and Timing Requirements

Peripheral blood smears, used to manually evaluate blood cells under a microscope, are prepared by taking a single drop of blood and smearing it across a microscope slide. A *thin* peripheral smear is the most common type of blood smear ordered. It is often used to assist with manual blood counts (manual *differentiation*, or *diff*) and to evaluate blood cells. A *thick* peripheral smear is less commonly ordered, and it is most often used (in conjunction with a thin blood smear) to detect the presence of *malaria* (a parasitic protozoa transmitted by mosquitoes). The primary difference between performing a thick and thin blood smear is the size of the droplet of blood used to prepare the slide. A thin smear requires a small drop of blood, while the thick smear requires a large drop of blood.

Blood samples for peripheral blood smear can be obtained via capillary or venous puncture. For a specimen collected by capillary puncture, the first drop of blood should be wiped to avoid potential contamination from alcohol or other residue from the capillary puncture process. With the next drop of blood, the phlebotomist touches the specimen slide to the drop, taking care to position the drop above the frosted edge and centered on the slide. Additionally, the phlebotomist ensures the slide touches only the blood droplet and not the skin. One drop (1–2 millimeters in diameter) is the appropriate amount for a thin blood smear. A thick smear requires 2–3 large drops to form a 1–2 centimeter sample. Blood smears using capillary samples should be performed immediately after placement on the specimen slide.

Venous samples are obtained by venipuncture and are placed into an EDTA tube. The specimen should be mixed for approximately two minutes to ensure the anticoagulant additive is evenly dispersed. Preferably, a drop delivery system (such as the DIFF-SAFE device) can be attached to the top of the tube and used to deposit a uniform drop onto the slide. Alternatively, a capillary tube or pipette may be used to collect the specimen from an opened EDTA tube. Blood smears using EDTA samples should be processed within an hour of collection to avoid changes to cells associated with the anticoagulant.

Techniques and Locations for Blood Culture Collections

The American Society for Microbiology (ASM) advises that two to four sets of blood cultures should be collected to ensure accurate identification of bacterial and fungal blood infections. Each set of blood cultures involves placing blood from a single venipuncture site into two separate bottles: an *aerobic* bottle (used to test for the presence of pathogens that need air to survive) and an *anaerobic* bottle (used to test for pathogens that thrive without air).

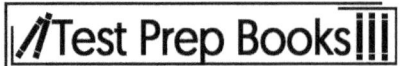

Special Collections

For situations that are very urgent, blood cultures are drawn from two to three venipuncture locations. Venipuncture collections occur back-to-back. Additionally, venipuncture locations must all be different, ideally using opposite arms. For patients with a *fever of unknown origin* (FUO; fever with no identifiable cause), the initial blood culture collection from two to three different venipuncture sites is performed. If the initial cultures continue to be negative after the first one to two days, another two sets of blood cultures might be indicated.

Phlebotomists can directly impact the chances of successful blood culture detection in many ways. Paying close attention to the timing of a blood culture order can be important because blood cultures are often ordered at times when fever or other infection signs have spiked, which means that pathogen levels are often higher at the time they are ordered. Ensuring blood cultures are drawn as close to that time as possible increases success rates. Careful preparation (skin preparation, sterile technique, appropriate order of draw) can help phlebotomists positively influence the outcome of a blood culture. Use of appropriate sample volumes is another critical way that phlebotomists ensure successful detection after blood culture collection.

Equipment Needed for Blood Culture Collections

When preparing to collect blood cultures, first consider how many sets of blood cultures have been ordered. Depending on the weight of the patient, select the appropriate number and size of collection bottles. General venipuncture equipment includes venipuncture needle, needle safety device, transfer device, tourniquet, gauze, alcohol prep pads, and bandages. Specific to blood culture collection, the phlebotomist should also obtain an appropriate skin cleanser (i.e., iodine tincture, chlorhexidine, or povidone/ethyl alcohol cleanser) and consider the use of sterile nitrile gloves.

The method utilized for inoculation of blood culture bottles will require additional equipment. Direct inoculation will require the use of adaptors or needle holders used in conjunction with butterfly sets. Delayed inoculation will require applicable syringes and transfer devices to transfer specimens after collection. If inoculation is to be performed by the lab after transport, appropriate collection tubes will need to be used.

If available, the phlebotomist can also utilize an *initial specimen diversion* (ISD) device to reduce the risk of sample contamination. This device isolates the first 1.5–2 milliliters of blood obtained from a venipuncture site, which has been found to contain an overwhelming majority of contaminants (e.g., skin cells, surface microorganisms) that impact the accuracy of blood culture results. ISD devices have mechanisms to isolate the initial blood while opening a second sterile channel for the attachment and transfer of the blood specimen used for blood culture collection.

Skin Preparation for Blood Culture Collections

A major area for concern regarding blood culture collection is the risk of sample contamination with normal skin flora. In response to this risk, it is essential for phlebotomists to meticulously cleanse the venipuncture site prior to collecting blood cultures. If normal bacteria contaminate a sample, the laboratory is required to report these findings. The physician must interpret the results and make decisions about whether a noted microorganism is normal or harmful (*pathogenic*). Contamination of a sample can risk delayed or inappropriate treatment, which can have detrimental patient outcomes.

Although it is impossible to achieve an absolutely sterile venipuncture site, phlebotomists use sterile techniques to eliminate as many microorganisms as possible and prevent sample contamination.

Special Collections

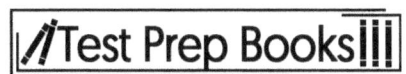

Principles of sterile technique include scrubbing the venipuncture site for 30–60 seconds. Antiseptics recommended for use in blood culture collection include iodine tincture, chlorhexidine, or a povidone/ethyl alcohol combination. When using ampules of chlorhexidine or iodine tincture, place the swab where the planned venipuncture will be performed and make concentric circles until an area of approximately 2.5 inches x 2.5 inches is covered. When selecting the appropriate cleanser, it is important to confirm whether a patient is allergic to shellfish or iodine before using iodine tincture. Chlorhexidine is the recommended cleanser for infants (2 months and older) as well as for patients with iodine allergy. Additional sterile measures used for blood culture collection include careful setup and handling of supplies used during the collection process.

Volume Requirements for Blood Culture Collections

The bottles used for blood culture collection are unique in that they contain a special nutrient *medium* (or *broth*) that promotes the growth of microorganisms. Bottles are differentiated by color and include descriptions. Pink-capped bottles are the smallest, having a recommended fill volume of 1–3 milliliters (no less than 0.5 milliliter). Blue-capped bottles are aerobic (contain air) and have a recommended fill volume of 8–10 milliliters (no less than 3 milliliters). Purple-capped bottles are anaerobic (do not contain air) and have a recommended fill volume of 8–10 milliliters (no less than 3 milliliters).

Use of appropriate fill volumes is one of the most important factors to successful pathogen detection. The American Society of Microbiology (ASM) makes volume recommendations based on patient weight. For NICU patients and infants weighing less than 18 pounds, the recommendation is for a single set of blood cultures using 1 milliliter of blood in a single pink-capped bottle. For patients between 18–29 pounds, two sets of blood cultures should be obtained. Each set is a single 3 milliliter specimen in a pink-capped bottle. For patients weighing 30–88 pounds, two sets of blood cultures—10 milliliters placed into a blue-capped aerobic bottle—is recommended. Lastly, for patients weighing greater than 88 pounds, two sets of blood cultures are recommended with each set including 10 milliliters placed in a blue-capped aerobic bottle and 10 milliliters placed in a purple anaerobic bottle.

Order of Draw for Blood Culture Collections

The order of draw for blood culture collection can have a direct impact on the accuracy of pathogen detection. Mistakes made regarding order of draw could potentially result in sample contamination. Incorrect order can also impact the ability for the bottle and growth medium to facilitate growth of certain microorganisms.

For this reason, it is important to always draw blood cultures first if they are ordered along with other laboratory testing. This reduces the risk of contamination from the other tubes. Additionally, if the total volume of blood needed for a set of blood cultures is less than required, prioritize filling of the aerobic (with air) bottle completely, then inoculate the anaerobic bottle with the remaining volume. The reason for this is that it has been found that the majority of identified bacterial and fungal pathogens are *aerobic* (need oxygen to survive) or *facultative* (they can survive with or without oxygen). This means that the aerobic blood culture bottle is most likely to be the medium that grows any identified pathogens.

It is also important for phlebotomists to recognize differences in order of draw when utilizing different inoculation techniques. When directly inoculating blood culture bottles (butterfly set connected directly to bottle), the aerobic bottle is filled first. The reason for this is that air present in the butterfly tubing is pushed into the collection bottle prior to the blood specimen beginning to flow. Conversely, if

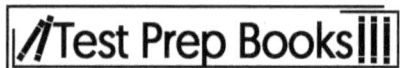

Special Collections

inoculation occurs just after collection, via syringe transfer, the anaerobic bottle is filled first. This is to ensure that the air bubble at the end of the syringe does not get added to the anaerobic bottle.

Blood Culture Bottle Preparation Procedures

Adding blood specimens to blood culture bottles (called *inoculation*) can occur immediately during collection or following collection. Direct inoculation can be achieved via butterfly set and specialized adaptor. Using this method, the aerobic container is filled first due to there being air in the butterfly tubing set. Prevention of backflow is achieved by keeping the collection bottle and tubing below the venipuncture site. For this method, it is important to ensure that blood culture medium does not come in contact with the stopper or needle while the collection is in progress (including not agitating or mixing the bottle until after it has been removed from the adaptor housing).

If inoculation is completed following collection, a common method involves syringe transfer to blood culture bottles. This will require the use of a safety transfer device. With this method, first inoculate the anaerobic blood culture bottle by connecting the bottle to the transfer device, followed by the aerobic bottle. Take care to closely monitor the volume of blood being drawn into the bottle, disconnecting the transfer device once the appropriate volume level has been reached. Never push the plunger to force blood into the blood culture bottles, as this can cause hemolysis of the specimen and can also lead to blood spray (aerosolization) upon removing the transfer device from the blood culture bottle. Another delayed inoculation technique involves collection of the specimen in a special collection tube to be transferred to the lab for inoculation.

Equipment and Transfer Procedures

When assisting another healthcare professional with specimen collection, one task the phlebotomist may perform is transferring the collected blood sample from syringes to the appropriate tubes. The phlebotomist reviews the patient's orders and gathers the appropriate equipment. This may include gloves, collection tubes, syringes, and an appropriate transfer device. The phlebotomist will accompany the other healthcare professional to the patient care location, and they will introduce themselves and perform hand hygiene prior to confirming the patient's identity.

The phlebotomist will don clean gloves and stand by while the healthcare professional performs the steps necessary to access and withdraw the required volume of blood into a syringe or syringes. The phlebotomist will have the appropriate tubes and syringe transfer device nearby ready to receive each filled syringe. Being mindful of asepsis, the healthcare professional and phlebotomist must coordinate handoff of the filled syringe, by direct handoff or by setting the syringe onto a prepared work surface. If direct handoff is performed, the phlebotomist must ensure they do not touch the healthcare professional to avoid contamination. Additionally, any needles should have safety mechanisms activated prior to handoff to avoid accidental needle stick. The phlebotomist should immediately attach the appropriate transfer device to each syringe and fill the tubes in the appropriate order of draw. Upon completion of the procedure, the phlebotomist thanks the patient, assists with proper disposal of biohazards and other waste, and removes gloves before performing hand hygiene.

Techniques to Collect Blood on Filter Paper/Guthrie Cards

Testing for inborn errors of metabolism is ideally performed within 24–72 hours of birth via blood spot collection. A *blood spot collection* is completed by taking a few drops of blood and applying them to

Special Collections

spots on a *Guthrie card* (a card with filter paper that is used to perform dried blood spot testing). Heel puncture is the recommended avenue for newborn blood spot collection.

To appropriately complete the collection process, each circle must be filled. This is accomplished by touching each circle on the *front* surface of the card to the large drop of free-flowing blood on the patient's heel. It is held in place until the blood absorbs to fill the circle, saturating both sites of the card. All the circles should be filled completely.

After filling each circle, the card must be allowed to air dry. The card should be placed horizontally and away from sunlight or heat. Hanging a specimen card could result in the specimen bleeding onto the lower part of the card, which impacts the validity of the testing. After the specimen fully dries, it can be packaged and sent for testing.

It is also important to take care to avoid contaminating the filter paper prior to specimen collection. This includes avoiding touching the filter paper with ungloved hands or allowing the paper to contact potential contaminants that can impact test results. Alcohol, urine, lotions, and powders have all been shown to impact accuracy of test results.

Standards for Blood Donation

Blood donation (the process of collecting blood from donors to be used for medical transfusion) involves rapid withdrawal of a unit of blood, which is approximately 450 milliliters of blood. Due to the volume of donation, blood donors are first given a health screening to assess their overall fitness for blood donation. Ideal candidates are between 17–66 years old, and they weigh at least 110 pounds. Some states allow 16-year-old individuals to donate if they have written consent from their guardian. Individuals between 66–76 years old require the consent of a blood donation physician, and those over 76 years old require written consent from their own physician. Donors are asked to provide a thorough health history and are also physically evaluated to ensure they are healthy enough for donation. Point of care testing is performed to ensure donors have a hemoglobin level greater than or equal to 12.5 g/dL (for female donors) and 13 g/dL (for male and non-binary donors).

Following collection, donated blood products are processed. The donated blood may remain as whole blood or be separated into components. Any blood or component is federally required to be documented and traceable to the donor and any recipient. In cases where a blood recipient experiences an infection that could potentially be associated with a transfusion, the blood bank would be notified to begin an investigation. This includes notification and testing for the blood donor as well as any recipient who received their blood. Any remaining blood products associated with that donor would be removed from inventory.

Pediatric Volume Calculations

Blood volume calculations are a way for phlebotomists to estimate the total volume of blood for pediatric patients. The reason this is important is that pediatric patient blood volumes vary widely with age groups as well as with weight. For premature infants, for instance, there is an estimated 115 milliliters of blood for every kilogram of body weight. Newborns have between 80–100 milliliters of blood for each kilogram of weight. Infants and children, similarly, have between 75–100 milliliters of blood per kilogram of body weight.

To calculate pediatric total blood volume, find the patient's weight in kilograms. This is calculated by taking the weight in pounds and dividing that by 2.2. For example: A patient weighing 22 pounds would be 10 kilograms.

Next, the weight in kilograms is generally multiplied by 100 milliliters to get the estimated total blood volume in milliliters. Blood volume is typically represented in liters, so the last step would be to divide the total blood volume in milliliters by 1000. That gives you the total blood volume in liters.

General guidelines are that patients should have no more than 3% of total blood volume taken in a single draw and no more than 10% of total volume drawn in a month. An easy and conservative calculation the phlebotomist can use to estimate maximum volume for a single draw is to take the patient's weight (in kilograms) and multiply that by two to get the safe volume limit. For example: A patient weighing 10 kilograms can safely have 20 milliliters of blood drawn in a single session.

Equipment and Techniques for Performing Non-Blood Specimen Collection

Non-blood specimens include various substances that are produced by the body. Examples of non-blood specimens include tissue, hair and nail samples, urine, stool, breath, and sweat. As with blood specimens, non-blood specimens are considered potentially infectious and should be handled appropriately.

Outpatient urine testing (covered in Patient Preparation) is typically self-collected by the patient. A clean urine container may be used for many routine or timed urine collections. For clean-catch specimens, cleansing wipes are also used to reduce the risk of contamination by skin microbiome. A clean graduated urine collection pan may be placed into the toilet to assist patients who have difficulty with midstream urine self-collection. For 24-hour urine collection, the patient takes a large container home to collect urine produced during a 24-hour period. They are instructed to keep the container in the refrigerator until returned to the lab.

Stool samples are generally collected into wide mouth containers. Special tests like the *fecal guaiac blood test* or *fecal immunochemical test* are performed by placing a small amount of stool onto a special card that contains a point of care (POC) test for bleeding in the intestines. DNA stool tests are another newer screening test to detect markers associated with colon cancer.

General guidelines for obtaining non-blood specimens includes confirmation of patient identification and labeling of the specimen. Specimens should be labeled with date and time of collection. They may also need to be labeled with the location and the type of specimen collected, depending on the specimen being tested. Additionally, special considerations may need to be taken to process and store non-blood samples.

Skin Preparation for Blood Alcohol Level Collection

Blood alcohol level testing, also called ethanol (or ETOH) testing, is a test to measure the amount of alcohol in the bloodstream. In some cases, the results of this test are used only to assist with medical treatment. Alternatively, ETOH may be ordered and used in forensic cases. As always, it is important for the phlebotomist to take measures to minimize the chances of errors during the collection, processing, and transportation of specimens.

As mentioned previously, one major consideration associated with blood alcohol testing is the method of preparing the skin for venipuncture. Cleansers containing alcohol can impact the results of the test

Special Collections

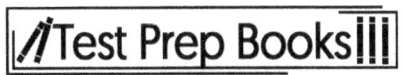

and should, therefore, be avoided. Most of the common skin prep products contain alcohol. These include isopropyl alcohol prep pads, methanol, and ethyl alcohol. Iodine tincture also contains alcohol and cannot be used for blood alcohol collection. The most common product that can be used is aqueous benzalkonium chloride (BZK). Aqueous povidone-iodine is a second choice that can safely be used in this situation. If neither of these products are available for use, the site may be cleansed using soap and water.

Processing

Prepare Specimens for Testing or Transport

Collecting and testing bodily fluids and other specimens for diagnostic testing requires strict adherence to guidelines and protocol to avoid contaminating or compromising the sample. Slight alterations to the sample can cause results to be erroneous. Any specimen collected should be delivered to the laboratory for testing as soon as possible. All staff involved in the testing and transporting process should have knowledge of the general guidelines for proper storage based on specimen type.

Any specimen that is to be transported must be labeled to identify the patient and the test that is being completed. Lab requisition forms are used to communicate the specific test order, ordering provider's name, patient's name, date of birth, age, health record identification number, and the date and time that the collection occurred.

The label should be adhered to the sample so that it is readable. Certain laboratory specimens may require the label to be placed in a particular way for the diagnostic testing equipment to be able to read the label for processing. For specimens such as swabs or tissue samples it is important that the site and the initials of the healthcare staff are marked and clearly legible on the label. This is to indicate where the specimen was obtained from for comparison with the order and to provide a contact for any questions or concerns from the laboratory staff.

Maintain Integrity of Specimens Based on Handling Requirements

Maintaining the integrity of specimens begins with education about the entire laboratory collection process. This includes how to ensure correct patient identification, appropriate collection methods and techniques, knowledge of laboratory tests, and preservation and handling requirements.

Laboratory, nursing, and healthcare provider leadership must create succinct policy for staff guidance on the standard operating procedures for collection, handling, and transport methods to ensure that specimen integrity is managed. Staff involved with lab collection must stay competent and adept with accreditation and nationally recognized standards.

Adhere to Chain-of-Custody Guidelines When Required

Chain of custody is a process used for certain testing types, such as drug testing. This process includes an official document that provides a record of each individual who has handled a specimen, and the document may be used as screening for employment eligibility or as court evidence. This ensures the collection is accurate, reliable, and conforms to the legal requirements of the court.

The form typically includes sample collection details, transporting information, receiving confirmation, and signatures of all parties involved. The form includes all pertinent information of the donor, such as name, date of birth, social security number, and any special collection methods that are unique to that test (such as blue dye in toilet prior to sample collection). The sample collection details are to include the time and date of collection, the name of the individual that collected the sample, and a description that may include size, weight, type of sample, and process used to collect the sample. Transportation information includes the time and date of transport, name of individual transporting the sample, and the method of transportation such as personal delivery, mail, or courier service. Receiving information includes the name of the individual who has accepted the sample, the time and date that the sample was received, and the condition of the sample when delivered.

In the case of deviation from the standard collection process, the form may also document refusal by the donor, attempts to adulterate the test, or the inability of the donor to produce a sample.

Coordinate Communication Between Non-Laboratory Personnel

Laboratory specimen collection and processing is a multi-disciplinary process. Depending on the type of test, specimen collection may occur within inpatient units, outpatient clinics, provider offices, surgical areas, or clinics designed solely for sample collection (i.e., Covid swabbing). Effective communication is essential to ensure that the laboratory diagnostic sample is safely collected and preserved. Communication between all parties should remain professional, clear, and concise. Poor communication may lead to misunderstanding, unclear expectations, and risks to patient safety. Communication tools such as avoiding assumptions and using simple language all support understanding within a multidisciplinary team.

All staff that will be part of the collection or transport process related to laboratory samples must have sufficient education to protect themselves against contracting an infectious disease due to exposure. Communication is essential to provide the details needed by collecting staff on type of collection method, container, and storage needs. This must be conveyed to the staff that are transporting, especially if via courier. Any special requirements, such as temperature management will need to be understood.

Input and Retrieve Specimen Data Using Available Laboratory Information System

Electronic health records (EHRs) are used to digitally provide access to patient's health information, including laboratory values. There may be a separate software system that is often referred to as the laboratory information system (LIS). This is an electronic system that manages, records, and stores patient data related to clinical and pathological diagnostic testing. These systems may be used separately from the electronic health record. Within these systems, accession numbers are used to keep track of when an order is received, link to the patient record with identifying information, and track the sample transport, as well as provide a record of staff that have handled it through its testing cycle.

Laboratory staff are trained to access these systems to verify provider orders, upload values, and review data. According to the Joint Commission, two unique patient identifiers should be used to verify the identity of the patient, specimens, and correct input of documentation. Those identifiers are typically the patient's name and date of birth, but other choices for identifiers are listed in the Patient Identifiers section of this guide.

Recognize and Report Critical Values for Point-of-Care Testing

Point-of-care (POC) testing indicates that the sample may be taken from a patient and processed without being sent to a lab. Results are typically available within fifteen minutes, and some, such as those of a blood glucose test, are available within less than a minute. Point-of-care testing has provided a reliable and relatively simple method to identify and monitor chronic disease conditions or active infection and deliver results in a short time frame. This dissolves care barriers by providing improved access to care, expedited treatment, and convenience to the patient.

Other types of POC testing include drug screening, pregnancy testing, pH levels, urine strip testing, fecal occult blood analysis, infectious disease diagnostics, and rapid cardiac, coagulation, and blood gas monitoring. Providing monitoring of disease progression or improvement is possible with testing for cholesterol levels, hemoglobin, and diabetic markers such as blood glucose levels and HgbA1C.

Common lab values of these tests may be visually posted for reference with critical parameters indicated for reporting results that are outside reference points. These values are reviewed further along in this section. While point-of-care testing is safe and accurate, values that are critically outside of reference ranges may need to be verified with a blood test. For example, point-of-care to test blood glucose via a finger stick uses capillary blood. Exceedingly high values should be verified with a whole blood test. Check with facility policy for further guidance.

Distribute Laboratory Results to Ordering Providers

Distribution of laboratory results will vary depending on the facility, office, or healthcare establishment that the order came from. Requirements for reporting to more than one provider or specialty for one patient may also exist. Lab reports may be sent via secure fax, mail, electronic messaging systems, or verbally over the telephone.

EHRs can improve the safety and ease of identifying and reporting critical lab values. Any lab values that are marked as a STAT order and/or results that are critical or life-threatening are prioritized to be reported out first. Standard lab values are typically completed and reported within twenty-four hours. It is important to report out lab values in a timely manner to facilitate patient care.

Centrifuging Procedures and Techniques

Centrifugation is a technique that separates particles from a solution based on shape, size, medium viscosity, density, and speed of rotation. To achieve this, the specimen is suspended within a liquid medium then transferred to a centrifuge tube. A motorized rotor spins the tube at a set speed.

Hazards related to use of a centrifuge include aerosolization and mechanical failure. Due to this, safe procedures must be established and followed per facility guidelines. All operators of the centrifuge must have competency training prior to use. Lab personnel must maintain a log for checking the rotors for expiration dates and verify that the rotors, tubes, and spindles remain dry and clean. O-rings should be replaced if found to be missing, cracked, or worn. Centrifuge tubes should be filled three-quarters full or less and caps must be secured onto the tubes prior to centrifuging.

As the centrifuge operates via rotating, the system must be balanced to prevent vibration or noise. An unbalanced load can cause damage to the centrifuge and/or samples. Any time there is noticeable drift, shaking, or vibration, the centrifuge should be stopped immediately.

For bodily fluid samples or potentially infectious material, the following safety procedures must be observed:

- A biohazard label must be placed on the centrifuge in use.

- Gloves are to be worn at all times when handling rotors or tubes.

- Celluloid tubes are not preferred for use with biohazardous material; however, if they are required, disinfectants must be used to decontaminate. This is because celluloid tubes are

Processing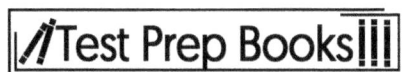

not able to be autoclaved due to their high risk for flammability and that they are prone to shrinking with use over time.

- Equipment made from glass, stainless steel, polypropylene, and polycarbonate are safe for autoclave processing.

- Safety cups, buckets, and sealed rotors with O-rings should be used as secondary containment when possible.

- A biological safety cabinet should be used, when available, with filling of centrifuge tubes, loading of rotors, removal from rotors, and opening of tubes.

- Prior to loading the rotors or buckets, the exterior of tubes and bottles should be wiped down with disinfectants.

- After this is completed, gloves should be changed and the specimens transported to the centrifuge.

Once the centrifuge has completed spinning, allow ten minutes to pass for aerosols to settle prior to opening. If a spill or leak has occurred, refer to facility protocol for management of biohazardous materials. The centrifuge interior and accessories must also be decontaminated if tube breakage occurs.

This technique is commonly used for the separation of plasma and serum from whole blood. Plasma is an anticoagulated specimen while serum is coagulated. Anticoagulation additives prevent the formation of fibrin. It must be determined which is being collected in order to use appropriate draw tubes and allow serum to clot for thirty minutes to one hour prior to centrifugation. Both plasma and serum must be separated within two hours of being collected.

Aliquoting Procedures and Techniques

Aliquoting is the process of separating a larger sample into one or more smaller portions for chemical analysis. This is typically completed for plasma, when gel is not available to separate plasma from cells, and when a specimen requires stability during transport. It is important that the process for aliquoting is standardized and consistent between performing laboratory staff as deviations from practice can lead to results that are not uniform and lacking quality standards.

To aliquot a specimen:

1. The initial tube must be centrifuged first.
2. Then, with a pipette, the fluid floating at the top is removed only. Avoid collecting or disturbing the settled cells.
3. To utilize the pipette, the bulb is depressed to remove air and create suction.
4. The tip of the pipette is placed in the upper specimen.
5. The bulb is then released, and the fluid will backflow into the pipette.
6. This fluid will be transferred to a secondary aliquot tube.
7. Store and label according to facility protocol and specimen type.

Handling, Storage, Transportation and Disposal Requirements for Specimens

Proper storage and handling is required to maintain the integrity of samples. The type of specimen will indicate the environmental conditions that should be maintained to prevent compromise. Staff that collect samples must deliver the specimens timely when drawn within facilities that have laboratory capabilities to avoid any breakdown of the sample. Certain samples may need to be placed on ice immediately, such as blood gas sampling, even when transport may be mere minutes. This is because this slows metabolic processes, use of oxygen by cells, and stabilizes the analyte. Other types of specimens are more accurate when kept at body temperature, 98.6 °F (37 °C). This may be achieved by using a pediatric heel warmer, or a portable incubator in the case of transporting a larger number of specimens. Light may also affect the results of a test, and the specimen should be transported so it cannot be penetrated by light. Bilirubin is an example of a light-sensitive test.

Pneumatic tube systems are often used for transporting items between units and floors. Ensure caps are tightened and place biohazard items within sealed bags. Care should be taken with fluid samples to prevent leaks; products that place a covering film to seal the container's lid should be used when available. Sufficient packaging material to cushion samples within the pneumatic tube container is required to prevent any damage.

When the sample is drawn outside of a healthcare facility with laboratory processing capabilities, samples may require certain handling and conditions. Always refer to laboratory test parameters and guidance from policy and accrediting bodies for specifications.

To safely transport specimen samples, appropriate packaging must be clean. Sturdy containers with lids that can be secured are required. Packaging materials, such as bubble wrap or padded envelopes may be used to separate containers and cushion against motion or jarring that may otherwise cause tubes and containers to be knocked together which may lead to cracking and leaking. Ice packs are required to maintain samples that are temperature sensitive and need to be kept below room temperatures. Tubes and containers should be placed upright when possible.

It should be ensured during the packaging process that any biohazardous material or chemicals are sealed within leak-proof and puncture-resistant containers.

Bacterial culture specimens should be transported at room temperature. Viral culture specimens must be transported on ice to maintain integrity. The caps and tops of the specimen containers must be secured prior to testing or transport. Any manipulation of the containers should be completed using standard precautions. This is to prevent spread of infection from the sample as well as to prevent any potentially colonized or transient bacteria transfer from the healthcare or laboratory staff hands. Standard precautions consist of the use of the following: gloves, gown, respiratory etiquette, hand hygiene, and safe sharps practices.

Serum samples require a cool container that is maintained between 1 °C and 10 °C if it will be delivered to the laboratory within twenty-four hours. If the transportation time will be beyond this timeframe, the sample should be frozen to −20 °C. Whole blood may be stored at 4 °C to 8 °C for twenty-four hours but must never be frozen.

Urine samples are kept at 2 °C to 8 °C. Always be cautious with twenty-four-hour urine collection systems as the solution contains preservatives including boric acid, acetic acid, and/or hydrochloric acid, which may cause chemical burns when handling. Stool samples are often collected via home kits and brought in by patients. Samples are valid for four hours at room temperature and twenty-four hours when refrigerated. Any stool sample collected should be sealed well to prevent any leakage.

According to the Centers for Disease Control and Prevention (CDC), evidence does not show that medical waste is more infectious than regular household waste; however, regulatory guidelines categorize the appropriate disposal of waste based on type. This includes microbiology laboratory waste, pathology and anatomy waste, blood products and specimens, and other body-fluid specimens. The U.S. Environmental Protection Agency has published the *Manual for Infectious Waste Management* to provide guidance that coincides with individual State regulations. This and facility policy should be referenced for the disposal of regulated and non-regulated medical waste for proper and legal waste disposal procedures.

Chain-of-Custody Guidelines

In order to maintain the purpose of the chain of custody, standardization of the process and education for all individuals who are part of the chain must occur. Guidelines from regulatory agencies must be adhered to for the process to be legal and legitimate. Each sample must have succinct and clear identification that includes the subject being tested and each sample should be marked clearly with a distinct identification code on the label.

Each step of the process must be documented with information regarding the handlers. When used as intended, the chain of custody should be able to answer where the sample is at all stages of processing, who has had possession of the sample and at what time/date, locations the sample has been, and who is currently in possession of the sample.

Information that is collected within a chain of custody must be documented and accessible for review by authorized agents.

Internal and External Databases

Detailed information regarding specific laboratory tests may be found within internal and external databases. Internal databases are purchased by the healthcare organization or facility and are often integrated within the EHR software. An internal database is a resource for healthcare providers, clinical staff, and laboratory professionals for knowledge of test types, clinical indications, parameters for normal and critical values, and specifications for collection, storage, and transport. Patient education may be drawn from these databases for teaching purposes and inclusion on discharge and care instructions.

External databases, accessible for free and at cost, publish information from international, peer-reviewed journals and leading healthcare education and data organizations. These are much more expansive than the internal databases, which have a limited amount of information. Popular examples of external databases include CINAHL, ClinicalKey, Cochrane Library, and CDC. Data such as morbidity and mortality reports, legal cases, critical pathways, research results, and clinical trials may be searched related to specific diagnostic laboratory tests. This knowledge may be utilized to drive and guide patient care.

Critical Values for Point-of-Care Testing

Point-of-care testing is rapid blood or other diagnostic testing that can be completed within a short amount of time. The quick turnaround for results provides the opportunity for providers to act on the lab values while the patient is available for discussion and modification of their care plan. As results are dependent upon the individual patient and their current health status, any values outside of normal limit reference ranges for point of care testing should be relayed to the primary care team for awareness. This may alter the course of care for the patient. Communication should be timely and well documented.

The following are some of the most common point-of-care tests with normal reference ranges:

HgB

- Twelve years old to adult (male) — 13.8–17.2 g/dL
- Twelve years old to adult (female) — 12.1–15.1 g/dL

Cholesterol

- >200 mg/dL

Glucose, serum (fasting)

- 70–110 mg/dL
- Results of less than 50 or greater than 250 mg/dL should always be reported

HgbA1C

- < 5.7% (any value over 6.5% has an increased risk for patient health complications)

Activated clotting time

- Reference ranges vary with patient care, but the normal range is within 70 to 180 seconds. Clinical therapeutic values range from 130 to 600 seconds.

Macroscopic Urinalysis

- pH: 5–8
- Protein: Negative
- Glucose (Qualitative): Negative
- Ketones (Qualitative): Negative
- Bilirubin (Qualitative): Negative
- Urobilinogen: 0.2–1.0 Ehrlich units/dL
- Nitrites: Negative
- Leukocyte Esterase: Negative
- Specific gravity values range between 1.003–1.040 and can be affected by hydration levels. Out-of-reference results should be referred to the ordering provider.

Fecal Occult Blood

- Normal test results for infants and adults are negative.

Gastric Occult Blood

- Normal test results for infants and adults are negative.

Rapid HIV

- Normal test results are negative/non-reactive.

This list is not comprehensive, but an overview of commonly used point-of-care tests within physician offices and healthcare facilities. The healthcare entities policy on reporting of critical values should always be referred to for guidance of what values have reporting requirements.

Basic Protocol to Distribute Laboratory Results

Facilities housing laboratories must create policies and protocols to establish the distribution process for laboratory results, especially if the laboratory is analyzing samples for multiple establishments. Care should be taken to report results within a timely manner, with consideration given to clinical and community care sites that operate within limited office hours.

Lab values that are within normal limits may be reported within the standard reporting timeframe and venue that is standard for the operating procedure. Values that should be escalated include those that are outside reference ranges or if the lab value returned deviates significantly from previous values or what is expected.

The general guideline, per nationally accrediting bodies and national guidance organizations, advises that there should be a tiered process set in place to define laboratory values and their reporting urgency and requirements. Of note, it remains the responsibility of the ordering provider to provide the mode of reporting, contact information, and if any other provider should be notified of results.

Tests may be ordered with an expedited definition attached, such as STAT (urgent) or As Soon As Possible. STAT labs will be reported within six to twelve hours, depending on delivery of labs and type of test being ordered. In the case of a critical care emergency or life-threatening condition, healthcare providers must call directly to speak with laboratory staff to ensure that the test is run immediately and the results are called back to the ordering provider or department (i.e. critical care nursing department). Each facility should develop a list of laboratory tests along with the expectations of time to analyze and deliver results to prevent confusion or a delay in communications.

Laboratory Requirements

Laboratories are an integral part of the healthcare continuum and have unique requirements due to the nature of exposure to potential biological, chemical, and radioactive hazards. Numerous safety regulations at national, state, and local levels provide jurisdiction for operations and promote cultures of safety to protect staff as well as patients. The Occupational Safety and Health Administration provides general industry standards that include use of personal protective equipment, general environmental controls, and guidance for handling and use of hazardous and toxic substances. In addition, national and state associations set precedence of the use of ventilation to control and remove contaminant in the air. Heating, refrigeration, and air-conditioning standards are set, as are standards to protect from fire risk due to hazardous chemicals that are flammable and/or combustible.

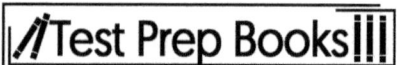

The Clinical Laboratory Improvement Amendments, under the Centers for Medicare & Medicaid Services, provides regulation of all laboratory testing completed on humans. Complaints are submitted via their state agency offices.

Practice Test

1. What commonly consumed chemical can cause changes in a wide variety of test results?
    a. Monosodium glutamate (MSG)
    b. Sodium chloride
    c. Aspartame
    d. Caffeine

2. Of the following patients, who would be at highest risk for developing anemia related to blood draws?
    a. A 3-year-old with orders for discharge labs following a recent hospital stay for respiratory distress
    b. A 19-year-old who has returns for the second time this week with orders for cholesterol level, complete blood count, and chemistry
    c. A 13-month-old with an order for a routine complete blood count following a recent 1-year checkup with their primary doctor
    d. A 68-year-old with an order for complete blood count and chemistry from their primary doctor

3. What is the total estimated blood volume for a 55-pound child?
    a. 12.1 liters
    b. 0.25 liters
    c. 2.5 liters
    d. 1.2 liters

4. A phlebotomist is preparing to perform a venipuncture on a patient. The patient sits in the chair and rolls their sleeve up to their upper arm. What type of consent is the patient giving to the phlebotomist?
    a. Verbal consent
    b. Written consent
    c. Given consent
    d. Implied consent

5. A nurse is preparing to collect a blood sample to send to the laboratory and calls the laboratory for assistance since they have never drawn this test before. How can the phlebotomist best support the nurse to ensure understanding of how to collect the sample correctly?
    a. The phlebotomist should go to the patient and collect the sample themselves.
    b. The phlebotomist should send the correct tube to the nurse.
    c. The phlebotomist should provide verbal instructions on the collection method, container, and storage needs for the test.
    d. The phlebotomist should email the nurse the policy on how to draw blood.

6. Which is NOT part of the phlebotomist's introduction?
    a. Name
    b. Role
    c. Consent
    d. Objective of appointment

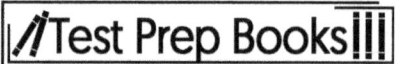

7. While preparing a thick blood smear from venipuncture, the phlebotomist anticipates using what equipment to deposit drops of blood onto the slides?
    a. Syringe
    b. Transport tube
    c. EDTA tube
    d. Pipette

8. Several laboratory values have resulted simultaneously. Which of the following laboratory results should be reported out first?
    a. STAT order that is within normal range
    b. Routine cholesterol panel
    c. Critical result of a cardiac marker
    d. Point-of-care glucose test at 100 mg/dL

9. According to the CDC/APHL Competency Guidelines, what do the cross-cutting technical competencies include?
    a. Quality
    b. Informatics
    c. Ethics
    d. Security

10. What can a phlebotomist use a requisition form for?
    a. Deciding what labs are necessary
    b. Verifying the provider/physician's information
    c. Contacting the insurance company for verification of coverage
    d. Verifying the patient's identity

11. Which of the following is a consequence to an employee for deviating from the guidelines and standards that are set by OSHA in order to increase efficiency?
    a. Disciplinary action
    b. Employee fines of up to $25,000
    c. Ineligibility to enroll in medical school
    d. Punishment by employer, but only if injury occurs

12. After attempting to perform a thin blood smear, the phlebotomist notices that the end of the smear appears jagged and uneven. This issue most likely originated from what?
    a. The blood drop size
    b. The phlebotomist's technique
    c. The spreader slide
    d. The preparation time

13. What type of language should be used to explain the procedure to the patient?
    a. Language that is at a tenth-grade level
    b. Language that is at a fifth-grade level
    c. Language that is at an eighth-grade level
    d. Language that is at a third-grade level

Practice Test

14. A phlebotomist has completed drawing blood on a patient and recaps the needle, accidentally sticking themselves in the thumb. What is the first action the phlebotomist should take?
    a. Ask the patient if they have AIDS.
    b. Call a supervisor.
    c. Flush the area with water and wash thoroughly with soap and water.
    d. Disinfect the area with an alcohol swab and continue working since the site isn't bleeding.

15. What does the HIPAA security rule encompass?
    a. Noncompliance
    b. Reporting
    c. Whistleblowing
    d. Protection of PHI

16. What determines transport and storage procedures for specimens?
    a. Type of specimen and what test is going to be completed
    b. Materials available for packaging
    c. Whether or not the specimen is hazardous
    d. Environmental temperature

17. Once a centrifuge has completed spinning, the lab staff wait before opening it for what reason?
    a. To allow contents of the tubes to settle
    b. To prevent aerosols from dispersing
    c. To allow for the centrifuge's cool-down period
    d. To equalize the pressure within the centrifuge

18. What is the main reason for temperature management and control on certain laboratory equipment?
    a. Reducing the cost of running equipment
    b. Ensuring that all lab samples are stable for several weeks
    c. Keeping it from overheating
    d. Maintaining integrity of samples, cultures, and reagents

19. What makes the order of draw so important to follow?
    a. Standardization helps the phlebotomist perform venipuncture correctly.
    b. It prevents the phlebotomist from forgetting to draw one of the tubes.
    c. It helps maintain a correct draw when an order comes in for a "rainbow."
    d. Additives can be moved from one tube to the next, possibly causing erroneous test results.

20. When performing a venipuncture on the dorsum of a hand, what is the recommended angle of needle entry into the skin?
    a. 20°
    b. 15°
    c. 10°
    d. 5°

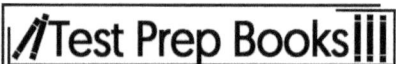

21. When anchoring the vein with the nondominant hand, how should the phlebotomist apply pressure and move the skin?
    a. Push down and pull the skin.
    b. Push down on the skin lightly.
    c. Pull the skin distally until taut.
    d. Push down so that the patient cannot move.

22. The leadership of a healthcare facility opts to reduce the supply of PPE for fiscal reasons although there have been complaints from laboratory staff that the current supply does not provide adequate protection or availability for use. What is NOT an expected outcome of this practice?
    a. PPE may be reused between patients.
    b. Staff will start providing their own PPE.
    c. Staff will use other sources of protection, such as waste bags, as coverage.
    d. Risk for transmission of microbial infections will be increased.

23. The phlebotomist is responsible for which of the following when using the chain of custody?
    a. Ensuring that the donor does not refuse the test
    b. Tracking the sample once given to the transport company
    c. Ensuring that sample collection details are included on the form
    d. Ensuring that the form is signed by all parties

24. As a phlebotomist is gathering a blood donation collection set, they recall that the liquid additive inside the collection bag serves all the following functions EXCEPT what?
    a. Anticoagulation
    b. Antisepsis
    c. Nourishment
    d. Stabilization

25. A phlebotomist overhears another coworker telling a patient's family member the results of a test, even though the patient has requested that any results be communicated directly with the patient and not family members. What act does this action willfully breach?
    a. Americans with Disabilities Act
    b. Health Insurance Portability and Accountability Act
    c. Family and Medical Leave Act
    d. Emergency Medical Treatment and Active Labor Act

26. What is an advantage of an electronic health record?
    a. It allows a patient to look up their results on healthcare facility computers.
    b. It increases the amount of paperwork that healthcare providers must complete.
    c. It manages, stores, and records patient data.
    d. It must be used with the Medical Administration Record.

27. Which of the following is the reason that quality control tests are completed on equipment?
    a. To ensure that staff is competent to utilize equipment
    b. To clean equipment
    c. To ensure accuracy of results
    d. To eliminate human errors when running tests

Practice Test

28. Which of the following is a part of therapeutic communication?
   a. Telling the patient about your children to distract them
   b. Listening completely without judgement
   c. Telling the patient that there is nothing to be worried about
   d. Telling the patient that it is silly to be scared

29. A phlebotomist is labeling a tissue specimen container. What information is important to include on this label?
   a. Patient's signature
   b. Room number
   c. Brand of swab used
   d. Laterality and site sample was taken from

30. A phlebotomist puts a tourniquet on a patient and finds a good vein to draw blood from. What should the phlebotomist do while assembling the equipment and cleaning the skin?
   a. Remove the tourniquet and reapply before venipuncture.
   b. Remove the tourniquet and draw the blood.
   c. Leave the tourniquet in place to not lose the vein.
   d. The equipment should have already been assembled; leave the tourniquet, clean the skin, and perform the venipuncture with the tourniquet in place.

31. The phlebotomist is preparing for blood specimen collection for an ethanol (ETOH) test. Which of the following would be acceptable to use in cleansing the skin prior to venipuncture?
   a. Soap
   b. Alcohol prep pad
   c. Iodine tincture
   d. Chlorhexidine swab

32. A patient arrives for a morning appointment to have his cholesterol (including triglycerides) test drawn. What question should the phlebotomist ask the patient before proceeding?
   a. "Are you well rested?"
   b. "Have you exercised in the past forty-eight hours?"
   c. "Have you had any food or drink besides water since midnight?"
   d. "Do you have a full bladder?"

33. What should be done before a tourniquet is placed on a patient?
   a. Prepare iodine to clean the patient's arm.
   b. Check for the appropriate vacuum in the evacuated tubes.
   c. Prepare all equipment.
   d. Label all tubes.

34. Which of the following is considered PHI?
   a. Point-of-care blood glucose level
   b. Type of vehicle the patient drives
   c. Patient's pet's name
   d. Research information that has been de-identified

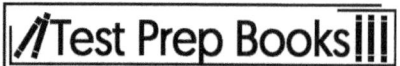

35. What should the phlebotomist do if a patient declines the venipuncture as the procedure is beginning?
    a. Assure the patient and continue as planned.
    b. Ask the patient for consent again.
    c. Stop the process immediately.
    d. Finish the venipuncture as quickly as possible.

36. The phlebotomist is performing blood culture collection. The patient has allergies to penicillin and shellfish. Which of the following cleansers would be most appropriate for skin prep?
    a. Alcohol prep pad
    b. Iodine tincture
    c. Betadine swab
    d. Chlorhexidine swab

37. A patient arrives for their appointment and expresses their anxiety around needles. Which of the following is NOT an intervention for a patient with a needle phobia?
    a. Performing the venipuncture as quickly as possible
    b. Topical anesthesia to numb the area
    c. Distraction
    d. Different body positions

38. What information is NOT needed when introducing yourself to a patient before a venipuncture?
    a. Education
    b. Name
    c. Title
    d. Task

39. What is the first action that should be completed before any other task when performing a venipuncture on a patient?
    a. Verify the patient's identity.
    b. Introduce yourself and state your role.
    c. Obtain consent.
    d. Verify orders on the requisition form.

40. How can all laboratory and non-laboratory personnel protect themselves from infectious disease while handling lab specimens?
    a. Cover their mouth when sneezing or coughing.
    b. Take a Covid test every day.
    c. Adhere to standard precautions.
    d. Encourage patients to use hand sanitizer prior to obtaining sample.

41. Which is NOT part of the explanation of the procedure that is given to the patient?
    a. Tell the patient that a small needle will be used to draw blood for the tests.
    b. Tell the patient that they will verify their information on the lab labels.
    c. Tell the patient that the results will be sent to them.
    d. Tell the patient that the results will be sent to their provider.

Practice Test

42. Approximately how many laboratory tests are completed in the United States each year?
    a. 10 million
    b. 100 million
    c. 1 billion
    d. 300 million

43. Competency is paramount to ensuring phlebotomy staff collect samples appropriately. Which of the following supports ensuring integrity of samples?
    a. Following the rules that have always been in place at the lab
    b. Placing labels the same way each time, regardless of container
    c. Reviewing standards from accreditation bodies and nationally recognized guidelines
    d. Searching the internet for instructions on unfamiliar lab orders

44. Light blue tubes are used for coagulation studies. What is one aspect of this evacuated tube that the phlebotomist must consider?
    a. The light blue tube must be filled to the fill line.
    b. The light blue tube can be attached directly to a butterfly needle and transfer device.
    c. The light blue tube additive should not be used before other tubes are filled.
    d. The light blue tube can be replaced with the royal blue tube.

45. What is NOT protected under HIPAA?
    a. Health information on paper
    b. Cancer diagnosis
    c. Patient's address
    d. Social Security number

46. A patient has orders for a lab draw. The orders include a type and cross, a rapid blood collection, and a hematology study. What is the correct order of draw for this patient?
    a. Red serum tube, orange tube, pink tube
    b. Orange tube, red serum tube, pink tube
    c. Red serum tube, pink tube, orange tube
    d. Orange tube, pink tube, red serum tube

47. A phlebotomist is concerned that quality testing is not being followed and refers to the Joint Commission's standards. What publication would provide the best reference?
    a. Healthcare facility policy
    b. OSHA requirements for phlebotomists
    c. *Comprehensive Accreditation Manual for Laboratory and Point-of-Care Testing*
    d. Manufacturer's recommendations

48. When looking for a vein on a patient for venipuncture, what is a critical safety question to ask the patient?
    a. "Which side do you prefer for me to use?"
    b. "Where does the phlebotomist normally stick you?"
    c. "Do you have any restrictions on which side I can use for venipuncture?"
    d. "Are you right-handed or left-handed?"

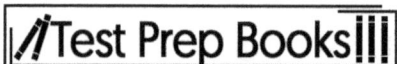

49. Older adults have specific characteristics that make their veins more difficult for venipuncture. What is one intervention that the phlebotomist can use to make the venipuncture more likely to succeed?
    a. Use light pressure with the tourniquet.
    b. Keep the tourniquet on while the needle enters the skin.
    c. Use a blood pressure cuff instead of a tourniquet.
    d. Occlude the vessel above the site of venipuncture.

50. Which of the following would increase the risk of compromising a specimen sample?
    a. Ensuring the label is adhered to collection container
    b. Using bubble wrap to secure containers before using the pneumatic tube system
    c. Immediately placing the sample on ice to preserve it
    d. Inverting tubes with additives several times once the sample is collected

51. The phlebotomist is reviewing their scope of practice and acknowledges that they have practiced outside of their scope. Which of the following practices would NOT violate this standard?
    a. Assisting a patient to transfer to a bedside commode
    b. Giving a patient a website that explains test results
    c. Drawing an arterial blood sample
    d. Collecting and processing a CLIA-waived test

52. What is the purpose of a phlebotomist introducing themselves to the patient before venipuncture is done?
    a. To become friends before the venipuncture
    b. To inform the patient of what to expect during their testing
    c. To verify their identity
    d. To inform the patient of who the phlebotomist is and what their role is

53. What action must be completed prior to drawing a blood sample, to prioritize patient safety?
    a. Checking the patient's blood type
    b. Verifying the patient with unique identifiers
    c. Introducing oneself and explaining tests that are to be drawn
    d. Applying antiseptic on skin to allow for dry time

54. What activity should be avoided for twenty-four hours prior to laboratory testing?
    a. Exercise
    b. Dining out
    c. Working
    d. Being sedentary

55. When providing instructions to a patient with orders for a 2-hour postprandial urine sample collection, the phlebotomist informs the patient they will perform urine collection 2 hours after which action?
    a. Eating
    b. Waking
    c. Drinking
    d. Exercising

Practice Test

56. Which site is the BEST choice for a dermal puncture when checking a patient's glucose?
   a. Dominant hand, index finger
   b. Nondominant hand, index finger
   c. Dominant hand, ring finger
   d. Nondominant hand, ring finger

57. Which of the following is the primary reason for explaining the procedure of venipuncture to a patient?
   a. To obtain verbal or implied consent
   b. To inform the patient of what test will be drawn
   c. To verify the patient's identity
   d. To determine what color tubes to draw

58. Which of the following are CLIA-waived tests?
   a. High-risk tests
   b. Tests without a small window of error
   c. Tests used to guide diagnostic treatment
   d. Tests where erroneous results do not carry high risks

59. When drawing labs and following the order of draw, what tube/test should be drawn before any other?
   a. Light blue tube for coagulation studies
   b. Red tube for hematology
   c. Light yellow tube for blood culture
   d. Gray tube for lactic acid

60. Who is responsible for ensuring that employees are provided training on workplace safety measures?
   a. OSHA
   b. Employee
   c. Government
   d. Employer

61. After the centrifuge has stopped spinning, how much time should be allotted prior to opening?
   a. Five minutes
   b. Ten minutes
   c. Twenty minutes
   d. One hour

62. How can facilities best uphold safe practice expectations for all employees?
   a. Assign educational modules to the employees with the most risk.
   b. Test employee knowledge of safe practices quarterly.
   c. Focus on one safe practice measure to improve.
   d. Promote a culture of safety.

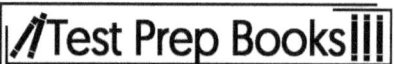

63. When performing a venipuncture in the antecubital area, what angle should be used when the needle enters the skin?
    a. 10–20°
    b. 15–30°
    c. 20–35°
    d. 5–35°

64. In the outpatient setting, what should be used to verify the patient's name and date of birth?
    a. The patient's name and date of birth as well as their state-issued identification card
    b. The patient's name and date of birth on the requisition form and the information on the appointment card
    c. The patient's stated name and date of birth and information on the hospital armband
    d. The patient's stated name and date of birth and the name and date of birth on the requisition form

65. Which method should be avoided when anchoring a vein to protect the phlebotomist's safety?
    a. C method
    b. Two-finger hold
    c. Two-handed stick
    d. B method

66. What is the first step when a phlebotomist begins skin preparation on a patient for venipuncture?
    a. Apply gloves.
    b. Ask the patient to wash their arms up to the elbow.
    c. Cleanse the patient's arm with chlorhexidine gluconate in a circular motion.
    d. Cleanse the patient's arm with povidone-iodine in a circular motion.

67. What is NOT an advantage of a point-of-care test?
    a. It decreases barriers to care.
    b. It is convenient.
    c. It provides more accurate results.
    d. The results are often available within fifteen minutes.

68. Which of the following is NOT a type of consent required for venipuncture?
    a. Verbal consent
    b. Express consent
    c. Implied consent
    d. Informed consent

69. Which location should be used for an infant under the age of 12 months?
    a. Nondominant hand ring finger
    b. Inner or outer heel
    c. Dominant hand ring finger
    d. Middle of heel

Practice Test

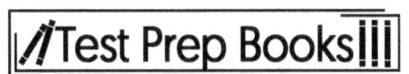

70. The phlebotomist is performing blood culture collection and has trouble obtaining the total recommended volume for both bottles. Which of the following would be the most appropriate action for the phlebotomist to take?
  a. Divide the blood specimen equally between the aerobic and anaerobic bottles.
  b. Inoculate the aerobic bottle and perform a second puncture to fill the anaerobic bottle.
  c. Dispose of that sample and repeat the procedure using a different venipuncture site.
  d. Inoculate the aerobic bottle fully before inoculating the anaerobic bottle with the remainder.

71. After cleaning the patient with a 70% alcohol wipe, what should the phlebotomist do to prevent pain to the patient?
  a. Continue with venipuncture.
  b. Place a tourniquet to help locate the vein.
  c. Ask the patient if they are ready.
  d. Let alcohol air-dry before performing venipuncture.

72. A phlebotomist is drawing a lab in a hospital, and the patient has an intravenous line in their left antecubital area. Where should the phlebotomist look for a vein to perform the venipuncture?
  a. Left dorsal hand
  b. Right median cubital vein
  c. Left forearm
  d. Right basilic vein

73. The phlebotomist is preparing to perform a venipuncture for a patient admitted to the medical surgical floor of the hospital. They note that the patient has a heparin well on the inner aspect of their left forearm, just below the elbow. The patient also has a peripherally inserted central catheter on the right upper arm. Which of the following locations is acceptable for the phlebotomist to perform venipuncture?
  a. The right median antebrachial vein
  b. The left median cubital vein
  c. The right dorsal vein
  d. The left metacarpal vein

74. Which of the following is an example of a deviation from standard collection process during chain of custody?
  a. Verifying patient information and order prior to drawing the ordered laboratory sample
  b. Donor adulteration of the test
  c. Sample size is adequate per test collected
  d. Collection container is personally delivered by phlebotomist

75. When cleaning with an alcohol wipe, what actions should the phlebotomist perform?
  a. Start above the site of venipuncture and wipe in downward motions.
  b. Start on one side and wipe side to side for at least three wipes.
  c. Start at the site of venipuncture and use at least three circular motions.
  d. Start below the site of venipuncture and wipe up using five different strokes.

76. After a sharps injury, when should post-exposure prophylactic treatment be initiated?
    a. Once the patient's labs have returned
    b. In twenty-four hours
    c. Within seventy-two hours
    d. Immediately

77. For which test would it be appropriate to follow the chain-of-custody process?
    a. Hemoglobin test
    b. Point-of-care blood glucose test
    c. Cardiac markers test
    d. Drug test

78. The requisition form provides the phlebotomist with the information that they will need to complete the venipuncture and prepare the specimens for the lab. What information is NOT provided on the requisition form?
    a. Priority of tests
    b. Special considerations
    c. Order of draw
    d. Tests to draw

79. What can happen to a blood sample if the tourniquet is left in place for an inappropriate amount of time?
    a. Hemodilution
    b. Erroneously elevated potassium
    c. Hemoconcentration
    d. Erroneously decreased potassium

80. A spill of a chemical solution has occurred. What is the best resource for the laboratory staff to access information regarding this solution?
    a. Poison control hotline
    b. MSDS
    c. Manufacturer of chemical
    d. Supervisor

81. Which safety hazard should be addressed immediately before a patient is led into an exam room for phlebotomy?
    a. Phlebotomy chair arm being up and locked
    b. Trash can next to the entry door
    c. Alcohol wipe on the floor
    d. Phlebotomy supplies lying out on the counter

82. Which of the following materials cannot be autoclaved?
    a. Celluloid
    b. Polypropylene
    c. Stainless steel
    d. Polycarbonate

83. What must a patient be informed about under HIPAA rules?
   a. The rights of the healthcare facility
   b. The ways in which patient information is used and disclosed
   c. Whether a facility is for-profit or not-for-profit
   d. The cost of the bill for uninsured patients

84. When inserting the needle into the patient, what direction should the bevel face?
   a. Right
   b. Down
   c. Left
   d. Up

85. Which of the following free webinars would be most beneficial for a facility that has a goal to improve biohazard waste disposal?
   a. Approaches to Reducing Errors at the Point of Care
   b. Planning for Laboratory Operations During a Disaster
   c. Principles and Procedures for Blood Culture
   d. Protection of Laboratory Workers from Occupationally Acquired Infections

86. What phlebotomist error can cause an evacuated container to lose its suction?
   a. Preparing the needle and transfer device with the evacuated tube within reach
   b. Placing the tube on the transfer device before the needle enters the skin
   c. Observing a crack in the tubing of a butterfly needle
   d. Ensuring there is a flash in the needle before placing the evacuated tube on the transfer device

87. A phlebotomist is drawing a lab and finds that one of their tubes has no vacuum. What does the phlebotomist suspect is the problem?
   a. The tube rolled off the counter.
   b. They switched from an ETS system to a butterfly system.
   c. Storage temperature logs are in compliance.
   d. The rubber stopper looks intact.

88. A patient with a mastectomy on the right arrives for her venipuncture. The phlebotomist knows that the venipuncture must be done on the left side to avoid which complication for the patient?
   a. Phlebitis
   b. Lymphedema
   c. Infiltration
   d. Bleeding

89. How often, at least, are calibration tests to be completed per the Clinical Laboratory Improvement Amendments of 1988?
   a. Once every six months
   b. Every day
   c. Biweekly
   d. Monthly

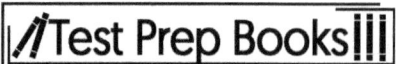

90. Where can training and consultation for laboratory roles, functions, and workflow be obtained?
    a. Centers for Disease Control and Prevention
    b. OSHA
    c. Digital transformation in healthcare
    d. CMS laboratory fee schedule

91. How often is it recommended that standard sharps training occurs for staff with high exposure to bloodborne pathogens?
    a. At hire and annually
    b. When deficiencies are noted
    c. Once every two years
    d. Every three months

92. A phlebotomist overhears a family member telling the patient that the treatment costs too much and they should leave. What would be the best option for the phlebotomist to take?
    a. Tell the family member to leave.
    b. Bring up the concern at the next ethics committee meeting.
    c. Call security.
    d. Report the concern to the immediate supervisor.

93. What is acceptable for patient identification in the hospital setting?
    a. Patient's stated name and date of birth and requisition form
    b. Patient's stated name and date of birth and hospital identification band
    c. Patient's hospital identification band and patient's nurse verification
    d. Requisition form and patient's stated name and date of birth

94. Phlebotomists have a very high risk of exposure to bloodborne pathogens. Which of the following is best practice to prevent needlesticks?
    a. Recap needles before putting into sharps container.
    b. Utilize safety devices on sharps.
    c. Use sterile gloves with all venipunctures.
    d. Throw away biohazardous materials in red bags.

95. Which of the following is an example of verbal consent given by a patient?
    a. "Okay, let's get this done."
    b. "Can you tell me what will happen again?"
    c. "I don't know if I am ready for this."
    d. "I'm not sure if I can do it."

96. During the centrifugation process, when should the exterior of tubes and bottles be wiped down with disinfectants?
    a. After the sample is collected from the patient
    b. After the centrifuge has stopped spinning
    c. Prior to serum coagulation
    d. Prior to loading the rotors or buckets

Practice Test

97. What does anchoring a vein do to assist in venipuncture?
   a. Stabilizes the vein
   b. Keeps the patient from jumping
   c. Holds the patient's arm from twitching
   d. Helps guide the dominant hand for venipuncture

98. A fingerstick blood glucose test is completed on a patient. The value returns at 400 mg/dL. What should the phlebotomist expect to be one of the next steps?
   a. Receive an order to draw a whole blood sample to test blood glucose level.
   b. Enter the results in the chart and go to the next patient.
   c. Check when the patient ate last.
   d. Redo the point-of-care test, as it must be inaccurate.

99. If a phlebotomist is seeking more information on the handling of biohazardous materials, under what Code of Federal Regulations would they look?
   a. Title 42
   b. USC 5705
   c. Title 29
   d. Public Law 106-430

100. Which cleanser should be used when drawing blood cultures?
   a. Povidone-iodine
   b. Alcohol wipes
   c. Chlorhexidine gluconate
   d. Alcohol swabs

101. A patient presents with obesity. What vein does the phlebotomist know will likely be the easiest to access?
   a. Basilic vein
   b. Median cubital vein
   c. Dorsal metacarpal vein
   d. Cephalic vein

102. Which of the following techniques for preparing blood cultures would NOT be appropriate?
   a. Use syringe and transfer device to inoculate the aerobic bottle and then the anaerobic bottle.
   b. Mark the minimum and maximum fill volumes on each bottle with pen or marker.
   c. Scrub the selected venipuncture site with a chlorhexidine swab for 30 seconds.
   d. Cleanse the stopper of each bottle with alcohol prep pad prior to inoculation.

103. A phlebotomist is reviewing a requisition form. They find that the information is not complete. What missing information will require a confirmation with the ordering provider?
   a. Insurance information
   b. Lab processing time
   c. Patient's phone number
   d. Patient's gender

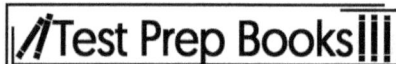

104. Which is NOT part of a basal state testing requirement?
    a. No food or drink for twelve hours
    b. No alcohol for twenty-four hours before testing
    c. Patient should be well rested
    d. Testing should be early in the morning

105. A phlebotomist enters a hospital room to perform a venipuncture. They notice that the patient's table is covered with crumbs and water. What is the most appropriate thing to do before placing the needed supplies on the table?
    a. Cleanse the area with disinfectant.
    b. Dust off the crumbs with a paper towel.
    c. Place the supplies on the bed instead.
    d. Clean the area with soap and water.

106. When a phlebotomist is having difficulty finding a vein, what is one thing that they should NOT do?
    a. Apply a warm blanket or heel warmer to the skin.
    b. Lightly rub the area.
    c. Allow the arm to dangle so that the veins will swell.
    d. Smack the patient's skin to cause the veins to swell.

107. A phlebotomist has been working within a healthcare facility for one month. They are currently still in orientation, which is progressing as expected. The new employee observes their preceptor preparing to draw blood without first sanitizing the patient's skin. What should they do?
    a. Stop the line and pass the preceptor an alcohol swab before venipuncture occurs.
    b. Notify the supervisor.
    c. Wait and remind the preceptor to use antiseptic on the next patient.
    d. Tell the patient that the preceptor is not following infection prevention guidelines.

108. When labeling collection containers, two unique patient identifiers should be used. Which identifiers are best practice?
    a. Full name and date of birth
    b. Last name and last four digits of Social Security number
    c. Social Security number and name of street that patient lives on
    d. Spouse's middle name and phone number

109. How many identifiers are required to verify a patient's identity?
    a. Two
    b. Three
    c. One
    d. Four

110. Laboratory staff must interact within a multidisciplinary team. Which type of communication tools would best to enhance understanding?
    a. Making assumptions
    b. Passive listening
    c. Using clear and concise statements
    d. Relying on email only

111. A patient comes to the lab for venipuncture. They have orders for coagulation studies, a chemistry panel, and a hematology panel. Which order should these labs be drawn in?
   a. Light blue tube, lavender tube, green tube
   b. Light blue tube, green tube, lavender tube
   c. Green tube, light blue tube, lavender tube
   d. Green tube, lavender tube, light blue tube

112. Which of the following is not considered a sharps instrument?
   a. Needle with safety device
   b. Lancet
   c. Blood-filled syringe without needle
   d. Pipette

113. What can be used instead of a tourniquet for a patient?
   a. Coban wrap applied tightly around the arm
   b. Blood pressure cuff inflated to less than systolic blood pressure
   c. Reusable automatic cuff
   d. Blood pressure cuff inflated to less than diastolic blood pressure

114. How can the phlebotomist confirm the patient's identity when the patient is unable to speak for themselves?
   a. Use just the patient's requisition form.
   b. Call the provider for verification.
   c. Ask the caregiver to verify the patient's identity.
   d. Search the patient for an identification card.

115. What is the maximum time for which a tourniquet should be left on an arm, according to CLSI?
   a. 1 minute
   b. 3 minutes
   c. 2 minutes
   d. 5 minutes

116. A nurse asks the phlebotomist if they could assist them by transporting a specimen to the lab. Which is the most appropriate response by the phlebotomist?
   a. Review the patient's lab orders before accepting the sample.
   b. Notify the nurse that you are unable to transport the specimen.
   c. Sign the appropriate documentation before accepting.
   d. Confirm the specimen is properly labeled before accepting.

117. If available, what safety device should be used when filling centrifuge tubes?
   a. High-pressure syringe
   b. N-95 mask
   c. Digital Geiger counter
   d. Safety cabinet

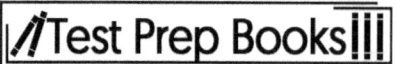

118. A patient arrives at the facility and tells the phlebotomist that they are there to get tests. What does the patient need to give to the phlebotomist?
    a. Requisition form and informed consent
    b. Informed consent and a state-issued ID
    c. Prescription and an insurance card
    d. Verbal order and the name of their healthcare provider

119. When inspecting equipment for a venipuncture, the phlebotomist knows that they should dispose of the equipment if they observe which of the following?
    a. A wrinkled package
    b. A hole in a package
    c. A package that expires the following day
    d. An unrolled tourniquet

120. What is the proper placement of the nondominant hand when anchoring the vein?
    a. Place the index and middle fingers 2 inches below the insertion site.
    b. Place the thumb 2 inches below the insertion site.
    c. Place the index and middle fingers 3 inches below the insertion site.
    d. Place the thumb 3 inches below the insertion site.

Answer Explanations

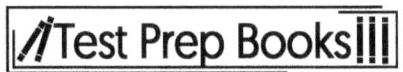

Answer Explanations

1. D. Caffeine can cause many laboratory result changes because it alters the metabolism of the consumer. It can change ionized calcium, blood glucose concentration, and non-esterified fatty acids. Choices *A*, *B*, and *C* are not known to alter lab results.

2. A: Hospitalized children are one of the most at-risk groups for iatrogenic anemia from blood draws. Choice *B* is incorrect because this young adult who has had a second blood draw this week would not necessarily be at high risk for iatrogenic anemia. Choice *C* is incorrect because the infant having routine CBC for their one-year checkup would be less at risk than a recently hospitalized patient. Lastly, choice *D* is incorrect because this older adult receiving routine bloodwork from a primary doctor would not necessarily be high risk for developing iatrogenic anemia.

3. C: This is calculated by taking the patient's weight (55 pounds) and dividing by 2.2, which would be 25 kilograms (kg). 25 kg is multiplied by 100 mL to get 2,500 mL of total blood. The total estimated blood volume is represented in liters, so 2,500 mL is divided by 1,000, which equals 2.5 liters of total blood volume. Choice *A* is incorrect because it was calculated by erroneously *multiplying* the patient's weight in pounds by 2.2 instead of dividing. Choice *B* is incorrect because the patient's weight in kilograms was incorrectly *divided* by 100 and then *multiplied* by 1,000. Choice *D* is incorrect because weight in kilograms was incorrectly calculated and then divided by 100.

4. D. The patient is implying consent by exposing their arm in a way that allows the phlebotomist to perform the venipuncture. Choices *A* and *B* are incorrect; verbal and written consent were not obtained in this situation. Choice *C* is incorrect; this is not a type of consent used in phlebotomy.

5. C: Choice *C* provides comprehensive information on the process for collecting this blood sample and educates the nurse. Choice *A* does not provide learning opportunities for the nurse. Choices *B* and *D* are incorrect, as this does not explain if there are any special requirements from collection, storage, or transport.

6. C. Patient consent is not part of the phlebotomist introduction. Consent will be obtained after explaining the venipuncture procedure. Choices *A*, *B*, and *D* are all part of the phlebotomist's introduction.

7. D: The phlebotomist would use a pipette to drop 2-3 large drops of blood onto the slide. Choice *A* is not correct, as syringes are not used to place drops of blood onto slides for blood smears. Choice *B* is incorrect because transport tubes are used for moving samples between locations (e.g., from a facility to a testing lab). Lastly, choice *C* is not correct because the EDTA tube (lavender-top, anticoagulant-containing test tube) would not be used to deposit drops of blood onto a slide.

8. C: Choice *C* must be reported first because it is the most concerning of the options to expedite patient care. Choice *A*, although a STAT value, would be reported second since it did not result in an urgent or critical value. Choices *B* is not a lab test that would have life-threatening or critical decision-making consequences if reported routinely. Choice *D* is within the expected range for this test.

9. B: The cross-cutting domain is composed of safety, surveillance, and informatics. Choices *A*, *C*, and *D* are not correct; these competencies fall under the base domain.

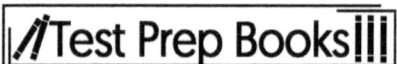

Answer Explanations

10. D. The requisition form is used to verify the identity of the patient when compared to the patient's stated name and date of birth. Choice *A* is incorrect. The phlebotomist does not decide what labs or tests are necessary. Choice *B* is incorrect because the phlebotomist doesn't need to verify the provider's information. Choice *C* is incorrect; the phlebotomist does not verify coverage with health insurance companies.

11. A: Blatantly and knowingly not following guidelines set by OSHA to cut corners may result in consequences such as additional training, disciplinary action, and termination from employment. Choice *B* is not correct; OSHA standards are followed in order to prevent harm to patients and employees, but deviating from them will not lead to employee fines. Choice *C* is not correct; not following standard practices is insubordination and may result in a range of disciplinary action, from reprimands to practice improvement plans to demotion, but it won't affect eligibility to enroll in medical school. Choice *D* is incorrect; the employee may receive employer punishment even if injury does NOT occur.

12. C: A thin blood smear that ends in a jagged, uneven edge would likely be due to defects or chips in the spreader slide. Choice *A* is not correct, as blood drop size would impact the length of the smear and would not cause a jagged edge. Choice *B* is also not correct because issues related to technique would not cause jagged edges of a smear. Lastly, Choice *D* is not correct because the preparation time would not create a jagged edge.

13. B. When explaining the procedure to a patient, the phlebotomist should use language that is consistent with a fifth-grade level. This ensures that most patients will understand.

14. C: It is recommended that as soon as possible the site be flushed with water and then washed, if this is available. Choice *A* is not correct; this is unethical, and it should be left to the attending provider to investigate the risk of disease. The provider may decide to test the patient; however, that conversation should always be initiated by the patient's provider. Choice *B* is not correct; this step should occur after the area has been flushed and washed. Choice *D* is incorrect; soap and water with thorough flushing is the recommended treatment immediately after a needlestick or sharps injury.

15. D: The protection and securement of PHI are covered under HIPAA's security rule. Choices *A*, *B*, and *C* all fall under the Breach Notification rule.

16. A: The type of specimen and test to be completed, Choice *A*, determines the temperature, timing, and storage to keep it from being compromised. The type of materials available, Choice *B*, should not determine how the specimen is transported. Choice *C* is incorrect, as specimens have criteria for transport and storage whether or not they are hazardous. There may be additional measures to be taken for safety reasons if a specimen is hazardous. Choice *D* is not correct because it is the internal temperature of the specimen that must be controlled, not the effects of environmental temperature.

17. B: During the spinning process, aerosolization can occur even with small leaks that are not detected with the naked eye. Allowing any aerosols to settle prevents contamination and keeps workers from accidental exposure. Choice *A* is incorrect because the process of spinning separates the particles of the solution. Choice *C* is incorrect, as centrifuges have a built-in cooling system, and Choice *D* is incorrect, as centrifuges used within labs do not have pressure build-up with normal function.

18. D: One of the purposes for maintaining temperature controls on equipment is to ensure that the sample is not compromised. Choice *A* is not correct; temperature controls are not aimed at reducing the costs of processing samples but may have savings due to not requiring repeat testing. Choice *B* is not

Answer Explanations

correct; sample preservation is varied, and it is not accurate to say that all samples have a longevity of numerous weeks irrespective of maintaining a certain temperature. Choice C is not correct; temperature control is not always focused on cooling, depending on the type of equipment. For centrifuges and sterilization equipment, the temperature may require that a high temperature goal is met to separate some samples, eradicate certain microorganisms after testing, or prevent contamination.

19. D: Carryover—or additives being carried from one tube to the next—can occur between tubes, so it is important to use the order of draw to prevent erroneous results. Choice A is incorrect; standardization is good in any industry, but this is not why CLSI standardized the order of draw. Choice B is incorrect; the phlebotomist should be verifying they have all equipment before starting the venipuncture process. Choice C is incorrect; a phlebotomist should not accept an order for a "rainbow." Orders should be placed appropriately by a provider, and this has nothing to do with the order of draw.

20. C: The correct angle of entry into the skin is 10° when performing venipuncture on the dorsum of the hand.

21. C: The skin should just be pulled distally until taut; no pressure should be applied on the arm.

22. B: OSHA dictates that proper and adequate amounts of PPE will be available to employees. Employees should not be expected to provide their own PPE, and most likely would not. Choices A and D are not correct; this unsafe practice may start occurring, which would increase the risk of nosocomial infections. Choice C is incorrect; when staff are faced with shortages, other inappropriate methods of protecting themselves is likely, such as the use of a waste bag for a gown.

23. C: Choice C is the responsibility of the performing phlebotomist because they are the only individual who can confirm the details of collection. Choice A is either the donor's choice or may be enforced through legal proceedings. Choice B is the responsibility of the transport company once it is transferred to the shipping company or individual transporting the sample. Each individual party is responsible for documenting their signature on the form, Choice D.

24. B: The preservative solution within a blood donation collection set does NOT function as an antiseptic. Choice A would not be the correct choice because the preservative solution does contain citrate, which acts as an anticoagulant. Choice C would be incorrect because ingredients like dextrose within the blood collection bag provide nourishment to blood cells. Choice D would also not be correct because phosphate within the preservative solution functions to stabilize the pH of the blood.

25. B: HIPAA protects patients' rights in how their protected health information (PHI) is used and communicated. Choice A is incorrect; this act protects the rights of individuals with disabilities and the laws and obligations of state and local governments as well as the private sector. Choice C is not correct; the Family and Medical Leave Act put into place laws protecting individuals when taking unpaid leave for certain family and medical reasons to ensure their job and health insurance are protected. EMTALA, Choice D, is not correct, as this law ensures that individuals requesting medical care are able to receive emergency medical treatment regardless of their ability to pay or status.

26. C: An electronic health record (EHR) is able to provide digital access to patient data and information for ease of retrieval by healthcare providers and staff, Choice C. Choice A is incorrect because a patient may be given access to certain records via a patient portal; however, this is separate from the EHR. Paperwork is reduced, not increased—Choice B—by adopting an EHR. A Medical Administration Record may be part of or separate from the EHR, making Choice D incorrect.

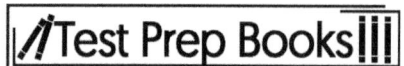

Answer Explanations

27. C: Quality control tests are performed to test if the equipment is functioning appropriately and providing results that are accurate and consistent. Choice A is incorrect. Education and simulation may ensure that staff are competent in the use of the equipment; however, quality control is completed to ensure that the equipment is functioning as expected. Choice B is not correct, as quality control does not clean the equipment; this should be done as a separate task according to manufacturer's guidelines. Choice D is not correct; lack of adherence to rules when using the equipment, or failure to follow the appropriate steps to prepare a sample, will not be corrected through quality control tests.

28. B: Listening to a patient without judgement is a critical component of therapeutic communication. Choice A is incorrect, as telling the patient about yourself is not therapeutic; asking the patient about themselves would be a better distraction. Choice C is incorrect, as it dismisses the patient and makes them feel like they are not being heard. Choice D is incorrect, as this option is demeaning to a patient.

29. D: Choice D is correct to ensure that the order matches the site that the sample was obtained from. The patient is not required to sign or initial the specimen container; however, if the procedure is invasive, they will need to sign a consent form. Choice B is incorrect; the room number is not pertinent information. Choice C is not the best choice because brand information should not affect the sample as long as it was the appropriate type to use.

30. A: The correct choice is to remove the tourniquet, ensure everything is ready and clean, and reapply the tourniquet for less than 1 minute while performing the venipuncture. Choice B is incorrect; the tourniquet should be placed back on the patient when ready for venipuncture. Choice C is incorrect; the tourniquet should not be left on for more than 1 minute to find a vein or for more than 1 minute to perform the venipuncture. Choice D is also incorrect; the tourniquet should be removed while prepping the patient for the venipuncture.

31. A: Soap and water is the best available choice for preparing the skin prior to collecting blood for a blood alcohol level test (ethanol, ETOH). Choices B, C, and D are incorrect because they all contain alcohol as an ingredient, which could falsely increase the test result.

32. C. The patient should be asked about fasting before the test. Triglycerides can become elevated after food or drink consumption. Choices A, B, and D are incorrect; these questions would not be needed for a cholesterol and triglyceride test.

33. C: The phlebotomist should prepare all needed equipment before placing a tourniquet on the patient. Choice A is incorrect, as iodine should not be used before venipuncture; alcohol wipes or swabs should be used instead. Choice B is incorrect, as checking for the appropriate vacuum in the evacuated containers will render them useless. The tubes should not be checked, and rubber stoppers should not be removed. Choice D is also incorrect; labeling should be done after the blood has been drawn and the information verified by the patient.

34. A: Choice A is a laboratory result and must not be disclosed except as defined by HIPAA law. Choices B, C, and D are not examples of information that is protected under HIPAA regulations.

35. C. The phlebotomist must stop immediately. This means that the patient is withdrawing their consent. The phlebotomist may talk to the patient and restart after the patient consents again (Choice B), but they must first stop the phlebotomy process immediately. Choices A and D are incorrect. These actions violate the patient's right to make their own choices and their right to withdraw consent.

Answer Explanations

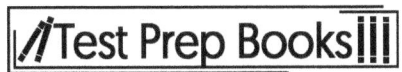

36. D: Chlorhexidine does not include any ingredients with a known patient allergen, and it is one of the recommended cleansers that can be used to prepare the skin before blood cultures. Choice A is not the best choice because alcohol prep pads alone have been shown to have less antiseptic effect than chlorhexidine cleansers. Choices B and C are incorrect because they contain iodine and should be avoided for someone with a known shellfish allergy.

37. A. Performing the venipuncture as quickly as possible can increase anxiety for the patient. Choices B, C, and D are the actions that should be taken instead. The phlebotomist should instead position the patient for comfort, use distraction, and numb the area prior to the venipuncture.

38. A. The phlebotomist's educational background is not required information when introducing themselves to their patient. Choices B, C, and D are incorrect. The phlebotomist's name and title and the task at hand should be told to the patient before proceeding.

39. B. The first task that should be completed for a patient is for the phlebotomist to introduce themselves and state their role. This is important for the comfort of the patient and should be done even before patient identity verification. Choices A, C, and D are incorrect. These tasks should be done, but they are not the first tasks to be done.

40. C: Using standard precautions, Choice C, with patients and when handling specimens is the best way to protect oneself from transmitting or contracting an infectious disease. Enhanced precautions should be used when a multidrug-resistant organism is known or suspected. Choices A and B help prevent the spread of infectious disease to other individuals. Choice D is best practice for prevention of contracting an infectious disease, such as respiratory infections, but is not applicable to laboratory personnel when handling specimens.

41. C. The patient's results will not be sent to the patient, although they may access them through a patient portal. Choices A, B, and D are all part of the explanation that will be given to the patient before their blood is drawn.

42. C: Over one billion laboratory tests are completed in the US each year. Choices A, B, and D are not correct, as the numbers underestimate the number of tests completed.

43. C: Accreditation bodies and nationally approved expert organizations will have up-to-date information that is evidence based. Choice A is incorrect, as outdated rules may no longer be valid. Labels are not always placed the same way on containers and may have certain placement based on the instrument they are processed on, making Choice B incorrect. The phlebotomist should ensure that valid, credible medical sources are used for verification of collection methods, making Choice D incorrect, since it may bring up results that are not from healthcare experts.

44. A: The light blue tube that is used for coagulation studies must be filled to the line. This is because the blood and the additive must be mixed at a certain ratio for accurate results. Choice B is incorrect; a tube with no additive should be attached to the butterfly needle and transfer device before the light blue tube to prevent a short draw. This is because air from the butterfly tube will fill the evacuated tube, and there will not be enough suction left to fill the tube to the line with blood. Choice C is incorrect; the light blue tube should be drawn first so that additives from the other tubes don't cause erroneous results. Choice D is incorrect; these tubes are not interchangeable.

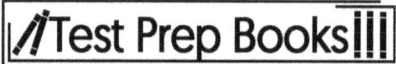

Answer Explanations

45. C: A patient's address, Choice *C*, is not considered directly identifiable information and is not covered under HIPAA. Choices *A*, *B*, and *D* are all health information examples that are protected under HIPAA laws.

46. A: The correct order of this draw is the red serum tube, then the orange tube, and finally the pink tube. Choices *B*, *C*, and *D* are all incorrect, as they do not follow the order of draw.

47. C: The Joint Commission provides guidance on quality standards and requirements within the *Comprehensive Accreditation Manual for Laboratory and Point-of-Care Testing.* Choices *A* and *D* are not correct; the facility's and manufacturer's policies may not align with the most up-to-date Joint Commission recommendations. Choice *B* is not correct; OSHA guidelines provide safe environmental standards, as well as standards for PPE use, cleanliness, and exposure prevention and management.

48. C: The phlebotomist should ask the patient if they have any restrictions on which side can be used for venipuncture. The phlebotomist must NOT perform a venipuncture on an arm that has a dialysis fistula or on the side of a mastectomy and lymph node removal. Ensuring that these restrictions are followed keeps the patient from harm. Choices *A*, *B*, and *D* are all reasonable questions to ask, but they are not critical to the patient's safety.

49. C. Using a blood pressure cuff instead of a tourniquet will reduce the pressure on the vein. This will reduce the chance of vein damage including a ruptured vein, bleeding, or hematoma. This will improve the chances of a successful venipuncture. Choices *A*, *B*, and *D* are incorrect. These actions should be avoided in older adults.

50. C: Not all lab specimens should be placed on ice. Refer to specific lab tests for reference on how to store for transport. Choices *A*, *B*, and *D* all uphold the integrity of maintaining specimen validity.

51. D: Phlebotomists are trained and able to obtain samples for CLIA-waived tests and process these tests for results. Choice *A* is incorrect; the phlebotomist is not trained to safely transfer patients and should refer to the nursing caregivers for the patient. Choice *B* is incorrect; the phlebotomist should refer all diagnostic and condition questions to the provider. Choice *C* is not correct; the phlebotomist is trained to perform venipuncture. Arterial blood samples may be drawn by trained respiratory and nursing staff.

52. D. Choice *A* is incorrect; it is not necessary to be friends with the patient. Choice B is incorrect; introducing themselves will not inform the patient about the visit, although this information will be given in the next step. Choice *C* is incorrect; the phlebotomist does not need to verify their identity to the patient.

53. B: Prior to completing any patient care, the patient must first be verified with two unique patient identifiers. Choice *A* is not correct; the patient's blood type will not change the process of drawing a blood sample. Choice *C* is not correct. Discussing diagnostic testing and disease processes is beyond the scope of the phlebotomist; these questions should be referred to the ordering provider. Choice *D* is not correct; the patient's identity must be verified prior to the patient being prepped for any testing.

54. A. Exercise should be avoided for twenty-four hours before labs are drawn because it can affect the results on many different tests. Choices *B*, *C*, and *D* do not need to be avoided for twenty-four hours prior to laboratory testing.

Answer Explanations

55. A: A 2-hour postprandial test evaluates urine that is collected 2 hours *after eating*. Choices B, C, and D are incorrect because postprandial testing is not scheduled around sleep, liquid intake, or physical activity.

56. D: The best choice for a dermal puncture is on the nondominant hand, using either the middle or ring finger. Choices A, B, and C are incorrect. The dominant hand should be avoided, and the thumb, index finger, and small finger should be avoided as well.

57. A. The primary reason to inform the patient about the procedure is to obtain consent from the patient. Choice B is incorrect; telling the patient what test will be taken is not the primary reason for explaining the procedure. Choice C is incorrect; the patient's identity should be verified before explaining the procedure. Choice D is also incorrect; the requisition form will be used to determine what color tubes will need to be drawn.

58. D: CLIA-waived tests are those that are not used for medical diagnosis or decision-making and will not have a significant impact on the patient's care. Choice A is not correct; low-risk, not-high risk, tests are included in the CLIA waiver. Choice B is not correct; CLIA-waived tests must be highly accurate and carry a small window of error. Choice C is incorrect; CLIA-waived tests may be used for monitoring but are not being used for diagnostic or treatment guidance.

59. C: The first tube that should be drawn is the light yellow tube, which is used for blood cultures. Cultures should be drawn before other labs and require extra preparation by the phlebotomist. Choices A, B, and D are incorrect, as these are not the first test that should be drawn.

60. D: The employer is mandated to provide employees sufficient and comprehensive education and training regarding safe working conditions. Choices A and C are incorrect; these regulating bodies establish, enforce, and regulate the laws and guidelines for workplace safety. Choice B is incorrect, as the employee is not responsible for organizing their own training for a job; however, they are responsible for completing and retaining the education to remain competent.

61. B: Ten minutes should pass prior to the opening of the centrifuge after it stops spinning. Choices A, C, and D are not the recommended time frames for this process.

62. D: A culture of safety increases psychological safety, speaking up about safe practices, and encouraging compliance with adhering to safety protocols. Choice A is not correct, as this only targets a certain group of employees. Choice B is not correct, as this only tests knowledge, not putting the knowledge into practice. Choice C is not correct, as this limits employee engagement to only one intervention.

63. B: The correct angle to enter the skin in the antecubital area is 15–30°. The angle should be closer to 15° for a shallow vein and closer to 30° for a deeper vein.

64. D. In the outpatient setting, the patient's name and date of birth should be cross-checked with the name and date of birth on the requisition form. Choice A is incorrect; this does not verify the patient's information with the information on the requisition form. Choice B is incorrect; the appointment information should not be used for patient identification. Choice C is also incorrect; the outpatient setting will not have hospital bands for patient identification.

65. A: The C method should be avoided because this positions the needle pointing at the phlebotomist's finger, exposing them to a potential needlestick event.

Answer Explanations

66. A: The phlebotomist should put on gloves before beginning to clean the patient's arm. Choices *B*, *C*, and *D* are incorrect. None of these options are the first thing that the phlebotomist should do. The patient does not need to wash their arms up to their elbows. Chlorhexidine gluconate and povidone-iodine are not the cleansers that should be used for a routine venipuncture.

67. C: Choice *C* is correct, as these tests are no more accurate or reliable than traditional collection and testing methods. Choices *A*, *B*, and *D* are all advantages for using point-of-care testing.

68. B. Express consent is usually reserved for invasive procedures, not for venipuncture. Choices *A*, *C*, and *D* are all types of consent that can be used in venipuncture. Choices *A* and *C* are incorrect. Verbal and implied consent are acceptable for venipuncture. Informed consent is required in venipuncture; this type of consent ensures that the patient understands the risks and benefits of the venipuncture.

69. B: Choices *A*, *C*, and *D* are incorrect. Dermal punctures should not be done on the hands of infants. In addition, the middle of the heel should be avoided to prevent harm to the infant.

70. D: It is recommended that in cases where the phlebotomist is unable to withdraw enough of a sample to appropriately fill both bottles, they should prioritize full fill of the aerobic bottle and inoculate the anaerobic bottle with the remainder. Choice *A* is incorrect because it is most important to prioritize filling of the aerobic bottle, as the majority of pathogens detected using blood culture are grown from the aerobic culture. Choice *B* is not correct because it would be inappropriate to use two different venipuncture samples for one set of blood cultures. Lastly, choice *C* is incorrect because it would be inappropriate to waste the first sample.

71. D: Allowing the alcohol to dry will prevent pain when the patient's skin is penetrated with the needle. The alcohol can cause a stinging or burning sensation if it is still wet when the venipuncture is performed. Choice *A* is incorrect; alcohol can cause pain if not left to dry. Choice *B* is incorrect; the tourniquet itself can be painful for patients. Choice *C* is incorrect; the patient stating that they are ready will not prevent pain if the alcohol is still wet.

72. B: The right median cubital is the best choice for venipuncture. Choices *A*, *C*, and *D* are incorrect. The left arm should be completely avoided because it has an intravenous line that can alter test results. The right basilic vein is not the preferred vein.

73. D: Choice *D* is the most appropriate site to perform venipuncture, as it is below the patient's heparin well. This location avoids potential damage to the indwelling catheter that could result from placing a tourniquet above the heparin well. This site also avoids potential blood sample contamination from performing venipuncture above a heparin well, and it prevents potential infusion injury due to puncture of a proximal vein. Choices *A* and *C* are incorrect because the phlebotomist should avoid venipuncture on the same arm as a peripherally inserted central catheter (PICC) line. Choice *B* is also incorrect because the left median cubital vein would be positioned above the heparin well and would not be an appropriate venipuncture site.

74. B: Adulteration, Choice *B*, is the purposeful compromise of a specimen sample to attempt to alter the results of the test. This is a deviation from standard collection practice. Choice *A* is the standard procedure when collecting any specimen from a patient. Choice *C* is best practice to ensure that the sample contains enough of the specimen to run the test. Choice *D* is allowed, provided that the phlebotomist documents and provides a signature that verifies they were the responsible party for both collecting the sample and providing the transportation.

Answer Explanations

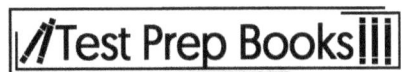

75. C: The correct action is to start at the site of the venipuncture and wipe in at least three circular motions from inside to outside. Choices A, B, and D are not the correct actions for the phlebotomist to perform.

76. D: There should be no delay in implementing post-exposure prophylactic treatment. Choices A, B, and C are incorrect, as they delay receiving treatment. It is most effective when initiated as soon as possible after exposure risk has occurred.

77. D: Chain-of-custody is used when a test must be accompanied by an official record that verifies collection methods and individuals involved, such as a drug test, Choice D. Choice A is a standardly collected and processed lab test that would not require such monitoring. Choice B is completed with the patient present, and results are available within minutes. Choice C is a lab that rules out cardiac stress and must be reported as soon as possible.

78. C. The order of draw is not listed on the requisition form. This information will be determined by the phlebotomist based on current recommendations. For example, a blue-top tube may be drawn before a green-top tube. Choices A, B, and D are all critical information that must be included on the requisition form.

79. C: Hemoconcentration can occur if a tourniquet is left in place too long, causing erroneous results.

80. B: Any product or substance utilized in a healthcare facility must be listed on a Material Safety Data Sheet that is kept in paper or digital form and is easily accessible to all staff. Choice A is incorrect; this public line is utilized for accidental ingestion or contact with a poisonous substance. Choice C is not correct; this would take additional time to contact the manufacturer for information. Choice D is not correct, as the supervisor should be referring to the MSDS for accurate and up-to-date data on the product.

81. C: An alcohol wipe on the floor should be addressed immediately, as it poses a slip and fall hazard due to wetness. Choice A is incorrect, as the phlebotomy chair's arm should be up and locked so that the patient can sit down. Choice B is incorrect, as the trash can next to the door does not pose a hazard. Choice D is incorrect because the phlebotomist will often get supplies ready by setting them on the counter.

82. A: Choice A, celluloid, cannot be autoclaved due to risk of shrinkage and flammability. Choices B, C, and D are all safe materials to be sanitized with the autoclave, as is glass.

83. B: HIPAA dictates that patients are informed about the type of healthcare information that is collected and how it is used in their care. Choices A and C are both facility-centered; HIPAA protects patient information and must be adhered to even if a facility is not-for-profit. Choice D is covered under the No Surprises Act of 2021, which says the facility must provide a good-faith estimate to the patient of fees for items and services.

84. D: The bevel of the needle should be facing up when entering the skin. Facing any other direction can cause damage to the vein and be more painful.

85. D: Of the choices, this webinar would offer information for lab workers to protect themselves against one of the higher biohazard risks with safe disposal. Choice A is not correct; this option would be better suited if the facility was focused on preventing repeat testing or reducing erroneous results with POC testing. Choice B is incorrect; this choice focuses on initiating a disaster plan, which would not be

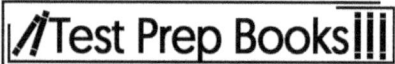

Answer Explanations

targeted toward the safe handling of biohazardous materials. Choice C is not correct; it may have a component of biohazard safety but would be focused on culture handling, and phlebotomists are exposed to broader areas of risk.

86. B: The phlebotomist placing the evacuated tube on the transfer device before puncturing the skin will cause air to enter the tube, eliminating its vacuum before blood is present. Choice A is not a phlebotomist error; having the evacuated tube within reach is appropriate and ensures equipment is ready. Choice C is incorrect; this is not an error of the phlebotomist. A crack in the tubing can cause the tube to fill with air, losing its suction, but it isn't due to the phlebotomist. Choice D is also not a phlebotomist error. The phlebotomist should check for a flash before placing the evacuated tube on the transfer device.

87. A: The likely cause of the tube not having a vacuum is that it rolled off the counter. Choice B is incorrect; changing needle systems would not cause a tube to lose suction. Choice C is incorrect, as temperature logs in compliance mean that storage has been within the normal range. Choice D is incorrect, as the rubber stopper should be intact to maintain the vacuum in the tube.

88. B. Lymphedema is a risk for patients who have had a mastectomy due to lymph node removal. Damage to any blood vessels on the affected side will increase the risk of lymphedema and infection. Choices A, C, and D are incorrect; these are not risks of a venipuncture after a mastectomy.

89. A: CLIA requires that calibration tests are performed at least every six months. The more frequent timeframes of Choices B, C, and D may be required per the healthcare facility; however, every six months is the standard set by CLIA.

90. A: The CDC provides free and fee-for-service training, consultation, and resources. Choice B is not correct; OSHA has a more concentrated focus on environmental workplace and employee safety rather than administrative functioning of a laboratory. Choice C is not correct, as this focuses on information regarding electronic health records and use of technology. Choice D is not correct; information regarding payment for services covered under Medicaid and Medicare is found within this document.

91. A: Best practice recommends that training occur at hire and once per year. Choice B is not correct; training should be proactive and occur to prevent deficiencies and unsafe practices. Choice C is not correct; this interval allows too much time to pass and will not ensure competencies are updated. Choice D is more frequent than the suggested timeline but may be required if staff are not adhering to policy or drift from safe practices.

92. D: The phlebotomist should refer to the chain of command and notify their immediate supervisor, as this is an ethical issue that may involve neglect or abuse. Choice A is not correct; the patient's nurse should also be advised to assess if the patient's family member is being disruptive to the patient or interfering with care. Choice C is not the best choice; while security may be required, unless the patient is in immediate danger, a supervisor should be involved to ensure that the patient's rights are being upheld. Choice B is incorrect; although this is an ethical situation, it should be addressed immediately, not at the next ethics meeting, because the patient may be coerced into not receiving treatment.

93. B. In the hospital setting, the patient's stated name and date of birth and the information on the hospital's identification band are used to verify the patient.

94. B: Utilizing safety devices on sharps reduces the chance for a needlestick. Choice A is not correct; needles should be immediately disposed of in a sharps container and should never be recapped. Choice

Answer Explanations

C is incorrect; not all venipunctures require the use of sterile gloves. Regular gloves are appropriate as long as the site is not touched after using antiseptic. Choice *D* is not correct; while that does prevent bloodborne disease exposure and potential for transmission, this question was specifically regarding preventing needlesticks.

95. A. The patient stating "Okay, let's get this done" is providing verbal consent for the venipuncture. Choice *B* is incorrect. In this situation, the patient needs more information before consenting. Choices *C* and *D* are both incorrect. In these situations, the patient is not yet providing consent but is showing hesitancy.

96. D: Prior to loading the centrifuge, tubes and bottles should be sanitized by wiping them down. Choice *A* is incorrect, as this will not wipe off any contamination that may have collected on the tubes during transport. Choice *B* may allow contamination to shift to other areas inside the centrifuge. Choice *C* is incorrect, as the sample must sit for thirty minutes to an hour prior to centrifugation and would not remove contaminants that may transfer to the tubes in that time.

97. A: Anchoring a vein helps stabilize the vein and keep it from rolling. Choices *B*, *C*, and *D* are incorrect. The phlebotomist should not try to hold the patient down. Anchoring the vein does not guide the dominant hand for venipuncture.

98. A: The phlebotomist would expect to verify the results with a whole blood test to check blood glucose levels. Choice *B* is not correct because it is a critical value and must be addressed. Choice *C* is incorrect because the range is so far outside of a normal result, this would not have affected the test. The value should be rechecked with a whole blood test, not Choice *D*, repeating the point-of-care test, as it is the best practice to verify critically high ranges.

99. C: The guidelines that determine, regulate, and enforce handling of biological hazards are published under 29 CFR 1910, also referred to as Title 29. Title 42, Choice *A*, is in regard to the public health code. Choice *B*, USC 5705, covers confidentiality of quality-assurance records. Choice *D* refers to the Needlestick Safety and Prevention Act.

100. C: Chlorhexidine gluconate should be used when drawing blood cultures. The cleanser should be used and allowed to dry completely before performing a venipuncture to avoid any contamination of the cultures. Choices *A*, *B*, and *D* are all incorrect; chlorhexidine gluconate is the cleanser of choice.

101. D. The cephalic vein is an appropriate site choice for a patient with obesity. The cephalic vein is frequently visible through the skin, more superficial, and is a good site to attempt in a patient with obesity. Choices *A*, *B*, and *C* are not the best choices in a patient with obesity.

102. A: Choice *A* is the correct answer because syringe inoculation should begin with the anaerobic bottle and end with the aerobic bottle so that any air at the back of the syringe will be injected into the aerobic bottle. Choices *B*, *C*, and *D* are not the correct answer because each of these choices represents an appropriate intervention for collecting blood cultures.

103. B. It is essential to know how fast the test should be run. The provider must decide if it is routine or STAT. The phlebotomist will need to call the provider for clarification. Choices *A*, *C*, and *D* can be missing from the requisition form without the need to contact the provider. This information can be obtained from the patient if needed.

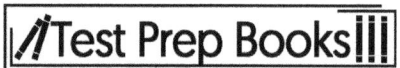

Answer Explanations

104. B. The patient should not have any food or drink for twelve hours. Alcohol falls into this group and does not have a longer abstinence requirement. Choices *A*, *C*, and *D* are all appropriate requirements of basal state testing.

105. A: The area should be cleaned with disinfectant before putting the supplies down. Choice *B* is incorrect; more must be done to clean the area besides moving food crumbs. Choice *C* is incorrect, as the equipment should not be placed on the bed with the patient; this is not more sanitary. Choice *D* is incorrect because soap and water is not the appropriate disinfectant.

106. D: The phlebotomist should NOT smack the patient's skin. This can cause venous damage and cause the patient pain. Choices *A*, *B*, and *C* are all actions that are appropriate to use when finding difficult veins.

107. A: As this appears to be the first time the new employee has observed this, it allows the employee to protect the patient and remind the preceptor of infection control practices. Choice *B* is not correct; the first action should be to protect the patient, and that requires speaking up. The supervisor should be notified immediately if this is a habitual practice and not a one-time mistake. Choice *C* is not correct; this still puts the patient at risk by not speaking up and preventing unsafe patient care from occurring. Choice *D* is not correct; this is disrespectful and is not a proactive solution to the infection control risk.

108. A: The Joint Commission, an accrediting body for best practice, advocates using two unique patient identifiers, which would include full name and date of birth. Choice *B* may not be unique, as the last four digits of a Social Security number may be the same as those of other patients. Choices *C* and *D* are not correct because they are not unique to the individual.

109. A. Two separate identifiers are required to verify a patient's identity. This usually includes their name and date of birth.

110. C: Choice *C* is the best tool to use to engage with a multidisciplinary team to enhance understanding and provide effective communication with a wide range of staff. Choice *A* is incorrect; making assumptions does not build trust and could create misunderstanding, leading to unsafe patient care. Active listening, not passive listening—Choice *B*—should be used. Choice *D* is incorrect because the method of communication must fit the situation and depends on who is receiving the message. A wide range of communication methods, such as verbal, fax, mail, electronic messaging, and email, may be considered.

111. B: The correct order of this draw is first the light blue tube, then the green tube, and finally the lavender tube. Choices *A*, *C*, and *D* are incorrect, as they do not follow the order of draw.

112. C: A syringe without a needle is a blunt device that will not puncture a container or pose a risk for a needlestick and should be disposed of in the appropriate biohazard bag. Choice *A* is not correct; even with the safety device activated, this device has the potential to puncture. Choice *B* is a small blade used to elicit blood and may cause injury if not disposed of in a sharps container. Choice *D* is not correct, as these are typically glass and have the risk for breakage.

113. D: Choice *A* is not a recommended replacement for a tourniquet. Choice *B* is incorrect, as a blood pressure cuff used for this purpose should not be inflated as high as the systolic blood pressure. Choice *C* is also incorrect; a tourniquet is not reusable and should not be an automatic cuff.

Answer Explanations

114. C. The caregiver accompanying the patient can verify their identity when a patient is unable to speak for themselves. Choices *A*, *B*, and *D* are incorrect. These choices are not appropriate ways to verify a patient's identity.

115. A: The Clinical & Laboratory Standards Institute recommends that a tourniquet should not be left on for more than 1 minute to prevent pain and harm to the patient.

116. D: The phlebotomist should ensure they check for appropriate labeling prior to agreeing to transport a specimen they did not personally collect. Choices *A* and *C* are not correct because the phlebotomist does not necessarily need to review the patient's lab orders or sign documentation unless advised to do so by their workplace. Choice *B* is incorrect because phlebotomists are permitted to assist with transport of specimens they did not collect, as long as they confirm proper labeling of the specimen.

117. D: Choice *D* should be used when available, as this protects the user, specimens, and lab from spillage, aerosolization, and cross-contamination. Choice *A* is incorrect, as high-pressure syringes may lead to splashing and overfilling. Choice *B*, an N-95 mask, is not required for all specimens and would not be effective against splashes. Choice *C* is used to detect radiation and would not have applicability for filling centrifuge tubes.

118. A. A requisition form from a provider and some type of informed consent from the patient are required to have lab testing done. Choices *B* and *D* are incorrect. The phlebotomist cannot do a venipuncture on a patient with only these items. Choice *C* is incorrect; in addition to needing informed consent, the phlebotomist needs a requisition form, not a prescription, to receive the correct information for the testing.

119. B: A package that has a hole should always be disposed of properly. This hole could cause the equipment inside to be contaminated. Choice *A* is incorrect; a wrinkled package is fine if it is still intact. Choice *C* is also incorrect; if the package has not passed its expiration date, it is okay to use. Choice *D* is incorrect; an unrolled tourniquet is okay to use if it is new and unused.

120. B: When anchoring a vein, the phlebotomist should place the nondominant thumb 2 inches below the insertion site.

Practice Test

1. What information does a peak draw provide?
    a. The least amount of medication in the blood
    b. The maximum amount of medication in the blood
    c. The amount of medication in the blood at a given time
    d. The amount of medication in the blood first thing in the morning

2. When loading a centrifuge, why is it important to ensure that the load is balanced?
    a. To reduce noise pollution
    b. To decrease time it takes to spin samples
    c. To reduce the need to clean the equipment
    d. To prevent damage to the equipment

3. The laboratory refrigerator log shows that the temperature for the last two weeks has been trending upward and has been above the recommended limit for the past three days. When a staff member finds the quality failure, what should they do?
    a. Notify the last person filling out the log so they can correct the numbers.
    b. Report the fallout to the supervisor and prepare to document and dispose of any samples.
    c. Turn the temperature of the refrigerator down.
    d. Visually inspect the specimens to ensure that they are not compromised.

4. A STAT specimen is drawn. When should it be transported to the laboratory?
    a. Immediately
    b. Within an hour
    c. Once the rest of the samples assigned to the phlebotomist are drawn
    d. There is no specification for delivering to lab

5. A patient faints and is breathing but continues to be unconscious. The patient remains unconscious for over 2 minutes. What is the phlebotomist's next action?
    a. Call 911.
    b. Apply a cold compress to the neck.
    c. Provide water to the patient.
    d. Keep the patient safe from falling.

6. Which needle system has a needle directly connected to a transfer device?
    a. Butterfly needle system
    b. Dermal collection system
    c. Evacuated tube system (ETS)
    d. Syringe needle system

7. Which blood collection device is best suited for fragile veins that easily collapse?
    a. Evacuated tube system (ETS)
    b. Butterfly method
    c. Syringe method
    d. Dermal puncture

8. When performing post-procedural care, what is the primary goal?
   a. Use minimal supplies.
   b. Achieve hemostasis.
   c. Discharge the patient.
   d. Clean the exam room.

9. What is completed with informed or express consent in comparison with implied consent?
   a. Identity verification
   b. Patient rolls up their sleeve
   c. Consent form
   d. Patient states they are ready

10. The phlebotomist is running a point-of-care test and notes that the result line is indicated; however, the control line is absent. What is the next best step?
   a. Repeat the test.
   b. Document the test result in the chart.
   c. Mark that the test is inconclusive.
   d. Tell the patient that the equipment is down and that they will have to return tomorrow.

11. What finding would indicate to the phlebotomist that the supply should be thrown away?
   a. 70% isopropyl alcohol wipe is dry
   b. Sterile packaging is wrinkled
   c. Tourniquet is unused and without damage
   d. Storage temperature has varied but stayed within an acceptable range

12. A refractometer is used to analyze what?
   a. Specific gravity
   b. pH level
   c. Osmolality
   d. Clarity

13. What is NOT a recommended part of the phlebotomy chair?
   a. Backrest
   b. Footrest
   c. Armrest
   d. Extended armrest

14. What pathogen is NOT effectively controlled via hand hygiene using alcohol-based hand sanitizer?
   a. MRSA
   b. Influenza
   c. Rhinovirus
   d. *C. difficile*

15. When should pressure be applied to the venipuncture site?
   a. As the needle begins to be withdrawn from the skin
   b. After the needle has completely exited the skin
   c. While the needle is halfway out of the skin
   d. After the tourniquet is removed

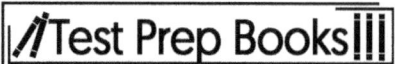

Practice Test

16. The phlebotomist is drawing blood from a patient in a double occupancy room. The neighboring patient requests that the phlebotomist assist with interpreting the results of lab values and their current treatment. What is the best response from the phlebotomist?
   a. "I am sorry; you will have to request this information through the medical records department."
   b. "I cannot interpret tests, but I will ask your nurse or healthcare provider to discuss them with you."
   c. "Sure, let me see the results."
   d. "This is a website I use to interpret results; it explains labs really well."

17. A patient is suspected of having tuberculosis. The phlebotomist is a new employee and recognizes that an N-95 mask is required. What should have occurred prior to donning an N-95 mask and entering the patient's room?
   a. Fit testing
   b. Prophylactic treatment
   c. Double gloving
   d. Finding another phlebotomist with more experience

18. A patient has orders for blood cultures, C-reactive protein (CRP), chemistry panel, and lactate level. Which would be collected first?
   a. Blood culture
   b. C-reactive protein
   c. Chemistry panel
   d. Lactate level

19. A phlebotomist is preparing to collect a twenty-four-hour urine sample. Why are special precautions required when handling this specimen?
   a. The solution may cause chemical burns.
   b. This test is used to test for multidrug-resistant organisms.
   c. The solution can release noxious gas.
   d. The sample has a higher risk for spilling.

20. A test that must be maintained at body temperature has been collected. How should this sample be supported?
   a. Place the sample in a pocket near the body.
   b. Sample may be kept at room temperature.
   c. Use a heel warmer or incubator.
   d. Transport the sample immediately so it does not have time to cool down.

21. Which is NOT required for the collection of a stool sample?
   a. The stool sample collected must be the size of a golf ball.
   b. The stool must be without the presence of urine or anything else.
   c. The stool sample should be delivered to the laboratory as soon as possible.
   d. The stool sample should be labeled or have the patient's name on the container.

22. Which of the following is a reliable source for patient education?
   a. Peer-reviewed databases
   b. Google search
   c. Medical textbook published fifteen years ago
   d. YouTube

132

23. For which age group would a phlebotomist perform a heel puncture to draw blood?
   a. Zero to six months
   b. Zero to three months
   c. Three to six months
   d. Zero to twelve months

24. What is the purpose of identifying the patient in two different ways?
   a. To ensure the correct patient receives the correct tests
   b. To ensure the correct order of draw
   c. To ensure the correct tubes are drawn
   d. To ensure the patient is who they say they are

25. What is the purpose of inverting the evacuated tubes?
   a. To mix the blood with the additives
   b. To keep the blood from clotting
   c. To separate the red blood cells from the plasma
   d. To ensure that the blood coats the inside of the tube

26. A newly hired phlebotomist is preparing a thin peripheral blood smear. Which of the following statements made by the new phlebotomist may require additional teaching?
   a. "I should place the drop of blood close to the frosted end of the slide."
   b. "I am making sure the blood goes all the way across the pusher slide before I move it."
   c. "I am trying not to put pressure on the pusher slide while I am doing the smear."
   d. "I can take my gloves off after the film has dried."

27. An older adult with fragile skin is receiving care post-venipuncture. What dressing should be used?
   a. Self-adhesive wrap
   b. Silk tape
   c. Hypoallergenic tape
   d. Transparent dressing

28. A phlebotomist has prepared a patient for venipuncture with antiseptic at the proposed insertion site. The phlebotomist answers an urgent call on a mobile device, removes the tourniquet from the patient, and steps out of the room for privacy. When returning to attempt to draw blood again, what should be the first step after performing hand hygiene?
   a. Re-apply antiseptic and allow it to dry.
   b. Access the vein since it has already been sanitized.
   c. Re-apply tourniquet and then apply antiseptic.
   d. Re-apply tourniquet and access vein.

29. Following the order of draw, what should be drawn first on a 6-month-old infant?
   a. Pearl evacuated tube for plasma molecular tests
   b. Lavender evacuated tube for hematology
   c. Gold evacuated tube for tuberculosis
   d. Green evacuated tube for blood gas collection

30. Which is NOT an acceptable way of verifying a patient's identity in addition to a requisition form?
    a. Stated name and date of birth
    b. Student identification card
    c. Caregiver-stated patient's name and date of birth
    d. Driver's license

31. A patient in the hospital is having severe tremors. The phlebotomist is struggling to hold the patient. What action should the phlebotomist take?
    a. Secure the patient's arm to the bed with a restraint.
    b. Hold the patient's arm down forcefully while performing the venipuncture.
    c. Delay the venipuncture until the next day.
    d. Ask for help from another phlebotomist or the patient's nurse or aide.

32. What is the standard needle gauge used in phlebotomy?
    a. 19 gauge
    b. 20 gauge
    c. 21 gauge
    d. 22 gauge

33. The phlebotomist is performing a CLIA-waived test. What is the reason that quality controls are completed on these types of tests?
    a. To ensure accurate results
    b. To verify accession numbers
    c. To reduce the spread of nosocomial infection
    d. To make sure that the test is being collected correctly

34. A requisition form is missing a critical piece. The phlebotomist knows that they must reach out to the provider's office prior to the venipuncture. What information was likely missing?
    a. The provider's office address
    b. The names of the labs ordered
    c. The patient's phone number
    d. The patient's insurance information

35. What type of urine sample requires the patient to clean their urethral opening and surrounding tissue before collecting a sample?
    a. Midstream urine collection
    b. Regular voided collection
    c. 24-hour urine collection
    d. Midstream clean urine collection

36. How soon after collection should plasma or serum be separated?
    a. Within thirty minutes
    b. Up to four hours
    c. Two hours or less
    d. Eight hours

Practice Test

37. A phlebotomist is preparing to enter the room of a patient with hepatitis B. What PPE should be applied to collect a sputum sample?
   a. Gloves, gown, and mask
   b. Gloves, gown, and N-95
   c. Nothing is required for hepatitis B
   d. Gloves

38. When would a specimen need to be rejected and require re-collection?
   a. The specimen is delivered on ice.
   b. The specimen has inadequate patient information.
   c. A family member of the patient drops off the lab sample.
   d. The chain of custody is used in a criminal case.

39. How many times should most tubes be inverted?
   a. 1–3
   b. 8–10
   c. 3–5
   d. 5–7

40. When observing a venipuncture site after drawing blood, the phlebotomist recognizes that a hematoma is forming. What is the best action to take next?
   a. Apply a bandage and notify the nurse.
   b. Wipe away any excess blood oozing and watch the site.
   c. Apply immediate, firm pressure to the site.
   d. Notify the ordering provider.

41. A phlebotomist is walking a patient out of the building. They ask a fellow phlebotomist to label the specimens they just drew. What would be the correct action?
   a. Go quickly and label the specimens before they leave the building.
   b. Label the specimens the next chance you get.
   c. Ask another phlebotomist if they will do it.
   d. Do not label the specimens in question.

42. What time of day is the best for a patient to produce a sputum sample?
   a. Evening
   b. Bedtime
   c. Afternoon
   d. Morning

43. A patient has a trough level ordered for an antibiotic that they have started taking a few days ago. What time would the lab be drawn?
   a. One hour after administration of the medication
   b. First thing in the morning
   c. Thirty minutes to an hour before the next dose
   d. Every six hours

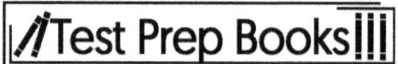

Practice Test

44. What is the correct site for a dermal puncture of a patient who is more than 1 year old?
   a. The side of the pad of the middle finger
   b. The middle of the pad of the ring finger
   c. The middle of the pad of the middle finger
   d. The side of the pad of the index finger

45. Which of the following is NOT used as a secondary containment within a centrifuge?
   a. Pipette
   b. O-ring
   c. Bucket
   d. Safety cup

46. When looking for a vein, for patient safety, what should the phlebotomist avoid?
   a. Birthmarks
   b. Intact skin
   c. Wounds or rashes
   d. Freckles

47. Tourniquets are single patient use. When using a tourniquet on the same patient, what would indicate that the tourniquet needed to be replaced?
   a. The tourniquet is hanging by the bed.
   b. The tourniquet is wrinkled.
   c. The tourniquet appears bright in color.
   d. The tourniquet has small cracks.

48. What is an important question to ask before performing a venipuncture on a patient?
   a. "Did you follow testing instructions?"
   b. "Do you have a full bladder?"
   c. "Did you drink a lot of fluids before arriving?"
   d. "Did you collect your sputum sample first thing in the morning?"

49. Which of the following is NOT a necessary component of patient information provided on the requisition form?
   a. Ordering physician
   b. Billing information
   c. Insurance
   d. Address of lab facility

50. What percent of alcohol is required in hand sanitizer to be effective at killing microbes per the CDC?
   a. 20 percent
   b. Greater than 40 percent
   c. At least 60 percent
   d. At least 50 percent

51. A phlebotomist is about to enter a patient's room to draw a lab sample on a patient. Outside the patient's door is posted a precautions sign stating that contact precautions are required. What PPE is recommended for contact precautions?
   a. No PPE required to enter as long as the patient is not touched
   b. Gloves and mask
   c. Gloves and gown
   d. Mask

52. Which of the following is considered a CLIA-waived test?
   a. Complete blood count
   b. Blood glucose monitoring
   c. PT/INR
   d. Potassium

53. Which tube must always be filled completely to the fill line?
   a. Red for iron studies
   b. Green for chemistries
   c. Light blue for coagulation studies
   d. Lavender for blood counts

54. Testing for inborn errors of metabolism is typically first performed when?
   a. 30–60 days after birth
   b. 7–14 days after birth
   c. 1–2 days after birth
   d. Immediately after birth

55. A new box of CLIA-waived tests that has been kept in storage is opened. What should be completed prior to distributing the tests for use?
   a. Perform QC according to manufacturer's directions.
   b. Check that the number of tests matches what is stated on the box.
   c. Check one test against a blood-drawn sample to ensure that it is accurate.
   d. Write the date that the box was opened on each test.

56. A serum sample will not be delivered to the laboratory for more than twenty-four hours. At what temperature should the sample be kept?
   a. Room temperature
   b. Below –20 °C
   c. 4 °C to 8 °C
   d. 1 °C to 10 °C

57. A patient loses consciousness while the phlebotomist is performing the venipuncture. The phlebotomist stops the draw immediately and notes the time. What is the phlebotomist's next action?
   a. Begin CPR.
   b. Apply a cold compress.
   c. Check the patient to ensure that they are breathing.
   d. Lower the patient to the floor.

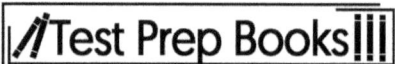

58. What features should the phlebotomy needle have in order to meet CLSI standards?
    a. Hollow and straight
    b. Hollow and nonbeveled
    c. Hollow and flared
    d. Hollow and beveled

59. What part of the arm should be inspected first for a good site for venipuncture?
    a. Hand
    b. Upper arm
    c. Antecubital fossa
    d. Wrist

60. Generally, the maximum volume of blood that should be drawn in a single session for a patient should be no more than what?
    a. 100 mL/kg of body weight
    b. 50 mL of blood
    c. 3 percent of total blood volume
    d. Double the body weight in kilograms

61. The phlebotomist notices their blood smear does not have a feathered edge. This is most likely due to which error?
    a. The blood drop was too small.
    b. The pusher slide was lifted too soon.
    c. There were contaminants on the slide.
    d. The smear was performed too quickly.

62. The phlebotomist explains the venipuncture procedure to help the patient with what complication?
    a. Difficult stick
    b. Consent
    c. Preparation
    d. Anxiety

63. When transporting bacterial or viral samples, what is important to ensure prior to transporting?
    a. Viral samples are kept at room temperature.
    b. Bacterial samples are transported on ice.
    c. Multiple samples are placed within the same biohazard bag.
    d. Standard precautions are used when packaging.

64. When using evacuated tubes, what should the phlebotomist do to ensure that the tube has enough vacuum to use?
    a. Ensure the tube fills completely while performing the venipuncture.
    b. Remove the rubber cap to ensure that it seals adequately.
    c. Test the suction using a needle and syringe before the venipuncture.
    d. Check the tube after the draw to ensure the tube is full.

Practice Test

65. Which of the following items is required to be on a requisition form?
   a. Physician's name
   b. Physician's practice name
   c. Patient's Social Security number
   d. Collection tubes required

66. To calculate an adult's total blood volume, multiply the patient's weight in kilograms by what?
   a. 115
   b. 100
   c. 80
   d. 70

67. Which of the following tasks would be outside the scope of practice for a phlebotomist?
   a. Recording temperature for freezers on a daily checklist
   b. Preparing a specimen for transport
   c. Completing a lab requisition form
   d. Collecting a tissue sample during a procedure

68. What is the purpose of a routine laboratory draw?
   a. To monitor the levels of antibiotic for therapeutic levels
   b. To determine the level of antibiotic first thing in the morning
   c. To monitor a patient's response to medication
   d. Regular medical management

69. Which of the following is NOT a characteristic of an ideal vein for venipuncture?
   a. The vein is visible without a tourniquet.
   b. The vein is a good size.
   c. The vein is straight.
   d. The vein can be felt with a tourniquet.

70. At what angle should the needle be removed from the patient?
   a. 30° after being inserted at 15° from the antecubital
   b. 15° after being inserted at 10° from the dorsum of the hand
   c. 10° after being inserted at 15° from the antecubital
   d. 25° after being inserted at 25° from the antecubital

71. The phlebotomist has drawn blood from a patient and, while affixing labels, finds that one of the tubes is expired by one month. What should the phlebotomist do?
   a. Since it is only a month, place the patient label over the date and send for processing as usual.
   b. Note in the chart that an expired tube was used.
   c. Redraw the patient with a tube that is verified to be within expiration time frame and send both.
   d. Discard the expired tube and draw another sample from the patient after explaining the reason for needing to redraw the lab.

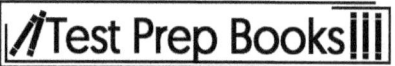

72. What is the most important reason that aseptic technique is utilized?
    a. To prevent community infection spread
    b. To decrease spread of nosocomial infection
    c. To reduce the need to use sterile supplies
    d. To encourage hand hygiene

73. Why must a standardized practice for aliquoting techniques be confirmed with all performing staff?
    a. It reduces the cost of supplies.
    b. Results may differ with even small deviations.
    c. Less gel may be used to separate plasma from cells.
    d. It prevents the spread of infectious disease.

74. A phlebotomist has developed a sensitivity to latex gloves; however, their employer refuses to provide nitrile gloves. What agency should the phlebotomist report this to?
    a. The Occupational Safety and Health Administration
    b. The Joint Commission
    c. The Centers for Disease Control and Prevention
    d. The Better Business Bureau

75. What is the standard length range of a phlebotomy needle?
    a. 0.5–1 inches
    b. 1–1.5 inches
    c. 1.5–2 inches
    d. 2–2.5 inches

76. Which of the following statements best represents following standard precautions to prevent the spread of respiratory pathogens?
    a. Covering the mouth with a hand when sneezing
    b. Wearing a mask to cover the mouth only
    c. Washing or sanitizing hands before and after each patient encounter
    d. Coughing into a reusable handkerchief

77. Which of the following is NOT a requirement of basal state testing?
    a. No exercise for twenty-four hours
    b. No eating or drinking for twelve hours
    c. Must be done at the same time every day
    d. Must be done first thing in the morning

78. When the patient is sitting, what is required to meet national guidelines?
    a. Chair back
    b. Lab table
    c. Procedure tray
    d. Padded armrest

Practice Test

79. Which vein is situated between two muscles, making it easier to access and ensuring less risk of patient harm?
    a. Median cubital vein
    b. Basilic vein
    c. Cephalic vein
    d. Median antebrachial vein

80. What vaccination is required to be offered by healthcare facilities to phlebotomists and other healthcare providers at risk for bloodborne pathogen exposure per OSHA guidelines?
    a. Influenza
    b. Hepatitis B
    c. HIV
    d. Monkeypox

81. What is the correct procedure for processing a Guthrie card after completing collection?
    a. Hang the card in an area that is away from heat and sunlight.
    b. Place the card in the designated bin with other cards awaiting packaging.
    c. The card can be packaged immediately into its envelope for transport.
    d. The card should lay flat in a relatively dark, cool area.

82. When following the capillary order of draw, which should be the last tube drawn?
    a. Red serum evacuated tube
    b. Green evacuated tube
    c. Lavender evacuated tube
    d. Royal blue evacuated tube

83. For how long are stool samples valid at room temperature?
    a. Twenty-four hours
    b. Ten hours
    c. Four hours
    d. Eight hours

84. Which of the following is a task that is within the phlebotomist's scope of practice?
    a. Drawing a blood sample from an arterial line
    b. Calling the provider to report a critical value
    c. Placing an order to draw a lab panel
    d. Point-of-care testing

85. Which of the following is NOT a potential adverse event from venipuncture?
    a. Vasovagal response
    b. Nausea
    c. Headache
    d. Hematoma

86. What dictates which needle device is used in a hospital setting?
    a. Phlebotomist's comfort level with supplies
    b. Phlebotomist's consistent use of one type of supply
    c. Patient's request for certain supplies
    d. Available supplies in the hospital

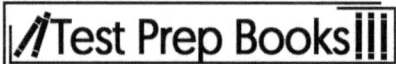

87. The phlebotomist is concerned that a patient's HIPAA rights are not being upheld. Which of the following is an example of a HIPAA violation?
    a. Asking the patient their name and date of birth prior to drawing blood
    b. Providing privacy when discussing a patient's concerns
    c. Leaving a lab slip on a fellow phlebotomist's lab cart in the hall
    d. Referring the patient to the provider for interpretation of lab results

88. What is a good example of telling the patient that the venipuncture is going to begin?
    a. The patient doesn't need to know.
    b. "Get ready, I'm going to stick you."
    c. "Big poke coming your way."
    d. "Okay, here we go. 3, 2, 1..."

89. Which of the following positions is recommended for the patient?
    a. Prone
    b. Lateral
    c. Sitting
    d. Trendelenburg

90. What position is most appropriate for a patient with a history of fainting or becoming lightheaded during venipuncture?
    a. Sitting
    b. Trendelenburg
    c. Prone
    d. Supine

91. For how long, at minimum, should effective hand washing with an antibacterial soap occur?
    a. Ten seconds
    b. One minute
    c. Twenty seconds
    d. Thirty seconds

92. A patient was given orders for an 8-hour urine test. The phlebotomist anticipates providing which of the following instructions?
    a. Collect the first void upon waking in the morning.
    b. Do not eat or drink anything for 8 hours prior to collecting.
    c. Collect all voided urine during the 8-hour test window.
    d. Void at the specific time ordered by your physician.

93. When performing collection for newborn screening, the phlebotomist uses which of the following techniques?
    a. Uses a capillary tube to deposit a single drop to each circle
    b. Brings the card to the drop of blood, avoiding touching the skin to fill each circle
    c. Presses the card to the puncture site to deposit a drop of blood into each circle
    d. Allows the drops to fall onto the paper, filling each of the circles

Practice Test

94. The phlebotomist has drawn a blood gas sample. What step should be taken immediately?
   a. Place on ice.
   b. Maintain at room temperature.
   c. Shake the tube well to ensure it is mixed with additive.
   d. Personally deliver to the lab immediately.

95. Which type of consent is required for the phlebotomy process?
   a. Express consent
   b. Informed consent
   c. Written consent
   d. Implied consent

96. A phlebotomist is drawing blood and knows that they must follow the order of draw on their adult patient. The orders include a light blue, gray, and green tube. In what order would these be drawn?
   a. Green, gray, light blue
   b. Light blue, green, gray
   c. Light blue, gray, green
   d. Gray, light blue, green

97. What is a disadvantage of the pneumatic tube system?
   a. It may damage the specimen if improperly cushioned.
   b. It increases the temperature of the specimen.
   c. It adds oxygen to anaerobic samples.
   d. It decreases speed of delivery.

98. A phlebotomist is labeling evacuated tubes for a venipuncture. Which of the following is necessary when labeling?
   a. Label the tube with the label over the rubber stopper.
   b. Label the specimens before the venipuncture.
   c. Label the specimens with the patient in the room.
   d. Label the tubes so that the label looks like a flag.

99. Why must some specimens be placed on ice?
   a. To increase metabolism
   b. To increase chemical reaction of the analyte
   c. To speed separation of plasma from whole blood
   d. To slow metabolism

100. Which of the following is a blood collection device that has a specific type of needle attached to a tube that is approximately 5 inches long?
   a. Butterfly needle system
   b. Evacuated tube system
   c. Syringe method
   d. Dermal collection

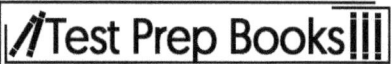

101. The laboratory staff member is preparing to aliquot a sample. What is the first step of the process?
   a. Transfer fluid floating at the top to a new tube.
   b. Place the tip of the pipette in the lower portion specimen.
   c. Centrifuge the first tube.
   d. Depress bulb of pipette to remove air.

102. A supervisor is notified that a phlebotomist has had a sharps injury after drawing a blood sample from a patient with suspected hepatitis B. Where is the best place that the supervisor can find best-practice information to guide treatment?
   a. PEPline
   b. MSDS
   c. Staff member's healthcare provider
   d. US Environmental Protection Agency

103. What is best practice for transporting multiple tubes to the laboratory?
   a. Laying the tubes on their side
   b. Inverting the tubes on the test tube rack
   c. Individually wrapping each tube in bubble wrap
   d. Keeping them upright with the lids tightly sealed

104. A phlebotomist has performed a quality control test prior to using the equipment. What is the next step the phlebotomist must take?
   a. Document the results in the logbook.
   b. Note the results in the patient's chart.
   c. Clean the equipment thoroughly.
   d. Have the immediate supervisor verify the results.

105. What is the purpose of the requisition form?
   a. Informs the phlebotomist of which order to draw labs
   b. Informs the phlebotomist of the medical reasons for the labs requested
   c. Informs the phlebotomist about the patient and what labs must be drawn
   d. Informs the phlebotomist about the physician's office and protocols

106. A phlebotomist is washing their hands before the start of their shift and finds a cut near their thumb. What is the best action to prevent the risk of contracting an infection?
   a. Check for a scab; if there is one, it does not need to be covered.
   b. Notify the supervisor that they cannot work in patient care areas.
   c. Cover the area with waterproof adhesive dressing.
   d. Wear a glove on that hand for the entire day and double-glove during patient care.

107. A phlebotomist is preparing to perform a venipuncture. When inspecting the tubes, they realize that one must be thrown out. What did the phlebotomist realize?
   a. The rubber cap appears untouched.
   b. The expiration date is tomorrow.
   c. There is fluid in the tube.
   d. The tube's label is torn.

Practice Test

108. Which color top tube is used for bacterial studies?
    a. Light blue tube
    b. Light yellow tube
    c. Green tube
    d. Gray tube

109. Which of the following is the correct location for a dermal puncture on an 8-month-old infant?
    a. Plantar surface of the foot in the middle of the heel
    b. Dorsal surface of the heel on the side
    c. Plantar surface of the foot on the side of the heel
    d. Ring finger to the side of the pad

110. What is the purpose of an accession number?
    a. To verify a patient's identity
    b. To provide a code for the healthcare provider to order tests
    c. To provide a unique number for cataloging purposes
    d. To track chain of custody for legal purposes

111. How can staff and patients prevent the spread of transient bacteria?
    a. Wearing gloves
    b. Using alcohol-based cleaners on all hard surfaces
    c. Performing proper hand hygiene
    d. Wearing a mask

112. What temperature should a semen sample be held at until it is delivered to the laboratory?
    a. Less than forty degrees
    b. Room temperature
    c. Body temperature
    d. Less than ninety degrees

113. What is centrifugation most commonly used for?
    a. To separate a sample into smaller portions for chemical analysis
    b. To process urine samples
    c. To grow bacterial cultures
    d. To separate plasma and serum from whole blood

114. A patient has very small veins that can be difficult to access. Which blood collection device should be used?
    a. Evacuated tube system (ETS)
    b. Butterfly needle system
    c. Syringe method
    d. Dermal puncture

115. While collecting a blood culture using a direct inoculation technique, the phlebotomist fills the aerobic bottle first. What is the reason for this?
    a. To ensure appropriate volume for the aerobic bottle
    b. To prevent syringe air bubbles from entering the anaerobic bottle
    c. To account for the butterfly set tubing
    d. To prevent cross-contamination between both bottles

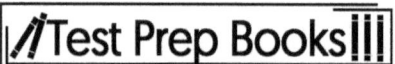

116. The phlebotomist is preparing to draw blood from a patient with a Do Not Resuscitate bracelet on. The patient suddenly slumps forward and has no pulse. What should the phlebotomist do first?
    a. Press the emergency call button.
    b. Do nothing, because the patient is DNR.
    c. Assist the patient back to a lying position.
    d. Leave the room to find the nurse.

117. A unit of donated blood is equal to approximately how many milliliters of fluid?
    a. 450
    b. 400
    c. 350
    d. 300

118. What priority should be given to a STAT order?
    a. First
    b. Last
    c. Second
    d. First in the morning

119. The phlebotomist is preparing to draw blood from a patient. Which of the following represents an aseptic technique?
    a. Ensuring that drying time for the antiseptic is followed per manufacturer's recommendations
    b. Using a clean field
    c. Taking off the glove to better feel for the vein after the antiseptic has dried
    d. Having the patient put their finger over the site to stop the bleeding

120. A patient is refusing to have their blood drawn. What is the best action by the phlebotomist?
    a. Leave the patient's room and ask another coworker to attempt later in the day.
    b. Document that the patient is refusing and notify the ordering provider.
    c. Tell the patient that the provider ordered it, so it must be completed.
    d. Ask the patient's family to hold the patient down so that a sample can be drawn.

Answer Explanations

Answer Explanations

1. B. The peak draw is taken one hour post medication administration and indicates the maximum amount of medication in the blood. Choices *A*, *C*, and *D* are incorrect, as they do not represent a peak level.

2. D: An unbalanced load can cause the centrifuge to malfunction and lab specimens to break. Choice *A* is not correct because although an unbalanced load may cause additional vibrational noise, this is not the most important reason. Choice *B* is not correct because balancing a load will not affect run time from standard processing. Choice *C* is not the best choice. An unbalanced load may result in broken tubes and leaks that will require additional cleaning; however, balancing a load does not reduce the need for regular cleaning.

3. B: The failure needs to be reported immediately and any samples reviewed for compromise. Choice *A* is not correct; QC logs should never be corrected or falsified. Choice *C* is not correct; while the refrigerator does require service to correct temperature issues, just turning it down will not ensure that the specimens kept within the fridge have been maintained for integrity. Choice *D* is not correct; visual inspection will not confirm whether the temperature was maintained sufficiently to prevent spoilage of samples, which will lead to erroneous results.

4. A: STAT samples are ordered urgently and require immediate results for treatment guidance on life-threatening patient conditions. Choice *B* would be appropriate for an urgent lab order. Choice *C* is for standard orders. Choice *D* is incorrect, as policy assigns an expectation with all labs, even non-emergent ones, to prevent breakdown of the sample.

5. A: The phlebotomist should call 911 if the patient is still unconscious after 2 minutes. Most fainting episodes are very short. Choices *B* and *D* are actions that should be completed immediately after fainting. Choice *C* is incorrect, as water (or anything) should not be given to a patient who is unconscious.

6. C: An evacuated tube system (ETS) is a needle directly connected to a transfer device.

7. C: The syringe method is best for fragile veins that easily collapse because it places less suction pressure on the vessel, allowing blood to be pulled out. Choice *A* is incorrect; the increased pressure of the ETS can collapse fragile veins. Choice *B* is also incorrect; the butterfly method also uses evacuated tubes, which create too much pressure. Choice *D* is incorrect and is not routinely used for phlebotomy on adults.

8. B: Achieving hemostasis and the prevention of bruising and bleeding is the primary goal after venipuncture.

9. C. A consent form is signed when informed or express consent is obtained. Choice *A* is not a part of the consent process; the patient identity should have been verified before consent was obtained. Choices *B* and *D* are incorrect; these options are examples of implied consent.

10. A: A control line verifies that the sample and testing equipment met standards. A test result that lacks the control line indicates an error with the process and will need to be repeated. Choice *B* is incorrect; a lack of control suggests that the test result will not be accurate. This test should be repeated and not noted in the chart. Choice *C* is insufficient, as the test still requires collection and processing;

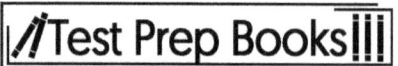

Answer Explanations

marking that it is inconclusive will not fulfill the order. Choice D is incorrect; it is inappropriate to tell the patient false information, and this can result in a delay in patient care. The sample should be re-collected, if necessary, and re-processed.

11. A: A dry alcohol wipe should be disposed of, and a fresh moist wipe used instead. Choices B, C, and D are all findings that indicate the supplies are usable.

12. A: A refractometer allows for physical examination of urine specific gravity. Choices B, C, and D are incorrect because these urine qualities are not evaluated using a refractometer.

13. B. A footrest is not a recommended piece of the phlebotomy chair. Choices A and C are recommended for patient safety to prevent any falls and to help the patient to be comfortable. Choice D is recommended, as the extended armrest goes to the front of the patient and keeps them from falling forward in case of fainting.

14. D: *C. difficile* is a spore that is not effectively sanitized with alcohol scrub. Soap and water should always be used for hand hygiene after contact with a patient who has *C. difficile*. Choices A, B, and C are microbes that are effectively killed with hand sanitizer as long as hands are not visibly soiled and the alcohol content is at least 60 percent.

15. B: Pressure should be applied after the needle has been completely removed from the skin. Choice D is incorrect, as the tourniquet should be removed as the final evacuated tube is being filled, not after the entire draw is complete.

16. B: Interpreting tests is outside the scope of practice of the phlebotomist. This answer is honest and provides an action to elicit the information and get it back to the patient. Choice A is not correct; the patient can receive results without going through medical records, and this response does not assist the patient in getting an answer. Choice C is not correct; the phlebotomist should not attempt to explain the patient's results, as they will not have the medical expertise to do so. Choice D is incorrect because it will not provide an explanation to the patient of how the lab results relate to the diagnosis and treatment plan.

17. A: All staff members involved in patient care must be fit tested for an N-95 mask prior to donning and providing care for patients who are in airborne precautions. This ensures that the N-95 mask will fit and provide effective protection.

18. A: Blood cultures should be collected first if other labs are ordered at the same time. This is to prevent potential contamination from the other tubes. Choice B, C, and D are incorrect, as they would not be first in the order of draw.

19. A: The solution used contains acids for preservation and may cause chemical burns if contact is made with skin. Choice B is not correct because this test is used to assess kidney function, not to test for organisms. Choice C is not correct, as it does not release any gases. This sample does not have a higher risk to spill than other fluid samples, so Choice D is incorrect.

20. C: To keep a sample at body temperature (37 °C), a heel warmer or incubator will provide the right temperature control for safe transport. Choice A is an unsafe option for the lab staff and has potential for transferring transient bacteria. Also, it may not be able to maintain the temperature sufficiently. Choices B and D are incorrect, as these will allow the sample to cool off. Average room temperature is 20 °C to 22 °C, well below body temperature.

Answer Explanations

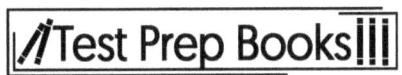

21. A. The stool sample only needs to be the size of a dime. Choices *B*, *C*, and *D* are steps that are required when obtaining a stool sample.

22. A: Patient education should always be derived from reliable sources that are peer reviewed, Choice *A*, and validated by health experts and accrediting bodies. Choices *B* and *D* are not regulated, and information cannot be confirmed as accurate unless it has been published by a trusted organization in healthcare, such as the Centers for Disease Control and Prevention. Choice *C* is an outdated source of information; healthcare staff should ensure that education is obtained from sources that are no more than five years old.

23. A. Zero to six months is the appropriate age for using heel sticks.

24. A. The identification verification process ensures that the correct patient is receiving the correct tests. Choices *B* and *C* are incorrect; these options are not the purpose of properly identifying a patient. Choice *D* is also incorrect; the purpose of verifying the identity of the patient is to ensure that no patient harm occurs due to a patient not receiving the correct tests or receiving someone else's tests.

25. A: The tubes are inverted to ensure that the blood is completely mixed with the additive in the tubes.

26. D: The preceptor may need to provide additional teaching after the new phlebotomist states, "I can take my gloves off after the film has dried." This is because blood smears are considered a potentially infectious biohazard until they are fixed or stained, and handling dried film without gloves could place the phlebotomist at risk for infection. Choice *A* would not require additional education, as the blood drop should be placed in the center of the slide near the frosted end (0.5-1 inches from the unfrosted end). Choice *B* would not require additional teaching because allowing the drop to spread the full width of the pusher slide helps to ensure the smear is not too narrow or thick. Lastly, Choice *C* would not need additional teaching because applying pressure to the pusher slide can lead to unacceptable film due to uneven distribution, streaking, or lines.

27. A: A self-adhesive wrap will prevent damage to the skin, including skin tears and blisters. Choices *B*, *C*, and *D* are not appropriate for this patient.

28. A: The site should be cleansed with antiseptic again to ensure sterility and reduce the risk for infection prior to venipuncture. Choice *B* is not correct; any field or surface that has been made sterile is no longer sterile once the phlebotomist has turned away from it. Choice *C* is not correct; a tourniquet should not be applied for more than a minute prior to venipuncture, for comfort and to limit numbness and poor circulation. Choice *D* is not correct; the area must be sanitized again before accessing the vein.

29. D: The green tube for blood gas collection should be collected first so that the infant's crying does not affect the test results. Choices *A*, *B*, and *C* are incorrect; these tubes are not first in the order of draw.

30. B. A student Identification card is not an acceptable way of verifying a patient's identity. Choices *A*, *C*, and *D* are included as one way to identify a patient.

31. D: The phlebotomist should ask available staff members to help hold the patient while they perform the venipuncture. Choices *A* and *B* are incorrect; these actions could be considered battery. Phlebotomists must not apply restraints, nor should they hold anyone down forcefully. Choice *C* is also

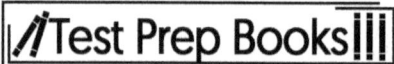

Answer Explanations

incorrect; the labs should not be delayed due to the phlebotomist's decision. This could be a safety issue for the patient.

32. C: The standard size of a phlebotomy needle is 21 gauge, although 23 gauge is also permissible for smaller veins.

33. A: QC tests are completed to verify that an expected range of values is consistently resulting when tests are run. Choice B is not correct; an accession number is used to track a sample through the electronic system and does not have any effect on quality control of test results. Choice C is not correct; infection control will reduce the spread of microbes, not quality control. Proper cleaning, following biohazard precautions, and effective hand hygiene offer the best protection against the spread of nosocomial infections. Choice D is not correct; the laboratory technician must be sure to follow local policy and the manufacturer's instructions to ensure correct collection of a laboratory test.

34. B. The names of the labs ordered are a critical piece of the information on the requisition form. Without this information, the phlebotomist will not know what test to collect. Choices A and C are not required on the requisition form. Choice D is also incorrect; while it is convenient for billing purposes, not all patients have insurance.

35. D. Midstream urine collection requires the patient to clean the urethral opening and surrounding area before collecting urine. Choices A, B, and C do not require the patient to clean before collecting a sample.

36. C: Plasma or serum must be separated via the centrifuge within two hours. Choice A is incorrect; the sample must first sit for thirty minutes to an hour prior to being placed on the centrifuge. Choices B and D allow the sample to sit for too long, which will compromise it.

37. A: While standard precautions are advised for hepatitis B, the phlebotomist should use critical thinking to determine the risk based on the task to be performed. Gloves, a gown, and a mask are appropriate for a task that involves the collection of bodily fluids and potential for spray. Choice B is not appropriate; collecting a sputum sample is a droplet risk, so a regular mask is appropriate unless the patient has an airborne respiratory disease. Choice C is not correct; this would not offer the phlebotomist any protection. Choice D is not correct, as this does not protect from the droplets that will be expected when collecting sputum due to coughing and spitting samples into a specimen cup.

38. B: A sample with a source that cannot be verified must be discarded, and the missing specimen must be identified and redrawn with the correct identifying information. Choice A is appropriate for certain samples and would be valid for processing. A sample that is collected at home may be dropped off to the lab by an agent of the patient (in this case, a family member), so Choice C is incorrect. Choice D indicates that the collection of the sample has not deviated from the standard, so this answer is incorrect.

39. B: Most tubes need to be inverted 8–10 times. The exceptions are blue, which only needs to be inverted 3–4 times, and red or SST tubes, which should be inverted 5 times. Inverting the tubes gently 8–10 times ensures that all tubes are inverted adequately.

40. C: The phlebotomist should recognize that a hematoma is blood pooling under the skin, as hemostasis has not been acquired. This requires immediate pressure over the puncture site to staunch

Answer Explanations

the bleeding. Choice *A* is not correct; a bandage will not stop the internal bleeding that is occurring. Choice *B* is not correct; applying immediate pressure will assist with preventing further bleeding beneath the skin that may not be evident from the puncture site. Choice *D* is incorrect; the phlebotomist should alert the nurse, not the provider, and continue to hold pressure. The nurse may elect to notify the provider after assessing the site.

41. D: The phlebotomist should never label a specimen that they did not draw.

42. D. The morning is the best time for a patient to produce a sputum sample. This time of day can result in a bigger sample size. Choices *A, B,* and *C* are incorrect; these options are not the best time to obtain a sputum sample.

43. C. A trough is drawn to determine the smallest amount of a medication in the blood. This is thirty minutes to an hour before the next administration of a medication. Choice *A* is incorrect; this is the time that a peak level would be drawn. Choices *B* and *D* are incorrect; these are different types of draws.

44. A: Choices *B* and *C* are incorrect, as the middle of the pad should be avoided. Choice *D* is also incorrect, as the index finger should not be used.

45. A: A pipette is used to transfer fluids between containers, not centrifuges. Choices *B, C,* and *D* are all appropriate secondary containment options to prevent leaks and spills within the centrifuge.

46. C: The phlebotomist should avoid wounds or rashes to prevent harm from coming to the patient. A patient with these issues is at risk because a needle could penetrate the area and introduce the infected or irritated tissues into the vein. Choices *A, B,* and *D* are all normal and do not need to be avoided.

47. D: The tourniquet should be replaced if it shows any signs of wear, including cracking along the edge. Choices *A, B,* and *C* do not indicate a need to replace the tourniquet.

48. A. The best question to ask the patient is if they followed the testing instructions. This will enable the labs to be drawn appropriately. Choice *B* is incorrect; venipuncture is not related to having a full bladder. Choice *C* is also incorrect; drinking extra fluids is not a typical requirement for venipuncture. Choice *D* is incorrect; sputum is unrelated to venipuncture.

49. D. The address of the lab facility is not required on the requisition form. Often, patients can choose their lab based on their preferences or on their insurance requirements. Choices *A, B,* and *C* are incorrect. The ordering physician, billing, and insurance information are required items on a requisition form.

50. C: The CDC recommends an ethanol alcohol content of at least 60 percent in hand sanitizer to ensure that microbial load is reduced. Choices *A, B,* and *D* do not ensure that the alcohol content is high enough to consistently and adequately kill microbes enough to prevent infection spread.

51. C: At a minimum, gloves and a gown are required upon entering a patient's room, if the patient is on contact precautions. Choice *A* is incorrect; appropriate PPE must always be donned prior to entering a patient's room if these precautions are ordered. Choices *B* and *D* are not correct; these options do not prevent potential spread from touch. Using only a mask would be appropriate for droplet precautions.

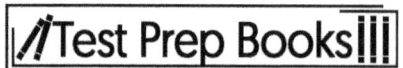

Answer Explanations

52. B: Blood glucose monitoring is a point-of-care test that is easily obtained, reliable, and accurate. Choices A, C, and D are all blood tests that require careful processing in order to ensure the accuracy of results.

53. C: Light blue tubes used for coagulation studies must always be filled completely. The blood/additive ratio must be exact.

54. C: Testing for inborn errors of metabolism occurs along with newborn screening, which typically happens 1-2 days after birth. Choice B is incorrect because 7-14 days after birth is the typical time when performing a second newborn screening test.

55. A: To check that the newly opened box of CLIA-waived tests has not been compromised during storage, it should have a QC test run, and the results should be compared against expected results, Choice A. Choice B is not correct; a QC check for quality is more important to verify prior to distributing. Choice C is not required; this would waste resources by running an additional test that is not required, and following the manufacturer's guidelines to complete a QC test is sufficient. Choice D is not correct, as the test should be completed to check for the quality and efficacy of the tests prior to marking so that they may be returned to the manufacturer for reimbursement if the QC test is off.

56. B: When serum is unable to be delivered within 24 hours, it must be stored below −20 °C. Choices A, C, and D would not preserve the sample for accurate results.

57. C: The phlebotomist should first assess the patient for breathing. This will determine the phlebotomist's next actions. Choice A is incorrect; the phlebotomist does not know if CPR is needed if breathing is not assessed. Choice B is incorrect, as a cold compress should not be applied before breathing is assessed. Choice D is also incorrect; the patient will only need to be lowered to the floor if they are not breathing and CPR is required. This decision cannot be made until the phlebotomist knows whether the patient is breathing.

58. D: The needle used by the phlebotomist should be hollow and beveled.

59. C. The antecubital fossa is the first place that a phlebotomist should inspect to find an appropriate venipuncture site. Choices A, B, and D are not the phlebotomist's first choice of location.

60. C: The general rule for maximum volume drawn in a single session is 3% of the patient's total estimated blood volume. Choice A is incorrect, as 100 mL/kg of body weight represents the calculation for pediatric total blood volume. Choice B is also incorrect, as 50 mL of blood will not be the appropriate amount for all patients. Choice D is incorrect because this represents an easy calculation to generate a conservative maximum volume in pediatric patients.

61. B: Lifting the pusher slide early results in a missing feather. Choice A is incorrect because a small drop would result in a short smear. Choice C is incorrect because contaminants on the slide would result in spots or streaks within the smear. Choice D is incorrect because not pausing to allow blood to spread across the pusher slide would result in a narrow smear.

62. D. Explaining the procedure to the patient can help reduce the patient's anxiety. Choice A is incorrect; a difficult stick cannot be helped through an explanation of the procedure. Choices B and C are also incorrect; these items are not complications.

Answer Explanations

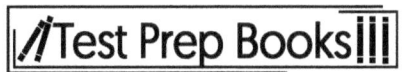

63. D: When transporting biohazardous material, standard precautions, Choice *D*, must be used to prevent infectious disease spread and prevent samples from being cross-contaminated. Choice *A* is not correct, as viral samples must be kept on ice during transport. Bacterial samples should be kept at room temperature, not on ice, Choice *B*. Each sample should be placed in its own biohazard bag to prevent transfer of organism between samples in case of leak or spillage.

64. A: While performing the venipuncture, the phlebotomist should ensure each tube fills all the way; if not, they should use another tube. Choice *B* is incorrect; the rubber cap should never be removed, as this will cause complete loss of vacuum. Choice *C* is incorrect; the tube should not be punctured before the venipuncture, as this will release the vacuum and could cause contamination. Choice *D* is incorrect; each tube should be checked as it is drawn so that a tube can be replaced as needed and the patient does not have to have a second venipuncture.

65. A. A physician's name is required on the requisition form. This verifies that the test was ordered by an eligible provider. Choices *B*, *C*, and *D* are not required on the requisition form.

66. D: An average adult has approximately 70 mL per kg of body weight. Choice *A* is incorrect, as this is the average volume per kg of a *premature infant's* weight. Choices *B* and *C* are also incorrect because 80 and 100 mL/kg blood volumes are associated with *newborns* (80-100 mL/kg), *infants* (75-100 mL/kg), and *children* (75-100 mL/kg).

67. D: A phlebotomist is not trained to obtain a tissue sample; this is completed by a specialized physician, such as a pathologist or radiologist, or a specialized technician. Tissue harvesting is outside the scope of practice of a phlebotomist. Choices *A*, *B*, and *C* are all within the scope of practice of a phlebotomist.

68. D. Routine lab draws are typically drawn for a primary care provider to monitor their patients. Choices *A* and *B* are incorrect; antibiotics draws are usually drawn as trough, peak, and random. Choice *C* is also incorrect.

69. D. The phlebotomist should not choose a vein based on the ability to feel the vein with a tourniquet. Choices *A*, *B*, and *C* are all options that should be considered when choosing an appropriate vein. A good-sized vein that is straight and visible without a tourniquet has the characteristics that a phlebotomist should look for.

70. D: The needle should be removed at the same angle at which it entered the skin and should be at the appropriate angle for the area where the venipuncture is performed.

71. D: Expired blood collection tubes should never be used or sent for processing, as the additive could be compromised, the loss of sterility could lead to fungal or bacterial growth, or the tube may underfill due to loss of vacuum seal, which will lead to suboptimal or incorrect results. Any treatment that is based on the results could be harmful. Choice *A* is not correct; expired tubes are not run in labs. If discovered, an expired tube would lead to a delay in patient care, as the sample will need to be re-collected. It is also unethical to knowingly try to hide the date. Choice *B* is not correct; documenting the use of an expired tube provides evidence of deviation from standards of care, and any sample that is run would still be at risk for erroneous results. Choice *C* is incorrect; this may cause confusion in the processing, leading to the possibility that the results from the expired tube may be the ones used to guide treatment.

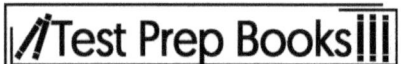

Answer Explanations

72. B: Aseptic technique is targeted at keeping patients safe, stopping microbial contamination, and preventing the spread of hospital-acquired infections. Choice A is not correct; aseptic technique will not prevent community spread. This is more effectively completed with hand hygiene and respiratory etiquette. Choice C is not correct; sterile supplies are a large part of an effective aseptic technique strategy to prevent infection. Choice D is not correct, as hand hygiene is only one facet of aseptic technique. It also consists of using sterile supplies and equipment, following strict infection prevention guidelines, and placing barriers to reduce the chance of pathogen transmission.

73. B: Results will not be uniform or accurate with deviations to the aliquoting techniques and may lead to erroneous values. Choice A is incorrect because the supply use should not change; technique refers to how the pipettes are filled and the contents transferred. Choice C is not correct, as aliquoting is used with plasma when gel is not available and would not be used in this process. Choice D is not correct because standard precautions are used to prevent infectious disease spread, not aliquoting technique.

74. A: OSHA enforces the rules mandating that healthcare facilities provide an adequate amount and type of PPE that is required to keep employees safe. Choice B will provide regulation, and Choice C will provide guidance on the type of PPE needed and when to wear it depending on the specific patient care or disease; however, neither agency has authority over enforcing employer obligations to employees. Choice D is not correct; this organization provides information to the public on complaints filed against companies for poor business practices.

75. B: The correct length range for phlebotomy needles is 1–1.5 inches.

76. C: Stringent hand hygiene before and after patient contact, after contacting items that may have the potential for nosocomial infection spread, and before and after eating is the number one way to prevent the spread of pathogens. Choices A and D are not correct; the proper technique is to cough or sneeze into the elbow or a tissue. The tissue should be immediately disposed of, followed by hand washing. Choice B is not the correct placement of a mask; the nose should also be fully covered to prevent droplet spread.

77. C. Testing at the same time every day is not part of basal state testing. Choices A, B, and D are all part of basal state testing. Basal state testing includes no exercise for twenty-four hours and no eating and drinking for twelve hours, and should be drawn first thing in the morning.

78. A. A back to the chair is required to meet national guidelines that are in place to keep patients safe. Choices B, C, and D are not required for venipuncture.

79. A. The median cubital vein is located between two muscles, is easier to access than the basilic vein, and has less risk for harm than the basilic vein. Choices B, C, and D are incorrect; these are not situated between two muscles with less risk of harm.

80. B: A series of three vaccinations administered over a set schedule provides protection to healthcare providers and staff from contracting hepatitis B due to exposure. Choice A is not correct; the flu vaccination is recommended but not required. Choice D is not correct; this vaccination is recommended for individuals who have been exposed to monkeypox or are at a higher risk, but the risk for healthcare providers is relatively low when standard precautions are followed. Choice C is not correct; there are no FDA-approved vaccinations available that prevent or treat HIV.

81. D: Guthrie cards should be allowed to dry in a horizontal position and away from heat and sunlight. Choice A is incorrect because hanging cards can result in bleeding of sample onto the lower part of the

Answer Explanations

card. Choice B is incorrect because cards should not touch other cards or be stacked due to risk of cross-contamination. Choice C is incorrect because the card must dry completely before being packaged in its envelope for transport.

82. A: The red (and gold) serum tubes should be drawn last, as the blood clots within these tubes, and capillary draws tend to clot quickly. All other tubes should be drawn first following the order of draw.

83. C: A stool specimen is valid for four hours at room temperature. Choices B and D are beyond the four-hour time limit, and samples should be refrigerated after that time for up to twenty-four hours. A stool sample beyond twenty-four hours, Choice A, is no longer able to be tested and must be re-collected.

84. D: The phlebotomist may perform point-of-care testing. Choices A, B, and C are all registered nurse duties and are outside the phlebotomist's scope of practice.

85. C: A headache is an atypical response to venipuncture. Choices A, B, and D are all potential adverse effects following venipuncture.

86. D: Facility policy and available supplies often dictate what phlebotomists can use. Choices A, B, and C are incorrect; a phlebotomist should use available supplies tailored to the patient's veins and their size and fragility. Using what they are most comfortable with, what they typically use, or what the patient requests may not be what is best for the patient.

87. C: Protected health information is exposed when left in a public area. Choice A is not correct; verifying the correct patient ensures that the right patient will have the results documented in the chart. Choice B is not correct; providing privacy allows the patient to be confident that their health concerns are not being heard or relayed beyond the appropriate healthcare team. Choice D is not correct; this upholds the phlebotomist's scope of practice, and there is no conflict with HIPAA.

88. D: The appropriate warning for a patient is, "Okay, here we go, 3, 2, 1..." Choices A, B, and C are all inappropriate patient interactions.

89. C. Sitting is the best position for the patient. This position will not influence test results and is usually comfortable for the patient. Choices A, B, and D are not recommended positions for venipuncture.

90. D. The best position for a patient with a history of fainting or becoming lightheaded during venipuncture is supine. This is the safest position to avoid a patient fall and potential injury. Choices A, B, and C are all incorrect, as these are not appropriate positions for a fainting patient.

91. C: The CDC recommends that hands are scrubbed for at least twenty seconds to effectively remove microbial load.

92. A: An 8-hour urine specimen (also called first-morning specimen) is collected using the first void of the day. Choice B is incorrect because although the test requires 8 hours since the last void, fasting is not explicitly required. Choice C is incorrect because only one void is collected after 8 hours. Choice D is also incorrect because the timing of the 8-hour specimen would depend on when the patient wakes and voids for the first time.

93. B: Proper technique for performing newborn screening is to carefully bring the Guthrie card to the drop of free-flowing blood and allow it to absorb into the filter paper. Choice A is incorrect because a

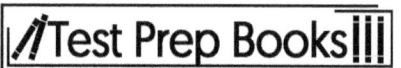

Answer Explanations

capillary tube is not used to perform this test. Choice C is incorrect because touching the skin should be avoided to prevent contamination and inaccurate test results. Choice D is incorrect because the blood should not be dripped onto the card.

94. A: All blood gas samples must be immediately placed on ice to prevent blood cells from consuming oxygen. Choice B is not correct because this may alter results. Choice C is not correct because when additives are used, the tube should be gently inverted several times, not shaken vigorously. Choice D is not necessary; the samples may be delivered within twenty minutes of draw for the most accurate results.

95. D. Implied consent is the required level of consent for a phlebotomist before a venipuncture. Choices A, B, and C are incorrect; these types of consent are not required for phlebotomy procedures.

96. B: The correct order of draw is light blue, green, and then gray.

97. A: If a specimen is not cushioned or packaged securely, the container may get damaged or leak, ruining the sample.

98. C: It is necessary for the phlebotomist to label the specimens in the room while the patient is still in the room. Choice A is incorrect, as the label should never cover all or part of the rubber stopper. Choice B is incorrect, as the tubes should not be labeled before the specimens are drawn. Choice D is also incorrect; the label should lie on the tube so that the barcode can be read, and it should be flat.

99. D: Placing the sample on ice slows metabolism to preserve the analyte. Choice A is incorrect; cooling blood slows down metabolism rather than speeding it up. Choice B is not correct because it is aimed at decreasing naturally occurring chemical reactions. Centrifugation, not temperature, separates plasma from whole blood, making Choice C incorrect.

100. A: The blood collection device with a tube approximately 5 inches long is a butterfly needle.

101. C: Before a sample may be aliquoted, the initial tube must first be centrifuged. Choice A is the second step of the process. Choice B is incorrect; the tip of the pipette should be placed in the upper portion of the sample. Choice D is completed when preparing to remove the top portion of the sample from the tube, which will occur after centrifugation.

102. A: The PEPline is a hotline managed by the CDC that offers guidance on treatment protocols for bloodborne pathogen exposures. Choice B is not correct; this resource is used for finding information about chemicals and solutions used within healthcare facilities. Choice C is not correct; this may cause a delay in receiving guidance depending on the availability of the provider to respond. Choice D is incorrect; this option would be better suited for chemical or radiation exposure.

103. D: Tubes should be kept upright with the lids securely tightened. Choice A is not ideal for multiple tubes, as they may bump against each other and break. Choice B is not correct, as inverting the tube may lead to leaking. Tubes should be maintained upright. Choice C is not practical because wrapping each tube would take a significant amount of time.

104. A: Results of QC must be documented immediately in a logbook to avoid gaps in the verification of quality checks. Choice B is not correct; QC results are used to verify the accuracy of equipment performance and are not specifically relevant to any patient's chart. Choice C is not correct; the QC process and cleaning procedures are two separate parts of laboratory operational standards and should be documented and performed separately. Choice *D* is incorrect; unless there is a deviation or trend of erroneous readings with a QC test, the results should be documented without the need for supervisory notification.

105. C. The requisition form informs the phlebotomist about the patient and the labs that are requested. The requisition form also informs the phlebotomist about the ordering provider and billing information. Choices *A*, *B*, and *D* are incorrect; these options are not part of a requisition.

106. C: Prior to each shift, the phlebotomy technician should thoroughly check their hands for any cuts, abrasions, or wounds and cover with a waterproof adhesive dressing. This dressing should be replaced as needed throughout the day. Choice *A* is incorrect; even with a scab, the skin is not intact and is vulnerable to scraping, tearing, or oozing. Choice *B* is not correct; the area does need to be covered, but, with glove use, the staff is safe to perform patient care duties with a small cut. Choice *D* is incorrect, as the glove may degrade or receive tears in it. Gloves should always be removed between patients, with appropriate hand hygiene between.

107. D: The phlebotomist should throw out the tube with a torn label. The label must be intact to know the expiration date and other details. Choices *A* and *B* are incorrect, as these are normal findings when inspecting supplies. Choice *C* is incorrect; there may be fluid in the tube, as some of them have additives that are liquid.

108. B: Light yellow tubes are used for bacterial studies or bacterial cultures.

109. C: The plantar surface of the foot to the side of the heel is the correct dermal puncture site location for an infant under 1 year old. Choice *A* is incorrect; the heel should never be punctured. Choice *B* is incorrect; the top of the foot should not be used. Choice *D* is incorrect; this site should not be used on infants less than 1 year old.

110. C: An accession number is used to link an order to the lab sample for tracking and cataloging purposes, Choice *C*. Choice *A* is incorrect because while it is a unique number, the patient's name and date of birth are safest to use for identification. Choice *B* is incorrect because once the healthcare provider orders the test and it is collected, the accession number is originated by laboratory staff. Choice *D* is incorrect because the accession process is not limited to the samples that are subject to the chain of command process.

111. C: Performing proper hand hygiene has been proven to be the most effective way of preventing the spread of transient bacteria and nosocomial infections. Choice *A* is not correct; wearing gloves without performing hand hygiene can still transfer bacteria. Standard precautions are to be followed. Choice *B* may help prevent the spread of some organisms on hard surfaces; but certain organisms, such as *C. difficile*, are not eradicated with alcohol-based sanitizer, and bleach must be used instead. A mask, Choice *D*, will prevent the spread of organisms spread via droplet, but will not decrease transmission via skin contact.

112. C. Semen samples should be kept at body temperature while being transported to the laboratory.

113. D: A centrifuge is most commonly used to separate the plasma or serum from whole blood. Choice *A* is the definition of aliquoting. Choice *B* is completed via dipsticks. Choice *C* is completed by growing the sample on a culture medium.

114. B: The butterfly needle system is best suited for small veins and veins that are difficult to access.

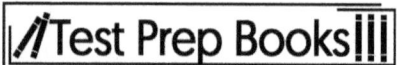

115. C: Air from butterfly set tubing will be pushed into the bottle as blood begins to flow. Choice A is incorrect because the aerobic bottle is only prioritized if insufficient volume has already been collected. Choice B is incorrect because direct inoculation uses butterfly set rather than syringe for specimen transfer. Choice D is incorrect because cross-contamination is not a primary concern when deciding which culture bottle to fill first.

116. A: While a DNR bracelet does indicate Do Not Resuscitate, this does not equate to "do not treat." The phlebotomist should call for help but should refrain from immediately initiating CPR. Choice B is not correct; a patient that has elected DNR may still be eligible or have preferences for other methods of emergency response beyond CPR, and the nurse should be notified immediately. Choices C and D delay care. The phlebotomist should stay with the patient and use the emergency call light or call out for help for nursing or a provider to assess the patient.

117. A: A unit of blood is, on average, equal to approximately 450 mL.

118. A. STAT orders are urgent; they should be completed first or as soon as possible. Choices B, C, and D are incorrect. These options do not prioritize the STAT lab as being done as quickly as it should be done.

119. A: In order to properly sanitize the skin and eradicate any current microbes, drying time must be followed. Choice B is not correct; sterile technique, not clean, is required. Choice C is incorrect; hands should be covered with clean or sterile gloves, and the site should not be touched once the site is cleansed. Choice D is incorrect; a clean cotton ball or gauze should be placed over the site and held, not a bare finger.

120. B: It is always the patient's right to refuse care; however, this does need to be noted in the chart. The provider that ordered the labs should be notified immediately for awareness and to address how this would change the patient's care plan. Choice A is not correct; this negates the patient's wishes and may delay needed care if the lab was ordered STAT. The ordering provider may be waiting for a result prior to the next phlebotomy attempt. Choices C and D are not correct; this is considered coercion and does not allow the patient to be autonomous with dignity in their care. Whether or not the patient is competent enough to guide their own care is not within the phlebotomy technician's scope of practice to determine.

Practice Test

1. Which of the following is a light-sensitive test?
   a. Hgb
   b. Arterial blood gases
   c. Chemistry panel
   d. Bilirubin

2. Which of the following choices indicates that the patient may be experiencing a complication during the venipuncture procedure?
   a. The patient is joking and laughing.
   b. The patient remains quiet.
   c. The patient says "Ouch!" during the stick.
   d. The patient begins to stare off and stops talking.

3. The phlebotomist has found a vein using palpation. What is the next step that the phlebotomist should take?
   a. Begin cleansing the area in preparation for the venipuncture.
   b. Slap the area to cause the vein to become enlarged and swell.
   c. Begin to gather the supplies needed for venipuncture.
   d. Palpate up and down the vein to find its direction.

4. Which of the following is NOT considered PPE?
   a. Gloves
   b. Mask
   c. Goggles
   d. Biohazard bag

5. A phlebotomist must create a label for an extra tube. What should the phlebotomist use to write the information?
   a. Pencil
   b. Pen
   c. Permanent marker
   d. Computer/typing

6. When should the phlebotomist inspect the needle safety device?
   a. On the way to the sharps container
   b. While filling the evacuated tubes
   c. After retracting the needle
   d. Before beginning the procedure

7. Using a blood pressure cuff instead of a tourniquet can help a venipuncture on what type of vein because of the lower pressure?
   a. Fragile vein
   b. Sclerosed vein
   c. Superficial vein
   d. Rolling vein

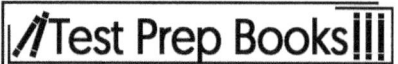

8. What information would NOT be found within a Material Safety Data Sheet?
    a. Spill and leak protocols
    b. Health and hazard information
    c. Special protection requirements
    d. Bloodborne disease facts

9. It is anticipated that splashing or splattering may occur while obtaining a specimen. At minimum, what type of PPE should be utilized?
    a. Gown and gloves
    b. Gown, gloves, mask, and eye protection
    c. Gloves and mask
    d. Gloves and eye protection

10. Which antiseptic should be used for routine venipuncture?
    a. Chlorhexidine gluconate
    b. 70% isopropyl alcohol
    c. Povidone-iodine
    d. 90% isopropyl alcohol

11. What must be followed when drawing test samples that are a part of a legal matter?
    a. Chain of command
    b. Chain of custody
    c. Subpoena
    d. Notary public signature

12. An outpatient laboratory manager is promoting continuous readiness to respond to a medical emergency. Which of the following actions would increase staff's ability to expedite emergency assistance to a patient or staff member collapsing?
    a. Review locations of fire extinguishers and AEDs.
    b. Hold in-service on use of emergency eye stations.
    c. Have staff demonstrate the emergency shut-down procedure.
    d. Create a chart of emergency numbers to post by the telephone.

13. Which of the following does the phlebotomist perform during the blood donation to prevent insufficient volume?
    a. Apply a tourniquet above the venipuncture site.
    b. Advise the donor to squeeze their fist.
    c. Assist the donor to a lying position.
    d. Encourage the donor to drink fluids.

14. When a patient does not provide a semen sample at the facility, how quickly must they deliver the specimen to the lab?
    a. Thirty minutes
    b. One hour
    c. Fifteen minutes
    d. Two hours

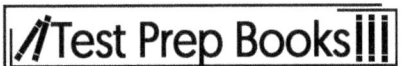

15. A patient is sent home with a stool sample kit. Which of the following statements by the patient indicates understanding of how to store the sample?
    a. "If it will be less than twenty-four hours before I can bring it back, I can leave it out at room temperature."
    b. "The sample should be refrigerated immediately."
    c. "I should not try to collect a sample unless I can deliver it within an hour."
    d. "If it will be over four hours before I can bring the sample back, it should be refrigerated."

16. Which of the following is the most common laboratory accident?
    a. Fire
    b. Spills
    c. Electrical shock
    d. Falls

17. Which governmental agency provides regulation through the Clinical Laboratory Improvement Amendments?
    a. Centers for Disease Control and Prevention
    b. Centers for Medicare and Medicaid Services
    c. Occupational Safety and Health Administration
    d. National Institutes of Health

18. How should a gown be donned?
    a. Tied in the front
    b. After mask and gloves have been donned
    c. Secured at back of neck and around waist
    d. With gloves under the sleeves

19. When should the tourniquet be removed during the venipuncture?
    a. After blood has entered the last evacuated tube
    b. After the needle has been removed
    c. Before the last tube has been attached to the evacuated tube system
    d. After the draw is complete but before the needle has been removed

20. After venipuncture, the patient bleeds through the provided cotton ball. The phlebotomist checks the site and sees that hemostasis has been achieved. What should the phlebotomist do next?
    a. Hold pressure for another 3 minutes.
    b. Apply self-adhesive wrap over the cotton ball.
    c. Add tape to the cotton ball.
    d. Apply a new cotton ball.

21. What is the first action to take when blood stops flowing during the venipuncture using the evacuated tube system (ETS)?
    a. Pull the needle out slightly.
    b. Move the needle slightly deeper.
    c. Stop the venipuncture and repeat.
    d. Move the needle side to side under the skin.

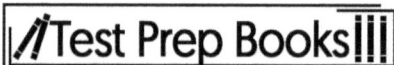

22. What is the most important factor in successful pathogen detection with blood cultures?
    a. Timely collection
    b. Taking 2-4 sets of cultures
    c. Order of draw
    d. Appropriate volumes

23. When should a sharps container be exchanged?
    a. When the expiration date is met
    b. Once the bin is full and will not hold more
    c. When the container is three-fourths full
    d. On a monthly basis

24. A phlebotomist is performing a venipuncture in the median cubital vein. What symptom would the phlebotomist expect if a nerve was inadvertently hit during the venipuncture?
    a. Swelling
    b. Bruising
    c. Numbness
    d. Sweating

25. A patient arrives to the lab in a wheelchair. How should the patient be positioned for venipuncture?
    a. Have the patient transfer to the phlebotomy chair.
    b. Draw the patient's blood while the patient is in their wheelchair.
    c. Have the patient transfer to a flat surface and lay supine.
    d. Have the patient put their arm on pillows after transferring to a chair.

26. Why should the needle enter the antecubital area with an angle between 15° and 30°?
    a. The angle of the vein
    b. The thickness of the vein
    c. The depth of the vein
    d. The proximity of the vein to the elbow

27. What information may a phlebotomist retrieve from external databases?
    a. Patient health record
    b. Clinical trial and research result information
    c. Medical care facility policies
    d. Human resource documents

28. A phlebotomist is about to enter a room to draw a STAT order, but the room has an isolation sign on a closed door. What should the phlebotomist do?
    a. Leave and come back later to check if the door is open.
    b. Enter the room and ask the patient what type of PPE is needed.
    c. Check with the nurse to learn the type of isolation requirements.
    d. Enter the room with gloves on and obtain the sample quickly, since it is ordered STAT.

29. What is the purpose of initial specimen diversion when collecting blood cultures?
    a. To regulate specimen temperature
    b. To reduce specimen dilution
    c. To remove air bubbles
    d. To prevent contamination

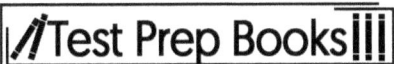

30. A patient has contracted MRSA due to exposure during their hospitalization. What is the term used for infections that are contracted from a healthcare facility?
   a. Colonization
   b. Community-acquired
   c. Nosocomial
   d. Idiopathic

31. Analytical communicators appreciate what type of communication?
   a. Broad information
   b. Information in sequence
   c. Facts and direct information
   d. Personal connection

32. A phlebotomist has finished performing a venipuncture and collected all the required tubes; however, they need one more label for a specimen. The phlebotomist is unable to print the extra label. What action does the phlebotomist take?
   a. Create a label out of tape with the patient's name and date of birth and put the tape on the tube.
   b. Write the patient's name and date of birth directly on the tube with a permanent marker.
   c. Create a label on paper with the patient's name, date of birth, and medical identification number, the date and time of the draw, and the initials of the phlebotomist.
   d. Let the patient leave, and use the computer to print a new label afterward.

33. How much blood loss, through either phlebotomy or trauma, can an older adult experience before it causes a decrease in hemoglobin and hematocrit?
   a. 50 mL
   b. 75 mL
   c. 100 mL
   d. 150 mL

34. What application method should be used when applying a tourniquet?
   a. Stopper knot
   b. Slipknot
   c. Square knot
   d. Half hitch

35. A patient arrives at the lab with a stool sample. What indicates to the phlebotomist that a new sample will have to be obtained?
   a. The sample is mixed with urine.
   b. The sample is quarter sized.
   c. The sample was delivered within three hours.
   d. The patient put their name on the sample container.

36. An anticoagulant prevents formation of:
   a. Calcium
   b. Platelets
   c. Potassium
   d. Fibrin

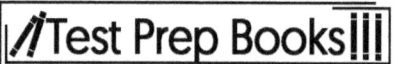

Practice Test

37. What is the limit for blood drawing for an infant within a 24-hour period?
   a. 50 mL
   b. 100 mL
   c. 1–5 percent of total blood volume
   d. 10 percent of blood volume

38. A patient who is undergoing a venipuncture suddenly becomes quiet. The phlebotomist recognizes this as a possible complication. What action should the phlebotomist take?
   a. Stop the venipuncture immediately.
   b. Ask the patient if they are okay.
   c. Apply a cold compress to the patient's neck.
   d. Call for assistance.

39. What should be verified in a patient that has no carotid pulse prior to initiating cardiopulmonary resuscitation?
   a. Absence of a DNR bracelet
   b. Femoral pulse
   c. Breathing
   d. Allergies

40. Point-of-care testing is used to monitor chronic disease. What disease is commonly monitored with an HgbA1C test?
   a. Heart failure
   b. Diabetes
   c. Cirrhosis
   d. Lupus

41. What allergy should the phlebotomist take notice of?
   a. Rubber
   b. Metal
   c. Plastics
   d. Latex

42. When assisting another healthcare provider, the phlebotomist can perform all the following duties EXCEPT what?
   a. Fill tubes using a transfer device on the access site.
   b. Provide feedback regarding proper order of draw.
   c. Transfer a blood specimen from syringe to tubes.
   d. Transport labeled specimens to the lab.

43. How should the needle be removed from the skin?
   a. Bevel down, smaller angle than entry
   b. Bevel up, smaller angle than entry
   c. Bevel down, same angle as entry
   d. Bevel up, same angle as entry

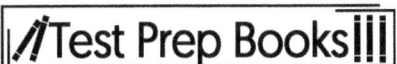

44. When performing capillary collection on an infant, in what order should a pink tube, gold tube, green tube (not blood gases), and red tube be drawn according to the order of draw?
    a. Pink, green, gold or red
    b. Pink, gold, green, red
    c. Green, gold or red, pink
    d. Gold, pink, green or red

45. What question should the phlebotomist ask the patient before a patient produces a sputum sample?
    a. "Did you perform hand hygiene before producing the sample?"
    b. "Did you perform hand hygiene after producing the sample?"
    c. "When was the last time you ate or drank?"
    d. "Have you cleaned your dentures and rinsed your mouth?"

46. A phlebotomist is talking with a patient and recognizes that the patient is a personal communicator. While the patient is listening to instructions, which of the following is the phlebotomist most likely to observe?
    a. The patient and the phlebotomist have built rapport.
    b. The patient asks a lot of questions.
    c. The patient is a direct communicator.
    d. The patient likes a broad approach.

47. The fecal immunochemical test (FIT) is a test that assists with identifying what?
    a. Parasites
    b. Blood
    c. Fat
    d. Cancer

48. The phlebotomist is preparing to send blood samples from a nursing unit to the laboratory. What should they be transported inside?
    a. A sealed plastic bag
    b. Bubble wrap
    c. A paper envelope
    d. Loose within the pneumatic tube

49. A patient arrives to the lab with a urine sample in a jar. They have a urinalysis ordered. What should the phlebotomist do to complete the test?
    a. Transfer the specimen to a lab-provided specimen cup.
    b. Label the specimen in its current container.
    c. Have the patient provide a fresh urine sample.
    d. Ask the patient if they cleaned thoroughly before urinating.

50. A phlebotomist technician has drawn blood and goes to dispose of the butterfly needle. The sharps container indicator shows that the bin is full. Which of the following actions is safest?
    a. Shake the container to make more room.
    b. Force this one sharp in.
    c. Dispose of the sharp in regular garbage.
    d. Dispose of the sharp in the nearest available bin and replace the full container.

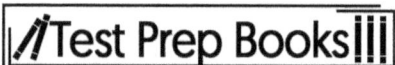

51. For a fasting lab, how long should a patient abstain from eating and drinking (except for water)?
    a. Six hours
    b. Eight to twelve hours
    c. Twenty-four hours
    d. Ten to twelve hours

52. The phlebotomist has reported a critical value to the ordering provider. What should the next step be?
    a. Tell the supervisor that they are ready for a break.
    b. Share the results with the patient.
    c. Document the date, time, and name of the provider it was reported to.
    d. Move on to the next lab value for processing.

53. If a phlebotomist uses an EDTA tube to collect a blood specimen for blood smear, how long do they have to prepare the slides?
    a. 1 hour
    b. 2 hours
    c. 3 hours
    d. 4 hours

54. Which of the following is NOT a risk for iatrogenic anemia?
    a. Menstruating female patients
    b. Underweight or malnourished patients
    c. Pediatric or infant patients
    d. Cancer patients

55. What should the phlebotomist do between cleansing the skin and performing a dermal puncture?
    a. Wipe the area with clean gauze.
    b. Rub the area vigorously to draw blood to the surface.
    c. Allow the cleanser to dry.
    d. Squeeze the area to draw blood to the surface.

56. When drawing blood using a butterfly needle, blood stops flowing. What is one of the actions the phlebotomist should take to restore blood flow?
    a. Push the needle in and out repeatedly until blood flow returns.
    b. Move the needle up and down in the skin in case it is against the vein wall.
    c. Palpate the site again, feeling for the vein in relation to the needle.
    d. Stop the venipuncture immediately.

57. A spill of a reagent has occurred within the laboratory. This would be considered what type of safety hazard?
    a. Chemical
    b. Physical
    c. Sharps
    d. Biological

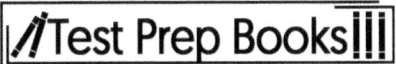

Practice Test

58. A patient with cognitive delay arrives for the venipuncture appointment. What is an appropriate action that will assist in achieving good communication?
   a. Talk slowly.
   b. Talk loudly.
   c. Use the normal verbiage of phlebotomy.
   d. Use words that the patient can understand.

59. What skin characteristic or location should be avoided when doing a dermal puncture for a capillary collection?
   a. Calluses
   b. The side of the pads of the fingers for a patient >1 year
   c. The side of the plantar heel for a patient <1 year
   d. Freckles

60. A phlebotomist has just finished a venipuncture. The patient suddenly becomes pale, cool, and clammy. After asking the patient if they are okay, the phlebotomist observes that the patient's breathing has become shallow. What is the next action the phlebotomist should perform?
   a. Call 911.
   b. Leave the patient to get assistance.
   c. Apply a cold compress to the patient's neck.
   d. Clear the area to prevent falls.

61. Which of the following describes the purpose of aliquoting?
   a. To transfer a sample to another container that contains a reactant
   b. To combine several samples into a larger container
   c. To separate a larger sample into one or more smaller portions
   d. To test a patient at the bedside

62. hen performing capillary collection on an infant, why should the venous blood gas be done first?
   a. It is a smaller tube.
   b. The additive expires faster after puncture.
   c. It prevents crying from altering the results.
   d. The green tube should be last.

63. What is NOT an intervention for a patient that is feeling faint?
   a. Loosen any clothing around the neck.
   b. Walk them to a more comfortable chair.
   c. Lower the patient's head.
   d. Instruct the patient to take deep breaths.

64. At what point in the procedure should the skin be anchored?
   a. Before cleansing the area
   b. Before applying the tourniquet
   c. After applying the tourniquet
   d. After the needle enters the skin

167

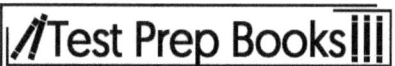

65. When would an emergency shutdown occur?
   a. Fire
   b. Needlestick
   c. Contained chemical spill
   d. Patient fainting

66. A patient arrives for a routine venipuncture. As the phlebotomist begins looking for a vein, the patient states that they have dialysis the next day. What should the phlebotomist do next?
   a. Ask the patient if they have a fistula.
   b. Ask the patient what their dialysis schedule is like.
   c. Look for a hemodialysis catheter on the patient's neck and chest.
   d. Look for a good vein to perform venipuncture.

67. Which of the following infection prevention measures protects patients and staff most effectively from spreading microbes?
   a. Handwashing
   b. Strict isolation precautions
   c. Wearing sterile gloves
   d. Antibiotic stewardship

68. Which of the following is the appropriate disposal method for solid biohazard waste?
   a. Flushed down a hopper
   b. Enclosed in a red biohazard bag
   c. In the red sharps bin
   d. In the regular trash, since it won't leak

69. In what order should PPE be removed?
   a. Gloves, goggles, gown, mask
   b. Mask, gloves, goggles, gown
   c. Gown, goggles, gloves, mask
   d. Goggles, mask, gloves, gown

70. A phlebotomist is drawing labs in the hospital. Before they leave the room, what should they do to ensure the patient is safe from harm?
   a. Ensure that no supplies are left in the bed.
   b. Dispose of unused supplies.
   c. Let the nurse know they are finished.
   d. Clean the room for the next patient.

71. A phlebotomist inserts a needle in the dorsum of the hand at 15°. What complication can occur from this action?
   a. Hemostasis
   b. Bleeding
   c. Pain
   d. Needle phobia

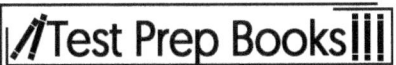

Practice Test

72. Which of the following is part of standard precautions?
    a. Wearing gloves, gown, and goggles
    b. Wearing gloves and an N-95 mask
    c. Re-capping all needles
    d. Asking the patient if they have any communicable diseases

73. Which is NOT an appropriate action to accommodate a blind patient?
    a. Assist the patient to the exam room if requested.
    b. Explain what is being done during the venipuncture.
    c. Proactively take the patient's hand to lead them to the exam room.
    d. Do not interfere with assistance devices, including guide dogs.

74. The phlebotomist is looking for information on the down-time process. What document would be most likely to have facility-specific practice outlined within it?
    a. National directive
    b. Joint Commission standards
    c. Standard operating procedure
    d. Peer-reviewed article

75. When attempting to draw blood from a patient, the phlebotomist notes that the patient starts holding their breath and bearing down in anticipation of pain. What medical event may occur from this action?
    a. Headache
    b. Fast heart rate
    c. Syncope
    d. Flushing

76. What acronym is used to describe the barriers, supplies, and clothing used to limit the risk of spreading infection?
    a. CMS
    b. OSHA
    c. PPE
    d. CLABSI

77. The phlebotomist receives a urine sample for urinalysis. How long after collection do they have to process the specimen if it remains at room temperature?
    a. 4 hours
    b. 3 hours
    c. 2 hours
    d. 1 hour

78. How long should a venipuncture be scrubbed with chlorhexidine gluconate for blood cultures?
    a. 30 seconds
    b. 45 seconds
    c. 60 seconds
    d. 90 seconds

169

79. Which of the following would be least likely to impact the results of a newborn screening?
   a. The phlebotomist forgot to wipe off the first drop of blood.
   b. The patient is currently receiving a blood transfusion.
   c. The phlebotomist's gloved finger touched one of the spots while performing the test.
   d. The blood sample was applied from the back side of the card.

80. A complication that can occur while a tourniquet is in place is small marks developing below the tourniquet. What is this complication called?
   a. Thrombosis
   b. Phlebitis
   c. Hematoma
   d. Petechiae

81. Negative pressure rooms and HEPA filters are utilized for what type of isolation precautions?
   a. Droplet
   b. Contact
   c. Nosocomial
   d. Airborne

82. Which of the following is NOT a characteristic of intuitive communicators?
   a. Broad approach
   b. May have many questions
   c. Want to know the result
   d. Detail oriented

83. What is the best position for the patient's arm to be in when drawing blood?
   a. Palm surface down with the forearm exposed
   b. Palm surface up with the wrist veins exposed
   c. Palm surface down with the top veins of the hands exposed
   d. Palm surface up with the antecubital fossa exposed

84. A provider has ordered a STAT test for a patient. They call the laboratory to ensure that the order was received and will be completed promptly. The lab staff verify that the order was received and notify the provider that the phlebotomist is on the way to the patient room to collect the sample. Which of the following best describes what type of communication this is?
   a. Professional
   b. Closed loop
   c. Active listening
   d. Passive-aggressive

85. A pediatric patient who weighs 8 kg has orders for a blood draw. If they have approximately 75 mL of blood per kilogram of body weight, what is the patient's total estimated blood volume?
   a. 600 L
   b. 0.6 L
   c. 1,320 L
   d. 1.3 L

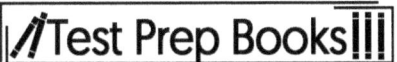

Practice Test

86. What is meant by an accrediting organization?
   a. A third-party educational and training center
   b. A third party that specifies the requirements to determine that competencies are met
   c. A third party that ensures that the facility can be a teaching hospital
   d. A third party that guarantees patients that safe care is delivered

87. Male blood donors should have a hemoglobin of greater than what?
   a. 12.5 g/dL
   b. 13 g/dL
   c. 13.5 g/dL
   d. 14 g/dL

88. A phlebotomist is talking to their patient, who is a known hard stick. What should the phlebotomist ask the patient before performing the venipuncture?
   a. "Do you have a full bladder?"
   b. "Where is the best spot to stick for your labs?"
   c. "When did you last exercise?"
   d. "Has it been 12 hours since you've last eaten or drank anything except water?"

89. Risk for development of iatrogenic anemia increases when monthly blood draws exceed what percentage of total blood volume?
   a. 3%
   b. 5%
   c. 8%
   d. 10%

90. Which needle should be used on the dorsal side of the hand?
   a. 18-gauge needle
   b. Butterfly needle
   c. 22-gauge needle
   d. Filter needle

91. The phlebotomist is finishing the venipuncture procedure on an older woman. What type of dressing should the phlebotomist use?
   a. Clear dressing
   b. Cotton ball and self-adhesive wrap
   c. Cotton ball and tape
   d. Band-aid

92. The phlebotomist is required to draw labs from a patient during a nuclear medicine test. What hazard is the most significant risk within this department?
   a. Physical
   b. Biohazard
   c. Radioactive
   d. Fire

93. A patient with a history of fainting comes to have their blood drawn. The venipuncture is performed without incident. How long should the phlebotomist observe the patient before they leave?
   a. Fifteen minutes
   b. Five minutes
   c. Thirty minutes
   d. One hour

94. Point-of-care testing for a coagulation test is completed on a patient. The result of the test is 400 seconds. What does this indicate?
   a. The value is within the clinically therapeutic range.
   b. This value is within normal limits.
   c. The patient is hypercoagulable.
   d. The test is out of range and must be re-run.

95. A patient arrives for a lab draw. What does the phlebotomist find that indicates they must use the opposite side?
   a. Superficial vein
   b. Bruising
   c. Sclerosed vein
   d. Dialysis fistula

96. What should the patient be instructed to do when performing a lab to determine the level of a home medication?
   a. "Take the medication right before bedtime."
   b. "Take the medication on the way to the lab."
   c. "Do not take the medication on the day of the test."
   d. "Take the medication at the same time every day."

97. What should lab personnel do to proactively ensure that the centrifuge continues to function as intended?
   a. Assign a weekly cleaning schedule.
   b. Call biomedical when there is a malfunction.
   c. Replace O-rings and rotors when they break.
   d. Maintain a log for checking the rotors for expiration dates.

98. What type of anemia is caused by medical interventions and treatments?
   a. Iatrogenic anemia
   b. Pernicious anemia
   c. Sickle cell anemia
   d. Hemolytic anemia

99. A patient arrives for their appointment at the lab. The phlebotomist realizes the patient is deaf. Which of the following is NOT an appropriate way to communicate with the patient?
   a. Talking loudly
   b. Through their caregiver
   c. Word charts
   d. Written word

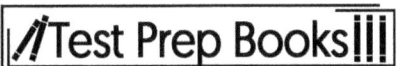

100. Which of the following does NOT go against laboratory and infection control standards?
    a. Wearing a wedding ring
    b. Having fingernails one-quarter inch long
    c. Wearing open-toed shoes
    d. Chewing gum

101. How often is it required for the Joint Commission to inspect and accredit a laboratory?
    a. Three times per year
    b. Once every two years
    c. Semiannually
    d. Every five years

102. Which of the following would be the most likely reason that a tube with an anticoagulant additive develops clotting within one minute of the draw?
    a. The tube was not mixed sufficiently.
    b. The patient is hypercoagulable.
    c. The tube was not delivered in a timely manner.
    d. There was not enough sample taken.

103. Which laboratory department would a culture be directed to?
    a. Hematology
    b. Microbiology
    c. Pathology
    d. Chemistry

104. A phlebotomist is assessing a patient's skin while looking for a vein. What skin characteristic would indicate that a site should be avoided?
    a. Thick hair
    b. Thin skin
    c. Scarring
    d. Loose skin

105. Which communicator style prefers a step-by-step approach to patient education?
    a. Analytical communicator
    b. Intuitive communicator
    c. Functional communicator
    d. Personal communicator

106. How many hepatitis B vaccination doses are required to provide efficacy to healthcare employees?
    a. One dose
    b. Four doses
    c. Three doses
    d. Five doses

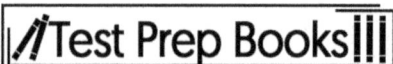

107. Which of the following bloodborne pathogens has the highest risk for transmission for healthcare workers?
    a. Hepatitis B
    b. Hepatitis A
    c. HIV
    d. Ebola

108. At what point during the venipuncture procedure should the needle's safety be engaged?
    a. After the patient's bandage has been applied
    b. Immediately after the needle leaves the patient's skin
    c. Before it is placed in the sharps container
    d. After hemostasis has been achieved

109. A patient arrives and tells the phlebotomist that they previously fainted during a lab draw. What position is best for the patient to be in prior to venipuncture?
    a. Sitting in a clinic recliner without an armrest
    b. Sitting in a phlebotomy chair with armrest down and locked
    c. Sitting in a phlebotomy chair with procedure table in front
    d. Sitting in a clinical recliner with an armrest attached

110. When the phlebotomist uses the principles of standard precautions, what does this assume about all patients?
    a. They are free from disease or microbes.
    b. They have potential for bloodborne disease.
    c. Contact precautions should be used for all blood draws.
    d. Gloves are only needed for patients in precautions.

111. A patient faints during venipuncture. The phlebotomist immediately stops and tries to rouse the patient. The phlebotomist is unable to wake the patient. What is the next action the phlebotomist should take?
    a. Use smelling salts.
    b. Give a sternal rub to the patient.
    c. Call 911.
    d. Get ice for the patient.

112. A patient is having a point-of-care glucose test completed by the phlebotomist. The phlebotomist uses a retractable safety lancet on the patient's finger pad. This does not puncture enough for the blood sample. What step should the phlebotomist take next?
    a. Retry using the same lancet.
    b. Immediately dispose of the lancet in the garbage.
    c. Set it aside and get a new lancet.
    d. Dispose of the lancet in a sharps container and cleanse the finger pad with alcohol.

113. A phlebotomist suspects that a lab sample being prepared for centrifuge is compromised. What should be the next step?
    a. Discard the original sample and have a new sample drawn.
    b. Continue to process the sample.
    c. Redraw, and then process both samples.
    d. Call the provider to see if the test order is actually needed.

Practice Test

114. Which type of test is acceptable for the widest range of urine lab orders?
   a. Clean catch
   b. Random
   c. 8-hour
   d. 24-hour

115. A phlebotomist with ten years of experience has started at a new hospital and is required to do all draws with an experienced preceptor. If they decide to draw blood from a patient without supervision, they would be doing which of the following?
   a. Showing initiative
   b. Showing incompetence based on facility policy
   c. Acting appropriately if the lab needed to be drawn
   d. Acting out of their scope of practice

116. A phlebotomist is inspecting the skin on a patient in the hospital. The patient has two IV lines, one in each antecubital space. Where should the phlebotomist look for a vein?
   a. 2 inches above the right antecubital area
   b. Dorsum of the hand
   c. 4 inches above either antecubital area
   d. Dermal puncture

117. A laboratory technician has never used a new piece of lab equipment and is nervous about operating it. What is the best way that the laboratory technician can avoid an accident related to new equipment use after hands-on training and education has been given?
   a. Wait until another technician has used it.
   b. Follow the manufacturer's instructions.
   c. Tell the manager that they are not comfortable using it.
   d. Troubleshoot if a failure occurs.

118. Bacterial and viral microorganisms are considered to be which type of hazard?
   a. Chemical
   b. Ergonomic
   c. Physical
   d. Biological

119. If a vein can be seen but cannot be felt, what does the phlebotomist know about the vein?
   a. It is large.
   b. It is sclerosed.
   c. It is superficial.
   d. It is usable.

120. What is the electronic system used to provide digital access specifically for clinical and pathological diagnostic testing?
   a. Medical Administration Record
   b. Electronic health record
   c. Laboratory information system
   d. Patient portal

Answer Explanations

1. D: Bilirubin must be protected from light for accurate results. Choice A is not correct because it is a part of the complete blood count and requires a tube with an anticoagulant. Choice B is not correct; this test requires ice for transport. Choice C is not correct because this test requires an anticoagulant in the tube.

2. D: Staring off and talking that stops suddenly are signs of a potential complication. Choices A, B, and C are not indications of complications.

3. D: The vein should be palpated up and down the arm to verify its direction. Choice A is incorrect; the phlebotomist has not reached that step yet. Choice B is incorrect; the phlebotomist should never slap or hit the area. Choice C is incorrect; the supplies should have been gathered before the phlebotomist started looking for an appropriate vein.

4. D: A biohazard bag is a waste management supply and does not provide personal protection to the employee. Choices A, B, and C are all types of personal protective equipment.

5. B: The correct choice is to write the information on the label using a pen. Choice A is incorrect, as this choice is not permanent and can come off the label. Choice C is incorrect, as a marker may smear and become illegible. Choice D is incorrect, as label creation is typically done on specific forms on which pens are used.

6. D: The phlebotomist should inspect the needle's safety device before beginning the procedure. This ensures that after the needle is retracted, they know how to engage the safety device to prevent accidental needlesticks. Choices A, B, and C are not the appropriate times to inspect the safety device.

7. A: A fragile vein will be less likely to rupture due to the lower pressure of a blood pressure cuff inflated to no more than the diastolic blood pressure. Choice B is incorrect; sclerosed veins are tougher and harder to puncture, so a tourniquet is a better choice for this type of vein. Choice C is incorrect, as a superficial vein should not be used at all. Choice D is incorrect, as a rolling vein will be easier to draw from if anchored well. A blood pressure cuff will not help with this.

8. D: An MSDS contains pertinent information regarding chemicals and substances that are used within a healthcare setting. It would not include information regarding bloodborne diseases; one should refer to infection control for pathogenic disease. Choices A, B, and C are all data that would be expected within the MSDS reference document.

9. B: Anytime a splash is anticipated, the phlebotomist should ensure that gloves, a gown, and face/eye protection are donned. Choice A is incorrect, as it does not offer any eye, mouth, or nasal membrane coverage. Choice C is not correct; this does not offer protection to clothing, eyes, mouth, or nasal membranes. Choice D is not correct; clothing, mouth, and nasal membranes are not sufficiently protected if an exposure from a splash should occur.

10. B: 70% isopropyl alcohol is the antiseptic used for routine venipuncture. Choice A is incorrect; this antiseptic is used for blood cultures. Choice C is incorrect; povidone-iodine should not be used. Choice D is incorrect, as this alcohol is stronger than the recommended strength.

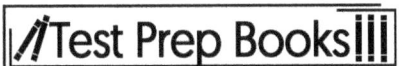

Answer Explanations

11. B: The chain of custody tracks all handlers of a specimen, including collection, transport, and processing. Choices *A, C,* and *D* are not correct descriptions of the legal record used for tracking a specimen.

12. D: This action decreases delays in staff knowing who to call in the case of an emergency. Choices *A, B,* and *C* all expedite the staff's ability to locate and utilize emergency equipment; however, these options do not improve the ability of staff to quickly identify the telephone numbers to request assistance.

13. B: Having the donor slowly make a fist periodically can help to promote ongoing blood flow during the collection process. Choice *A* is incorrect because the tourniquet should be removed after blood flow is established. Choices *C* and *D* are also incorrect because these interventions may be beneficial to donors but would not significantly impact ongoing blood flow during the donation process.

14. B. For the most accurate results, the sample should be delivered to the lab within one hour.

15. D: A stool sample must be refrigerated if it cannot be delivered within four hours. Choices *A, B,* and *C* do not reflect understanding that a sample can be left at room temperature if delivered within four hours or that it must be refrigerated if delivered between four and twenty-four hours.

16. B: Spills are the most common accident that occurs within the laboratory setting, whether with chemical or biohazardous materials. Choice *A* is incorrect; this accident ranks as the second most common accident in a lab, while an explosion is third. Choice *C* is not correct; while it is a risk, it is not as high and is mitigated by the mandated use of a ground fault circuit interrupter. Choice *D* is incorrect. Falls are an occupational risk; however, they are not as prevalent as spills.

17. B: The Centers for Medicare and Medicaid Services (CMS) is the regulatory authority for all laboratory testing done on humans, aside from research. Choices *A* and *D* provide information, education, and guidance on public health and research-based health topics. Choice *C* oversees occupational safety and sets industry standards for the nation.

18. C: The gown should be put on first, secured at the back of the neck, and then secured around the waist. Choice *A* is not correct; this would leave the gown open in the front, leading to a risk of contamination. Choices *B* and *D* are not correct; if the gloves are put on first, the wrists may be left exposed. The gown should tuck into the gloves for the most coverage.

19. A: The tourniquet should be taken off after blood has entered the final evacuated tube to be filled. Choice *B* is incorrect, as this could cause excess bleeding. Choice *C* is incorrect; the last tube should have blood in it before the tourniquet is removed.

20. D: The phlebotomist should apply a new cotton ball before using tape or self-adhering wrap on the patient. Choice *A* is incorrect, as the patient has already achieved hemostasis; the puncture site should be taped or wrapped to maintain light pressure on the site. Choices *B* and *C* are incorrect; the bloody cotton ball should be replaced before it is wrapped or taped.

21. B: The first step is to move the needle slightly deeper. Choice *A* is incorrect, as this is the second action if moving the needle deeper is unsuccessful. Choice *C* is incorrect, as actions can be taken to reestablish blood flow. Choice *D* is incorrect; the needle should never be moved side to side under the skin, as this can cause damage and pain to the patient.

22. D: Adequate specimen volumes is the most impactful variable of blood culture collection. Choice *A* is incorrect because timely collection may help get results faster but won't increase the success rate of pathogen detection. Choices *B* and *C* are incorrect because these are not the most important factors in the success of blood culture detection.

23. C: Sharps bins that are over three-fourths full have the risk of a stick when trying to add more biohazard sharps to them. Choices *A* and *D* are not correct, as the bin may be overfilled before this timeframe is met. Choice *B* is not correct; the bin must be replaced before becoming overfilled, as sharps and needles may protrude from the bin, causing harm.

24. C: When a nerve is hit during a venipuncture, the patient may experience numbness or "pins and needles." Choices *A*, *B*, and *D* are not signs or symptoms of hitting a nerve during venipuncture.

25. B. The patient in a wheelchair should not be asked to transfer out of their wheelchair. Accommodations should be made for the patient with physical disabilities. Choices *A*, *C*, and *D* do not allow for accommodation for the patient with disabilities.

26. C: The depth of the vein determines the angle of needle entry; the deeper the vein, the larger the angle. Choice *A* is incorrect; the angle of the needle is based on the depth of the vein. Choice *B* is incorrect; the thickness of the vein doesn't impact the angle of needle entry. Choice *D* is incorrect, as the proximity of the vein to the elbow has nothing to do with the angle of entry.

27. B: External databases are reliable sources of data that can provide information on morbidity and mortality reports, medical legal cases, and research studies. Choice *A* is not correct, as this information would be located within the electronic health record. Choices *C* and *D* are incorrect, as they would be found within the facilities internal database or intranet.

28. C: To protect themselves, the phlebotomist must know what type of PPE and precautions must be followed and should ask the patient's nurse. Choice *A* is incorrect because the order is STAT and this option would cause a delay in care. Choice *B* is not correct, as the patient may not know the type of PPE that must be used and how the precautions may affect procedures for the phlebotomist to safely continue. Choice *D* is not correct, as this will not sufficiently protect the phlebotomist and may cause spread of a microorganism via transmission from contact, droplet, or airborne factors.

29. D: Initial specimen diversion (ISD) removes the initial blood flow to reduce the chances of contamination from antiseptic cleanser residue, surface microorganisms, and other potential contaminants. Choices *A, B,* and *C* are incorrect, as the ISD does not address these issues.

30. C: An infection that has a direct link to being contracted during a hospital stay is termed a nosocomial infection. Choice *A* is incorrect; colonization is the occurrence of a pathogen, such as methicillin-resistant *Staphylococcus aureus* (MRSA), becoming a part of a patient's natural flora. Choice *B* is not correct; community-acquired infections are ones that have been contracted outside of a healthcare facility. Choice *D* is not correct; an idiopathic infection is one where the cause or source is not known.

31. C. Analytical communicators prefer to be informed using facts and direct information, as it is easier for them to understand. Choices *A, B,* and *D* are not ways that analytical communicators prefer to receive information.

Answer Explanations

32. C: The correct choice is to create a label with all the necessary information on it. The label should include the patient's name, date of birth, and medical identification number, the date and time of the draw, and the initials of the phlebotomist. Choices A and B are incorrect, as these choices do not meet labeling requirements. Choice D is incorrect; the specimens should be labeled before the patient leaves the exam room.

33. C. An older adult can lose up to 100 mL of blood before seeing a drop in their hemoglobin and hematocrit levels.

34. B: A slipknot is a knot that is easy to release with one hand and is used for tying tourniquets. Choices A, C, and D are not the appropriate knots to use for phlebotomy.

35. A. Stool samples that are mixed with urine are not testable, and a new sample must be obtained. Choices B, C, and D do not indicate a need for a new sample.

36. D: Anticoagulant additives are antithrombotic drugs that slow down clotting by reducing fibrin formation. Choice A is incorrect, as calcium is part of the clotting cascade and increases coagulation. Choice B is incorrect, as antiplatelets, not anticoagulants, prevent platelets from joining as part of clot formation. Choice C is not the correct answer since it is not directly affected by the anticoagulant; however, a sample that does clot will have a higher potassium result.

37. C. To avoid iatrogenic anemia, the maximum amount of blood that should be drawn from an infant is 1–5 percent of the infant's total blood volume. Choice D is the amount of total blood volume that can be drawn from an infant over an eight-week period—10 percent.

38. B: The phlebotomist should ask the patient if they are okay. This will help further identify any complications. Choice A is incorrect, as the phlebotomist has not fully assessed the situation. Choice C is incorrect, as a cold compress is applied when a patient faints or becomes lightheaded. Choice D is incorrect, as the phlebotomist does not currently need assistance.

39. A: When encountering a patient in respiratory or cardiac arrest, a quick assessment should verify the absence of a DNR bracelet prior to initiating CPR. Choice B is not correct; when assessing an adult patient for a pulse, the carotid pulse is sufficient. In children under two, a brachial pulse may be checked. Choice C is not correct; a lack of pulse is sufficient to initiate the CPR response and begin chest compressions. Choice D is not correct; this may cause a delay in care. Chest compressions should be immediately started with a lack of pulse unless a DNR bracelet is present.

40. B: HgbA1C evaluates the average blood sugars for the last three months in patients with diabetes. Choice A is not correct because cardiac markers are used to evaluate chronic heart conditions. Choice C involves the liver and would be evaluated with liver function tests. Choice D is diagnosed via a positive antinuclear body test.

41. D. Latex is a severe allergy that can end in anaphylaxis. It is important for the phlebotomist to take notice and ensure that the equipment they use is latex free. Choices A, B, and C are incorrect. These allergies are not as concerning.

42. A: Phlebotomists would not be permitted to withdraw blood specimens directly from an access device. Choices B, C, and D are all examples of ways the phlebotomist may assist other healthcare professionals.

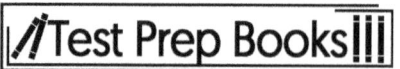

Answer Explanations

43. D: The needle should be removed with the bevel up and at the same angle at which it entered the skin.

44. A: The correct order for these evacuated tubes is pink, green, and then gold or red. Gold and red evacuated tubes have no additives and should go last.

45. D. The patient should brush their teeth or dentures and rinse their mouth with water before producing a sputum sample. This ensures that mouth bacteria do not contaminate the sample. Choices A and B are incorrect; while hand hygiene is important, it will not have an impact on the sputum sample. Choice C is incorrect because this is not a requirement for a sputum sample.

46. A. Patients who are personal communicators tend to make a connection with people while building rapport. Choices B, C, and D are not characteristics of personal communicators.

47. B: The FIT test detects the presence of hemoglobin in the colon and rectum. Choice D is incorrect, as detection of blood in the colon and rectum does not necessarily indicate the presence of cancer. Choices A and C are incorrect, as the FIT test does not detect parasites or fat in the stool.

48. A: All samples should be placed within a sealed plastic bag to contain any leaks or spills that might occur. Choice B may optionally be used, but this is not the correct answer, as the samples should still be placed within the sealed plastic bag. Choices C and D are not sufficient to prevent leaking and may lead to breakage of the tubes.

49. C. The phlebotomist should have the patient provide a fresh urine sample using the lab-provided supplies. A sample for urinalysis should be tested within fifteen minutes of urination for the most accurate results. Choice A is incorrect, as the sample from a non-sterile container should not be used. Choice B is incorrect; a new sample should be obtained and labeled. Choice D is incorrect, as the patient's sample is not acceptable.

50. D: The phlebotomist should first ensure safe disposal of the sharp that has recently been used and then replace the bin before leaving the patient care area. Choices A, B, and C are all examples of unsafe patient care and biohazard practices.

51. B. The correct amount of time for fasting before a lab is eight to twelve hours.

52. C: Any out-of-range or STAT values that are reported should be documented in a thorough and timely manner. Choice A is incorrect because the documentation should be completed prior to a break to prevent it from being missed. Choice B is outside the scope of practice for the phlebotomist role. The ordering or responsible provider should be communicating the results to the patient and the care team. Choice D is incorrect; the documentation for the current patient should be completed prior to moving on to the next result.

53. A: A blood smear using an EDTA specimen should be performed within an hour of collection. Choices B, C, and D are incorrect, as EDTA specimens processed after an hour have an increased risk of becoming distorted from the anticoagulant additives in the tube.

54. A. Menstruating females are not at a higher risk of iatrogenic anemia. Choices B, C, and D are high-risk populations. High-risk patients include underweight and malnourished patients, pediatric and infant patients, cancer patients, and older adults.

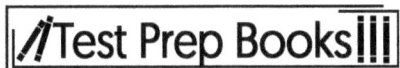

Answer Explanations

55. C: The cleanser should be allowed to dry completely. If not allowed to dry, the cleanser can cause pain, including stinging and burning, to the patient. Choice A is incorrect; the area should not be wiped after it has been cleansed. Choices B and D can cause irregularity with the draw and erroneous results.

56. C: The vein should be repalpated to see if it has moved off the needle. Choice A is incorrect; the needle should never be moved in and out repeatedly. Choice B is incorrect, as the needle should not be moved up and down under the skin. This can cause patient harm. Choice D is incorrect, as there are actions that can be taken to reestablish blood flow.

57. A: A reagent is a substance that is used to elicit a chemical reaction. This type of spill would be considered a chemical hazard. Choice B is not correct; an example of a physical hazard is a slip or fall. Choice C is not correct; this would be an accident such as a needlestick or cut. Choice D is not correct; biological hazards include exposure to materials or individuals that may cause pathogenic diseases.

58. D. The phlebotomist should use words that are small and easy to understand, as this will make communication easier. Choices A, B, and C will not make communication easier.

59. A: Calluses and any other cuts or irregularities should be avoided. Choices B, C, and D do not need to be avoided. Choice B and C are both appropriate locations for dermal puncture. Choice D does not need to be avoided.

60. A: This patient is exhibiting signs of shock. The first thing the phlebotomist should do is to call 911. Choice B is incorrect, as the phlebotomist should not leave the patient alone. Choice C is incorrect because this intervention is for syncope or fainting. Choice D is not the correct action; this can be used for patients who are lightheaded or faint.

61. C: Choice C correctly defines aliquoting as a method of breaking a large sample into smaller ones. Choice A is incorrect, as aliquoting does not necessarily transfer into a container that has a reactant. Choice B is the opposite of aliquoting and would better describe batch testing, such as a twenty-four-hour urine test. Choice D is incorrect, as it describes point-of-care testing, not aliquoting.

62. C: The blood gas should be drawn first because the puncture will likely cause the infant to cry, and that can alter the results. If it is drawn last, the amount of crying will increase, which also increases the chances of erroneous results. Choice D is incorrect, as a venous blood gas is typically collected in a green tube. When no blood gas is ordered, the green tube is not last in the order of draw.

63. B. The phlebotomist should not walk them to a more comfortable chair. While the patient is feeling faint, they are at risk for passing out and for falling. Choices A, C, and D are all appropriate interventions for a patient who feels faint.

64. C: Anchoring the vein should happen after all cleansing has been done, the tourniquet has been applied, and the phlebotomist is ready to insert the needle. Choice D is incorrect; anchoring needs to be done before the needle enters the skin.

65. A: During a fire, an emergency shutdown protocol would be appropriate in a laboratory. Power is eliminated to heat-producing and electrical equipment, and gas flow into the lab is stopped. Choice B is incorrect; when a needlestick occurs, the individual should immediately wash the site and notify the supervisor for further guidance. Choice C is not correct; since the chemical spill is described as contained, it would not need a full lab shutdown. The MSDS should be referred to for appropriate

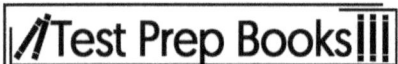

Answer Explanations

cleanup based on the chemical. Choice *D* is not correct; a rapid response should be initiated to seek medical attention for the patient.

66. A. The first thing the phlebotomist should do is to ask the patient if they have a dialysis fistula. This will reduce the risk of patient harm. Choices *B*, *C*, and *D* are not the first things that a phlebotomist should do after learning that the patient is on dialysis.

67. A: Hand hygiene reduces the risk of spread via contaminated hands that is inherent within healthcare organizations. Good hand hygiene practices have been found to reduce the number of microorganisms that can be passed, thereby reducing infection risk, poor patient outcomes, and nosocomial infections. Choices *B* and *C* are not correct; these measures protect healthcare personnel from contracting infections, but without hand hygiene, microbes may still be transferred. Choice *D* is not correct. Antimicrobial stewardship is crucial to limit the overuse of antibiotics, which leads to bacterial resistance and an inability to effectively control bacterial infections; however, this does not prevent the spread of viruses or bacteria in the hospital setting.

68. B: Biohazardous waste that is solid is appropriate to dispose of within a red biohazard bag. Choice *A* is not correct; depending on the amount of waste, solid waste may clog the hopper. Only fluids should be disposed of there. Choice *C* is not correct; anything other than sharps—such as gloves, plain syringes, or other material—should not take up room in the sharps bin. Choice *D* is not correct; while it may not leak, biohazardous material is processed to prevent exposure. Disposal in the regular trash may contaminate it or result in exposure to an infectious or hazardous substance.

69. A: PPE should be removed in the following order: gloves, goggles, gown, then mask. Choices *B*, *C*, and *D* increase the risk of contamination and exposure.

70. A: The phlebotomist should ensure that no supplies are left in the bed. Supplies that are left can be choking hazards for children or can cause wounds, including pressure sores, on older adult patients. Choice *B* is incorrect, as disposal of unused supplies does not keep the patient from harm. Choice *C* is incorrect, as it is not necessary to inform the nurse when the phlebotomist is finished. Choice *D* is incorrect, as this would happen in the outpatient setting. Phlebotomists are not responsible for cleaning the room in the hospital, although they should clean any mess that they make.

71. C: Using an entry angle greater than 10° into the dorsum of the hand can cause pain. In addition, it can cause harm to the patient. Choice *A* is incorrect, as hemostasis occurs when bleeding stops after a venipuncture. Choice *B* is incorrect, as bleeding is not associated with a greater entry angle of the needle in the hand. Choice *D* is incorrect, as the needle insertion angle does not have an impact on needle phobia.

72. A: Choice *A* reflects PPE that is used with standard precautions. Choice *B* is not correct because an N-95 mask would be a part of enhanced precautions. Choice *C* is an unsafe injection practice. Needles should never be re-capped unless it is a part of a safety cap mechanism. Choice *D* is incorrect, as it is not ethical to directly ask a patient; adhering to standard precautions will protect staff from exposure.

73. C. The phlebotomist should not assume that the person with blindness needs their assistance, and they should not touch the patient without permission. Choices *A*, *B*, and *D* are all appropriate ways to interact with blind patients.

74. C: The phlebotomist would find this information in the standard operating procedure. This document details a facility's alignment with the recommendations and requirements set by accrediting

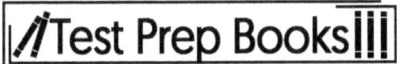

Answer Explanations

and regulatory organizations. Choices A, B, and D are not facility-specific but rather offer broader guidance.

75. C: In addition to fainting (syncope), pain, hematoma, and anxiety are common adverse effects from venipuncture. Choices A, B, and D are not typical symptoms related to venipuncture.

76. C: PPE, personal protective equipment, is used to protect oneself and patients from being exposed to microbial pathogens. Choice A is incorrect; it is the acronym for the Centers for Medicare and Medicaid Services. Choice B is not correct; OSHA is the acronym for the Occupational Safety and Health Administration. CLABSI stands for central line-associated bloodstream infection, so Choice D is not correct.

77. C: Room-temperature urine samples for urinalysis should be refrigerated or preserved if they cannot be processed within two hours of collection.

78. A: The phlebotomist should scrub the site with chlorhexidine gluconate for 30 seconds, back and forth, up and down, and allow it to dry completely before the venipuncture.

79. C: Touching the card or spots with a gloved hand would not contaminate the card. Choices A, B, and D are examples of variables that can impact the validity of newborn screening results.

80. D: Petechiae are small pinpoint bruises that can occur from normal use of a tourniquet or from leaving a tourniquet on for too long. Choices A, B, and C are incorrect, as these complications are not small marks below a tourniquet.

81. D: Airborne precaution orders include the use of HEPA filters and negative pressure rooms. As the pathogen is able to travel considerably otherwise, this prevents the microbe from filtering through passages to hallways and other rooms. Choice A is not correct; transmission of droplets is three feet or less, and simple masks offer sufficient protection. Choice B is not correct; transmission of this nature is through touch, so gloves and a gown are the appropriate PPE for contact isolation. Choice C does not describe a type of isolation precaution but rather refers to a type of infection that is contracted within a healthcare facility.

82. D. Intuitive communicators are not concerned with details. Choices A, B, and C all describe intuitive communicators. They are happy with broad information, want to get to the result, and may ask questions along the way.

83. D. The best place to begin the search for an appropriate vein is in the antecubital fossa. The veins here are larger and easier to access. Choices A, B, and C are not the best position or site to draw blood.

84. B: The laboratory staff received the provider's message and confirmed the answer. This is an example of communication that closes the loop and ensures that all parties understood and received the message. This type of communication is professional, Choice A, but that is not the best choice, as it does not specify that it is closed-loop communication. Choice C, active listening, is only a part of this interaction and does not aptly describe the interaction. Choice D is incorrect; the communication style was assertive and professional but would not be described as passive-aggressive.

85. B: $8 \text{ kg} \times 75 \text{ mL/kg} = 600 \text{ mL}$; $600 \text{ mL} / 1{,}000 \text{ mL per L} = 0.6 \text{ L}$. Choice A is incorrect, as 600 is the total blood volume represented in milliliters.

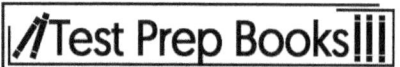

Answer Explanations

86. B: An accrediting organization is an establishment that provides assessment, evaluation, and guidance for meeting state and national standards of patient safety and care. Choice *A* is not correct; an accrediting organization is a third party that offers recommendations and assesses compliance with rules and regulations. It does not provide education or training to facility personnel. Choice *C* is not correct; the partnering school would be responsible for ensuring that faculty meet teaching certification requirements. Choice *D* is not correct. Ensuring patient safety is always a priority; however, meeting competencies and regulatory requirements does not promise that adverse events will never happen.

87. B: Choice *B* is correct per Food and Drug Administration (FDA) guidelines for safe blood donation. Choice *A* is incorrect because a minimum hemoglobin of 12.5 g/dL is required for *female* donors.

88. B. A patient who is a difficult stick will often know the best place to successfully have venipuncture. The patient should be asked before the phlebotomist begins the procedure. Choices *A*, *C*, and *D* are appropriate questions for certain patients and labs but do not relate to a patient being a hard stick.

89. D: General guidelines recommend that monthly blood draw volumes not exceed 10% of a patient's total blood volume. Choice *A* is incorrect because 3% represents the daily blood draw volume maximum.

90. B. A butterfly needle is the appropriate choice for the dorsal side of the hand due to its size and length. Choices *A*, *C*, and *D* are not the best choices for the dorsal side of the hand.

91. B: A cotton ball and self-adhesive wrap should be used to keep the patient's skin from tearing or becoming damaged. Choices *A*, *C*, and *D* are not the dressing of choice for this specific patient.

92. C: Nuclear medicine tests may involve the use of radiation or the injection, inhalation, or oral ingestion of radioactive drugs. Choices *A*, *B*, and *D* are also risks in this department; however, the risk of radioactive exposure is unique and higher within this department compared to other patient care areas.

93. A. The phlebotomist should observe the patient for fifteen minutes after the venipuncture to ensure that there are no complications.

94. A: This result is between 130 and 600 seconds, indicating that the value is within the therapeutic range. Choice *B* is incorrect, as the normal range is 70 to 180 seconds. Choice *C* is incorrect, as the activated clotting time indicates how long it takes the blood to clot, which indicates that this patient is hypocoagulable, not hypercoagulable. Choice *D* is incorrect; the high end of the range is 600 seconds.

95. D: A venipuncture should never be done on the same side as a dialysis fistula. Choices *A*, *B*, and *C* would indicate that another vein should be chosen, but it would not need to be on the opposite arm.

96. D. The patient should take the medication at the same time every day. Choices *A*, *B*, and *C* are not instructions that should be given to a patient.

97. D: Choice *D* is the only choice that represents proactive action to ensure the centrifuge parts continue to function. Choice *A* is incorrect, as cleaning needs to be completed on a more frequent basis. Choices *B* and *C* are retrospective and provide action only when a problem has already happened.

98. A. Iatrogenic anemia is anemia that is caused through the practice of medical interventions. It can be caused by drawing too much blood from a patient. Choices *B*, *C*, and *D* are not caused by medical interventions.

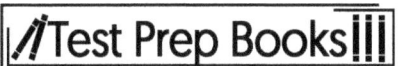

Answer Explanations

99. A. Talking loudly to a deaf patient will not help the phlebotomist and the patient communicate. Choices *B*, *C*, and *D* are appropriate ways to communicate with a deaf patient.

100. B: Nails should be kept trimmed to one-fourth of an inch or less, with no false nails. Choice *A* is not correct; rings and other hand jewelry are not recommended for healthcare workers who have direct patient contact due to colonization risk. Choice *C* is not correct; open-toed shoes expose skin to potential splashes and other risks. Closed-toe shoes are considered a part of personal protective equipment. Choice *D* is not correct; eating, drinking, and gum chewing is not allowed in areas where testing with chemicals, biohazardous materials, and toxic substances is present.

101. B: The Joint Commission is required to inspect laboratories for accreditation every two years, so Choice *B* is correct. Choices *A* and *C* are incorrect; these timelines are too frequent. Choice *D* is not correct; this timeline is too long between visits.

102. A: The tube must be inverted several times to thoroughly mix the blood with the additive anticoagulant. Choice *B* is incorrect; if mixed properly, the anticoagulant within the tube would be effective in preventing even a hypercoagulable patient's blood from clotting. Choice *C* is incorrect, as clotting does not begin to occur for at least an hour when mixed appropriately with the additive. Choice *D* is unlikely to result in clotting; however, the sample would be rejected due to an insufficient amount for testing.

103. B: A culture must be processed within the microbiology department of a lab. Choice *A* is not correct; hematology completes lab studies such as a complete blood count, plasma and platelet levels, and clotting times to assess anticoagulation therapy. Choice *C*, pathology, focuses more on blood dyscrasias, tissue sample testing, and identification of cancers and other chronic illnesses. Choice *D* is not correct; chemistry panels typically include electrolytes and blood sugar levels and assess function of hepatic and renal organs.

104. C: Scarring should be avoided, as it can cause pain and be difficult to push a needle through. Choices *A*, *B*, and *D* are all normal and do not need to be avoided.

105. C. Functional communicators like to get information in a logical and organized manner. Choices *A*, *B*, and *D* are not described by a step-by-step method.

106. C: The vaccination is administered as three doses spaced apart in intervals. Choices *A*, *B*, and *D* are not the correct number of doses required for efficacy and safety of the hepatitis B vaccination regimen.

107. A: Hepatitis B, at a 6–30 percent transmission rate, is the highest risk for healthcare workers. Choice *B* is incorrect; hepatitis A is not a bloodborne infection. Choice *C* is not correct; HIV has a 0.23 percent risk for transmission if exposed via a needlestick. Choice *D* is not correct; although the risk for transmission is extremely high with symptomatic patients, there have only ever been eleven people treated—and four that were laboratory confirmed—in the US, making the risk isolated and low.

108. B: The needle's safety should be engaged immediately after it has been withdrawn from the skin. Choices *A*, *C*, and *D* put the phlebotomist and patient at risk for needlestick injury.

109. B. The patient who faints should be seated in a phlebotomy chair with the armrest down and locked. Choices *A*, *C*, and *D* are not appropriate seats for the fainting patient.

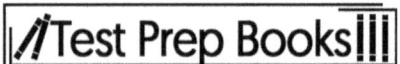

Answer Explanations

110. B: The use of standard precautions applies best practice and a standard level of infection control to all patients, regardless of known or unknown pathogen status. Choice A is incorrect. Patients are never assumed to be free from disease or microbes; practices are used to prevent contact, splash, and needlestick injury with any patient. Choices C and D are not correct; some patients may require the phlebotomist to don a higher level of PPE depending on the diagnosis and isolation precautions ordered.

111. C. The phlebotomist should call 911 if they are unable to wake the patient after fainting. Choices A, B, and D are not the next actions that the phlebotomist should take. Smelling salts are not an action the phlebotomist should take. Phlebotomists should not perform a sternal rub unless specifically trained to do so. Ice will not help the patient to wake.

112. D: A lancet is a sharp and must be disposed of properly to prevent injury. The site should be sanitized with alcohol again before retrying to prevent infection. Choice A is incorrect. Retractable lancets are intended to be used only once; attempting to use them again to puncture the patient's finger increases the risk that it may cause injury to the patient or phlebotomist. Choice B is not correct; the lancet must be disposed of in a sharps container. Choice C is not correct; the lancet should be immediately disposed of in a sharps container to prevent bloodborne exposure because it has made contact with the patient and should be considered contaminated.

113. A: In case of real or suspected compromise of a sample, the sample should automatically be redrawn. Choice B is not correct, as this could lead to erroneous results or results that have been contaminated. Choice C is not correct because there could be a discrepancy between the two values, leading to patient care that is not based on an accurate result. Choice D is unprofessional, and it would be inappropriate to suggest that a lab should not be redrawn for this reason.

114. C: An 8-hour (or first morning) urine specimen is going to be appropriate for many urine lab orders. Choice B is incorrect because random urine concentration can vary widely based on recent intake, as can timing. Choices A and D would not be appropriate for many urine labs.

115. B: The phlebotomist would not be competently trained to work within that facility prior to sign-off from the preceptor. Choices A and C are not correct because the phlebotomist has chosen to disobey the rules set by the facility. Choice D is not correct, as the phlebotomist is experienced and drawing blood is within their scope of practice; however, their facility policy requires further training.

116. B: The dorsum of the hand is the best choice. The venipuncture must be done distal to the IV lines. Choices A, C, and D are incorrect, as the venipuncture should not be done above the IV lines. A dermal puncture is incorrect.

117. B: The technician should refer to the manufacturer's instructions, which would align with the recent teaching. Choice A is not correct; delaying a patient test until a coworker needs to use the equipment is not appropriate. Choice C would be fiscally irresponsible and cause a delay in patient care. Choice D is not correct; the technician should not attempt to find workarounds or deviate from the recommendations of the manufacturer. Any issues should be reported to their supervisor.

118. D: Biological hazards include sources of infectious disease, molds, and natural toxic materials (such as plants). Choice A, chemical hazards, includes materials that are highly volatile and may cause acid burns, nausea, vomiting, or asphyxiation or lead to chronic health issues such as cancer. Choice B is incorrect; ergonomic hazards include those that are caused by unsafe work activities or wear on the body. Physical hazards, Choice C, may include excessive heat, radiation, or noise exposure.

Answer Explanations

119. C: The phlebotomist knows that when a vein can be seen but not felt, it is superficial and should not be used, as it is not large enough.

120. C: Choice *C* is a system dedicated to managing, recording, and storing patient laboratory information. Choice *A* is the record used to document medications administered to patients. Choice *B* is the electronic health record, which contains a patient's history, conditions, medications, and lab values. Choice *D* is incorrect, as a patient portal is where a patient may have access to certain medical records and lab values uploaded by the facility or provider.

Dear NHA Phlebotomy Test Taker,

Thank you for purchasing this study guide for your NHA Phlebotomy exam. We hope that we exceeded your expectations.

Our goal in creating this study guide was to cover all of the topics that you will see on the test. We also strove to make our practice questions as similar as possible to what you will encounter on test day. With that being said, if you found something that you feel was not up to your standards, please send us an email and let us know.

We would also like to let you know about other books in our catalog that may interest you.

CNA

This can be found on Amazon: amazon.com/dp/1637757832

CMA

amazon.com/dp/1637751729

We have study guides in a wide variety of fields. If the one you are looking for isn't listed above, then try searching for it on Amazon or send us an email.

Thanks Again and Happy Testing!
Product Development Team
info@studyguideteam.com

FREE Test Taking Tips Video/DVD Offer

To better serve you, we created videos covering test taking tips that we want to give you for FREE. **These videos cover world-class tips that will help you succeed on your test.**

We just ask that you send us feedback about this product. Please let us know what you thought about it—whether good, bad, or indifferent.

To get your **FREE videos**, you can use the QR code below or email freevideos@studyguideteam.com with "Free Videos" in the subject line and the following information in the body of the email:

    a. The title of your product

    b. Your product rating on a scale of 1-5, with 5 being the highest

    c. Your feedback about the product

If you have any questions or concerns, please don't hesitate to contact us at info@studyguideteam.com.

Thank you!

www.ingramcontent.com/pod-product-compliance
Lightning Source LLC
Chambersburg PA
CBHW061140230426
43663CB00027B/2983